DATE DUE

DEMCO 38-296

MAGILL'S HISTORY
OF
EUROPE

Magill's History
of
Europe

Volume 1

Edited by
FRANK N. MAGILL

Grolier Educational Corporation
Danbury, Connecticut

ISBN 0-7172-7173-0 (set)

Library of Congress Catalog Card Number 92-054832

REVISED EDITION

First Printing

Published 1993 by
Grolier Educational Corporation
Danbury, Connecticut, 06816

Printed in Mexico

PUBLISHER'S NOTE

Magill's History of Europe surveys, in chronological order, 288 events which shaped the Western world, from the promulgation of Hammurabi's code (c. 1750 B.C.) to the negotiations surrounding European economic union in 1992. Within this framework, "Europe" is construed broadly to refer to both Eastern and Western Europe, as well as those ancient civilizations (Middle Eastern, Mediterranean, and North African) which gave rise to many of the legal, social, and political institutions that have shaped Europe as we know it today.

The types of event addressed in these six volumes range from military clashes and revolutions to legal documents, from economic and religious developments to international organizations and treaties. All, however, have in common a political thread: The emphasis here is on the evolution of European (and, inevitably in the late twentieth century, international) governments, institutions, and laws. Items selected for inclusion therefore may have occurred outside the physical borders of today's Europe—most often the case in the earliest entries, which survey the evolution of nations and laws through the rise and fall of ancient Greece and Rome. Such representation also encompasses major military battles, from the Battle of Kadesh (1296 B.C.) through the Battle of Hastings (1066) and the Spanish Armada (1588) to the battles of World Wars I and II, the various uprisings and revolutionary movements during the Cold War era, and European involvement in the Iraq-Kuwait conflict of 1991. Economic developments are represented by the revenue laws of Ptolemy Philadelphius (259 B.C.), the rise of the Hansa and early European economic union (c. 1200), the first Soviet five-year plan (1928-1933), the formation of the Common Market (1957), and the recent efforts of the European Community to realize a true economic union (1992). Legal and constitutional developments are fully represented, from the codifications of Hammurabi (1750 B.C.) and Draco (620 B.C.), through Roman law (e.g., the Twelve Tables, c. 450 B.C.; Justinian's *Code*, c. A.D. 530), Magna Carta (1215), to NATO, the United Nations, and international agreements such as the Helsinki Accords (1975). Of course, the emergence and demise of nations is documented, from the ancient civilizations through the dissolution of the Soviet Union and the realignment of ethnicities, such as those of the former Yugoslavia, in the early 1990's.

The articles in this set of 288 appear in a standard format to enable the quick retrieval of information. Each entry opens with ready-reference data listing the *Type of event* (constitutional, diplomatic, economic, legal, military, political, politico-economic, politico-religious, religious, socio-political), the *Time* (the year and, where appropriate, exact date), the *Locale* (where the event took place), and the *Principal personages* involved. The first section of text, "Summary of Event," rehearses the event itself as well as providing some background and indicating the event's significance. Because a major purpose also has been to make available, along with the narrative summaries of the events themselves, scholarly evaluations of representative literature dealing with these occurrences, the second section, "Pertinent Literature,"

v

offers two in-depth reviews of notable works on the subject. Finally, a listing of "Additional Recommended Readings" provides sources for further study with brief annotations regarding the sources' contents and usefulness.

All the material was written by history professors and scholars from campuses throughout the United States. Reports of the events themselves average more than one thousand words in length, while the individual reviews of literature run about six or eight hundred words each.

At the beginning of each volume there appears a chronological list of events for that volume. Volume 6 includes the following four indexes: Alphabetical List of Events, Key Word Index, Category Index, and an alphabetized listing of Principal Personages. Each index gives both volume and page numbers. Because not all events lend themselves to a specific title universally applied, as do articles headed "Battle of . . . " or "Establishment of . . . ," the Key Word Index should enable the user to locate many events more readily than would an alphabetical list of events whose first word was arbitrarily assigned by the editors.

CONTRIBUTORS

Paul Ashin

Martin J. Baron

William D. Bowman

Kendall W. Brown

Byron D. Cannon

Mortimer Chambers

Frederick B. Chary

Thomas M. Coakley

Carl W. Conrad

Bernard A. Cook

M. Joseph Costelloe

Donald E. Davis

Martin L. Dolan

Samuel K. Eddy

Robert F. Erickson

Sarah M. Farley

Barry Faye

Miletus L. Flaningam

James H. Forse

John G. Gallaher

K. Fred Gillum

John H. Greising

Johnpeter Horst Grill

Manfred Grote

John J. Grotpeter

James M. Haas

William Harrigan

Fred R. van Hartesveldt

Hans Heilbronner

Howard M. Hensel

Kevin Herbert

James F. Hitchcock

Ronald K. Huch

Thomas H. Irwin

Mary Evelyn Jegen

Christopher J. Kauffman

Edward P. Keleher

Barry L. Knight

Felicia Krishna-Hensel

Shlomo Lambroza

Eugene S. Larson

Saul Lerner

John F. McGovern

Roderick McGrew

Roger B. McShane

Russell M. Magnaghi

Lynewood F. Martin

Johnathan Mendilow

George R. Mitchell

John H. Morrow, Jr.

Zola M. Packman

George M. Pepe

James W. Pringle

George F. Putnam

Carl F. Rohne

Joseph R. Rosenbloom

Frank Rusciano

José M. Sánchez

Wayne D. Santoni

Raymond H. Schmandt

Harold A. Schofield

Margaret S. Schoon

Michael S. Smith

Harold L. Stansell

James H. Steinel

Taylor Stults

Spencer C. Tucker

Carl A. Volz

Harry E. Wade

J. A. Wahl

Martha Ellen Webb

E. G. Weltin

Paul A. Whelan

Thomas P. Wolf

Richard J. Wurtz

Edward A. Zivich

List of Events in Volume One

MAGILL'S HISTORY
OF
EUROPE

PROMULGATION OF HAMMURABI'S CODE

Type of event: Legal: promulgation of amendments to current law
Time: c. 1750 B.C.
Locale: Babylon

Principal personage:
HAMMURABI, ruler of Mesopotamia c. 1790-1750

Summary of Event

That Hammurabi's laws are neither the oldest extant laws nor even a law code as popularly thought does not alter the fact that their promulgation and preservation constitute a landmark in history.

Hammurabi, who ruled from about 1790 to 1750 B.C., was the sixth Amorite king of a Semitic dynasty which had imposed its rule on the native Sumerian population of the territory within about a fifty-mile radius of Babylon some two hundred years earlier. Hammurabi himself, late in the course of a forty-three-year reign, extended his rule in the direction of Assyria and northern Syria. It was, at least in part, as a means of unifying this heterogeneous society that Hammurabi published what has come to be known as his code of laws.

An almost complete copy of the laws, engraved on a diorite column or stele about eight feet tall, was discovered in Susa in 1901. This stele is now in the Louvre, Paris. Apparently the laws were engraved on diorite, the most durable substance known to the Babylonians, so that a copy of the laws would stand as a public reference. Many fragments of other copies have been discovered and transcribed, and it is by comparing these that gaps in the Susa stele have been filled, providing a reasonably complete and accurate version of the laws promulgated close to the end of Hammurabi's reign.

The laws are introduced by a prologue in which Hammurabi, in the first person singular, describes his efforts to make law prevail in his lands. He states that the gods Anim and Enlil had appointed him, as a god-fearing prince, to advance the welfare of the people by promoting justice. He was to destroy the wicked and curtail the oppression of the strong over the weak. This divine commission would cause him "to rise like the sun over the black-headed people, and to light up the land."

Following the prologue, 282 articles or laws treat personal property, real estate, business, trade, agriculture, marriage, inheritances, adoption, contracts, and leases. The law also details penalties for injuries both to person and property. Finally, an epilogue recounts in detail Hammurabi's achievements and concludes with a list of blessings for those who keep the laws, and for those who violate them a much longer and more elaborate set of curses.

The collection of laws is not a code, but a set of amendments of existing laws. In the prologue, Hammurabi never calls himself a codifier or legislator. Instead, his aim seems to be to promote public order by making easily available current interpretations and applications of the existing law. This becomes clear when his laws are compared with earlier laws in use in Mesopotamia. Of these there remain sizable fragments of at least three antecedents of Hammurabi's work. The threefold division into prologue, the laws themselves, and an epilogue glorifying the lawgiver was a conventional form in Hammurabi's time.

Hammurabi's laws provide material for reconstructing the evidence of a remarkable civilization. What emerges is the picture of a society with a defined class system, well-developed agriculture, a viable economy based on foreign as well as internal trade, and a government with a strong judiciary.

At least three social classes are discernible in Babylonian society as reflected in the code: the highest class, including the king, civil and military officials, priests, landed proprietors, rich merchants, and manufacturers; a lower class comprising laborers and farmers, including many tenant farmers; and finally, a slave class made up of those captured in war, together with men who had lost their freedom through debt. Here it should be noted that in Babylon, as in Israel, a slave was not a mere chattel, as he became later in Roman law and practice. In the ancient Near East, there was little difference between the hired workman and the slave. Indeed, the Hebrew noun for "slave" means simply a "worker."

The role of women was significant in that the law accorded women marriage and property rights in advance of other societies of a considerably later time. Women could divorce, transact business, and inherit or bequeath property. The law recognized a clear distinction between the legitimate wife and the concubine. "If a man take a wife and do not draw up a contract with her, that woman is not his wife." However, even the harlot was protected from wanton exploitation, as were slaves and children. If a man handed over his wife, his son, or his daughter to the service of another, they must work only three years in the house of their purchaser or master; in the fourth year they secured their freedom.

In many respects the laws of Hammurabi appear excessively harsh. Criminal law follows the *lex talionis*, the vengeful principle of an eye for an eye. "If a man destroy the eye of another man, they shall destroy his eye. If he break a man's bone, they shall break his bone."

Undergirding the individual laws was an exalted ideal of justice and concern for the vulnerable members of society who were referred to in ancient literature collectively as "the widow and the orphan." In the prologue of his laws, Hammurabi declared that he was the agent of the gods, appointed to protect the weak by enforcing just laws. Again in the epilogue he stated that his purpose was to hinder the strong from oppressing the weak, to protect widows and orphans from injustice, and to affirm every man's right to equitable treatment.

The laws of Babylonia are significant because of the light they throw on the ways of life of an ancient civilization. However, in the case of Hammurabi's redaction, the importance transcends the geographic and historical boundaries of the ancient Near East. Hammurabi's laws coincide with the period which saw a considerable expansion of Babylonian civilization, though recent research shows that the influence was more by commerce than by conquest. Not only Egypt and the Eastern Mediterranean, but also the Aegean lands knew the influence of the Babylonian culture. A chief means of transmission of this culture was the law.

It was especially in the case of the Hebrews that this influence was felt, and it was primarily through the Hebrews that some of the political and legal concepts of Hammurabi's laws have become a fundamental part of the heritage of Western civilization and ultimately of the world. In some respects the Babylonian laws reveal a civilization in advance of that of the Hebrews; certainly this is true on the material and economic side. On the other hand, the Hebrew law implies a recognition of a fundamental human equality premised on a recognition of creation by one God, and from this developed a system of ethics far in advance of anything in the Babylonian law. Nevertheless, the historical connections between the two are direct and intimate, and Hammurabi's laws continue to be seen rightly as an early crystallization of some of man's deepest aspirations for social

justice and public order, and ultimately for the good life, conceived in much more than economic or even legal terms.

Pertinent Literature

Driver, G. R., and John C. Miles, eds. *The Babylonian Laws.* Vol. I. Oxford: The Clarendon Press, 1952.

Driver and Miles' work on Hammurabi's laws can be considered the standard English commentary. The first volume, after a disappointingly thin sketch of the background and antecedents of Hammurabi's laws, gives a massive and detailed historical and legal commentary on the laws themselves.

The authors explain that the laws are in no sense a code, but a series of amendments and restatements of laws in force at Hammurabi's time. The evidence indicates that Hammurabi simply chose for publication those particular laws he thought needed reemphasis by publication. In this respect, the laws are likened to the Anglo-Saxon *dooms* promulgated by rulers with the advice of their wise men. In neither case was there probably any conscious aim of constructing a code of law; rather, both Hammurabi and the Anglo-Saxons two-and-a-half millenia later were intent on declaring old customs and making amendments in matters of practical detail. Or again, Hammurabi's laws can be likened to a collection of decisions based on isolated individual cases. In studying Hammurabi's law, one is faced with the difficulty of dealing with a large number of amendments without access to the main body of the laws to which the amendments are related.

When due allowance has been made for these qualifications, however, it is still true that Hammurabi's work is built on recognizable principles of logic. The 282 articles are so grouped that they treat in turn: (1) offenses against the administration of justice; (2) offenses against property; (3) land and houses;

(4) trade and commerce; (5) marriage, family, and property; (6) assaults and talion; (7) professional men; (8) agriculture; (9) wages and rates of hire; and (10) slaves. The largest number of articles, eighty-eight, deal with marriage, family, and property. Among the important topics not touched upon are attempted murder, parricide, theft of chattels, and encroaching on a neighbor's land.

It is not known to what extent Hammurabi was personally responsible for the laws which bear his name. On the basis of extant letters which show Hammurabi's concern for matters of law and justice, however, Driver and Miles assume that his personal role was considerable and comparable to Napoleon's role in constructing the French code. Whatever the extent of Hammurabi's personal contribution, the laws themselves are remarkable for clarity and precision. The authors describe the compilation as a work of art in drafting, a model in its choice of accurate terminology with a pithy clarity.

In an attempt to help readers see Hammurabi's laws in Babylonian terms, the authors of the commentary make some keen observations on those particular matters where the ancient approach to law differs radically from our basic assumptions. Three points are particularly deserving of attention. First, the laws were not enforced by the Babylonian courts; they were more like rules or norms in which the spirit is more important than the letter. This conclusion is based on the fact that there is no evidence of any kind of verbal interpretation of Hammurabi's laws, nor any references to the exact wording of the laws in other Babylonian writings. It follows that the "laws" were not imperative; that is, parties to a dispute were free to make any agreements outside the law in an attempt to settle their differences. Second, the Babylonian documents dealing with property matters should not be seen as contracts, but as memoranda of transactions. The statements in the contract-like documents were liable to modification by oral evidence. Third, Driver and Miles make a distinction between ancient and primitive laws. While there are primitive elements in Hammurabi's law, some savage punishments, for example, in other respects the laws are in no sense a reflection of a primitive society.

Throughout the legal commentary, there are frequent comparisons between Babylonian and Hebrew law, a fact which adds greatly to the value of this work for the student of history of ideas or comparative cultures. For example, there are parallels between Hebrew laws and the form of Hammurabi's epilogue, with its list of blessings and curses.

A most significant contrast is in the law regarding treatment of slaves. Hebrew law (Exodus 21:20-21, 26-27) punishes a master who injures his own slave. It is clear that the Hebrew saw the slave as having a value higher than a mere piece of property. Hebrew law was interested in the slave himself, not only in the master's economic interests.

Both laws recognized talion, but probably accepted a compensation in place of an eye for an eye or a tooth for a tooth. Hebrew law (Exodus 21:15, 17) exacted a more severe penalty, death, for striking or cursing a parent, where Babylonian law was satisfied by mutilation.

Finally, it is worth noting that Driver and Miles take issue with the general view that the sculpture of the diorite stele, chief source of our knowledge of the laws, supposedly depicts the god Shamash handing the laws to Hammurabi. That some kind of homage is represented is clear, but according to Driver and Miles, this is all that can be deduced from the sculpture itself. Hammurabi himself claims to be the author of the laws. While he may have claimed divine sanction, there is no evidence that he presented the laws as divine revelation.

Speiser, E. A. "Authority and Law in Mesopotamia," in *Journal of the American Oriental Society.* Supplement 17, 1954.

While Speiser's article is not concerned solely, or even specifically, with Hammurabi's laws, it places the laws in their political and social context. The author's thesis is that it is a people's concept of state and law, much more than other institutions, which enable one to understand the distinctive features of a civilization.

Essential to any kind of penetration of Babylonian law is a grasp of the institution of kingship. An outstanding feature of kingship in ancient Mesopotamia was the ruler's subservience to the gods, played out in an elaborate ritual of interpretation of omens. In practice, this meant that the temple exercised a check on the court.

Another qualifying factor of the king's power lay in the assembly. Speiser shows that ultimate authority resided not in an individual ruler, but in a corporate assembly. There is literary evidence that Babylonians saw the king and assembly as complementary and as marking an advance over an earlier barbarous stage when they had no consultative government.

The laws of Hammurabi and the three earlier "codes" or fragments known to Sumerologists are to be understood, then, not as decrees issued by an autocratic ruler, but as expressions of consensus in a society where royal authority was limited by religion and by some kind of assembly.

Early Sumerian political and religious thought, which became normative for subsequent peoples who invaded or conquered the area between the Tigris and Euphrates, did not make a clear distinction between divine and human societies. Among the gods, as among their human counterparts, the Sumerians pictured a divine assembly as the ultimate source of authority. This notion of a divine assembly added to the significance of the assembly on earth. In Sumerian mythology, the cosmic body alone was competent to name the head of the pantheon, regulate the lengths of reigns, and to grant immortality to humans.

The legal system of Babylonian society as we have evidence of it in Hammurabi's laws had a double function: it reflected the concept of government here described; it also implemented it. Unfortunately, there is little or no extant data about the legal theory that underlay the law. A good case can be made that this is not a lacuna attributable to a loss of materials, but rather to the fact that the Babylonians of the eighteenth century B.C. had not devised a body of legal theory. However, there is much data about legal practice, so that it is possible to reconstruct something of the court system both as to structure and procedure. Legal theory, Speiser explains, can be deduced or reconstructed at least partially on the basis of two key concepts: *kittum*, which can roughly be translated "truth," and *mesarum*, or "justice."

Mesarum is a process of applying the law equitably, and this is one of the ruler's principal duties. To fulfill his role adequately, the ruler must not only supervise the application of the laws, but must also adapt them to contingencies. We can see, then, the meaning of the lengthy account of his exploits which Hammurabi gives in the epilogue to his set of laws. It is less a eulogy than an account of the conditions which provide a rationale for his selection and amendments of older and well-known laws.

An analysis of the concept *kittum*, or truth, shows that the king was not the source of the law, but only its agent. Here the Babylonian notion is close to the medieval idea that law is something discovered rather than something contrived or constructed. In the Babylonian value system, the cosmos is seen as founded on certain truths. The function of the law is to safeguard these truths, truths which bind the king as well as the lowliest slave. The ruler, therefore, is clearly under the law, not above it. Hammurabi himself succinctly expresses the meaning of *kittum* and *mesarum* when he speaks of himself as "the just king [*sar mesarum*], to whom Shamash [the sun-god] committed the truths."

The importance of statutes such as those known as Hammurabi's "code," a technical misnomer, now becomes clear. The collected statutes kept alive both the established traditions or customs, and also made possible the topical amendments to fit new circumstances.

Speiser concludes his treatment by reflecting that, together with the state, law was one of the unifying factors of Mesopotamian culture which influenced the Hittites, the Syrians, and ultimately many other peoples. On the negative side, he notes that the law was not conducive to ethical progress, and he attributes this to an underlying idea of the cosmos which saw ultimate authority, albeit collective, as arbitrary.

—*Mary Evelyn Jegen*

Additional Recommended Reading

Frankfort, Henri. *The Intellectual Adventure of Ancient Man.* Chicago: University of Chicago Press, 1946. A perceptive discussion of the Mesopotamian view of the function of the state.

Gadd, C. J. *Hammurabi and the End of His Dynasty.* Cambridge: The University Press, 1965. A fascicle of the revised *Cambridge Ancient History* containing a helpful bibliography.

Gordon, Cyrus. *Hammurabi's Code: Quaint or Forward-Looking?* New York: Holt, Rinehart & Winston, Inc., 1957. A brief study with a careful summary of the laws and a clear introductory essay.

Kramer, Samuel Noah. *The Sumerians: Their History, Culture and Character.* Chicago: University of Chicago Press, 1963. A treatise by a foremost Sumerologist on the cultural background of Babylonian civilization.

Pritchard, James B., ed. *The Ancient Near East—An Anthology of Texts and Pictures.* Princeton: Princeton University Press, 1958. A well-known collection containing translated fragments from antecedents of Hammurabi's laws and the text of Hammurabi's Code.

Wooley, Sir Leonard. *The Beginnings of Civilization.* New York: Harper and Row Publishers Incorporated, 1963. A part of the UNESCO *History of Civilizations* project, this book incorporates much recent research.

BATTLE OF KADESH

Type of event: Military: employment of ancient strategy
Time: Spring of 1296 B.C.
Locale: Southern Syria, about eighty miles northeast of modern Beirut

Principal personages:
MUWATALLISH, Hittite King 1310-1294
RAMSES II, Pharaoh of Egypt c. 1304-1237

Summary of Event

Carved on the walls and pylons of massive temples along the River Nile there remain pictorial and hieroglyphic reports of a military engagement between the Egyptians and the Hittites in 1296 B.C. which J. H. Breasted called "the earliest battle in history of which the strategy can be studied in detail."

Egypt had been intermittently at war with the Hittites in Syria for two hundred years, since Thutmose III in the early fifteenth century had extended his sway northward beyond the site of modern Lebanon. Later, however, Hittite kings had invaded Syria as far south as Kadesh, where the best routes inland from the Mediterranean Sea entered the valley of the Orontes River, chief passageway to the North and East. Thutmose III had once devoted an eight-year siege to conquer Kadesh, which now became the southern bastion of a widespread Hittite empire.

When Ramses II came to the throne about 1304 he desired to reassert Egyptian dominance in Syria. In the fourth year of his reign he sent troops north along the coast beyond modern Beirut to secure harbors, and then in his fifth year he personally led a large force through Palestine. His army was divided into four divisions named after the gods, Ra, Ptah, Amen, and Set, each division numbering about five thousand men. At the heart of this pharaonic army were professional charioteers, experts at using bows and spears.

Aware of the approach of Ramses, the Hittite King Muwatallish mustered a host of approximately equal size, between sixteen thousand and twenty thousand men, collected from vassal units of the Hittite empire, with at least half of his troops charioteers. Most Hittite chariots depicted in relief sculpture carried a driver along with two fighting men. With remarkable cunning Muwatallish concealed this large force from Egyptian scouts, and he sent several Bedouins to be captured by the Egyptians and to deceive Ramses about the location of the Hittites. Persuaded that the enemy was far to the north, Ramses allowed his army to straggle in their march with wide gaps between the divisions.

Only when the advance division, Amen, led by the Pharaoh himself, had crossed the Orontes River west of Kadesh did they discover, through the interrogation of new Hittite prisoners, that Muwatallish's main force was ominously near, just east of Kadesh. Alarmed, the Pharaoh hastily sent back a messenger and a staff officer to hurry forward the Ra division, next unit in line. But at this juncture Muwatallish, using the hill of Kadesh to screen his movement, launched his chariots in a surprise flank attack against the approaching Ra division. The Ra column was scattered in all directions.

Pursuing some Ra fugitives northwestward, Hittite chariots came upon the hill where Ramses with the Amen division was setting up camp; many of these Amen soldiers also broke and fled, leaving the Pha-

7

raoh with only a small bodyguard of chariots, encircled by the enemy. It was a perilous moment for the young Ramses. Nearly half his army had been slain or scattered, and the remaining units were far to his rear.

When the situation seemed desperate, according to eulogistic records carved later in Egypt, Ramses in his two-horse chariot charged into the midst of more than two thousand Hittite chariots and drove back the enemy. Emphasizing his personal heroism as divine, the sculptural accounts are vague about some timely aid which arrived in time to rescue Ramses. Modern historians generally credit these fresh troops, perhaps of the Ptah division, with rallying the scattered Egyptian forces, at a moment when Hittite charioteers were engaged in pillaging the Egyptian camp and chasing fugitives in several directions. The Hittites were driven back.

Muwatallish then brought into action another Hittite force of a thousand chariots and attempted six successive charges. However, these were driven off as additional Egyptian forces arrived on the battle scene, the Hittites suffering heavy losses. The next day Muwatallish may have agreed to a truce, once the entire Egyptian army had been assembled; the fresh division of Set had taken no part in the first day's battle. On the other hand Muwatallish had never used eight thousand foot soldiers stationed east of the river, perhaps because the swiftly changing strategy made less mobile infantry useless.

Even though Egyptian inscriptions claimed a triumph for Ramses, portraying the Kadesh plain as strewn with Hittite corpses, the Pharaoh's immediate retreat southward nevertheless evacuated the area as far as Damascus and left it in possession of the Hittites. More terse Hittite cuneiform inscriptions reveal that in their home cities the battle was reported as a crushing defeat for Egypt.

In the following years there were minor Egyptian campaigns into Palestine, but archaeologists have discovered both Egyptian and Hittite copies of a peace treaty drawn up fifteen years after the Battle of Kadesh between these two powers. The peace was sealed by a marriage of Ramses II to a Hittite princess, and we know of no subsequent battles between Egyptians and Hittites which compare in significance to the conflict at Kadesh. C. S. Ceram in his *Secret of the Hittites* calls the Battle of Kadesh one of the world's most important engagements because it "decided the fate of Syria and Palestine," and fixed the balance of power between Egypt and Khatti. Kadesh actually represented a truce between the two powers; it appears to have had a debilitating effect on the Hittites while it checked the rising glory of imperial Egypt. Both powers delineated their spheres of influence and became susceptible to the invading Sea Peoples shortly thereafter. The Pharaoh's retreat from the area and his marriage with the Hittite house does not really suggest the overwhelming victory recorded on the Egyptian inscriptions.

Pertinent Literature

Breasted, J. H. *The Battle of Kadesh.* First series, Vol. 5 of Decennial Publications. Chicago: University of Chicago Press, 1904.

This volume was the first detailed study in English of the numerous Egyptian inscriptions describing the Battle of Kadesh, and it was supplemented three years later by a more popular account in Breasted's *Ancient Records of Egypt.* Points of departure among scholars do not concern so much the battle itself as the records describing it. Breasted divides the inscriptions into three categories. First, there is what he calls the "Poem," a text not actually in poetic form which survives in hieroglyphic copies on towers at Luxor, on the walls of the huge temple at Karnak, and at Abydos, as well as in one hieratic manuscript. It provides a valuable account of Ramses' march north to Kadesh but only a confusing synopsis of the battle, focused on personal exploits of the Pharaoh.

Second, Breasted bases his reconstruction of the battle chiefly on what he calls "the Record," an inscription preserved at three different temples which gives a more consecutive narration about the battle than the "Poem." Third, Breasted publishes full-page drawings of many of the sculptured reliefs engraved in seven different versions on temple walls, one as far south as the great cliff sanctuary at Abu Simbel.

Breasted includes a review of geographical data along with detailed maps showing five stages of troop dispositions before and during the conflict at Kadesh. Critically analyzing evidence on the size of earlier and later Egyptian armies, he arrives at estimates of the forces of Ramses II at Kadesh, esti-

mates which have been generally accepted by later scholars. He then attempts to correlate literary and pictorial records so as to reconstruct the battle developments and strategies, offering hypotheses about obscure terms and sculptures.

While Breasted recognizes that the records leave vague the "recruits from Amor" who suddenly relieved Ramses in his most perilous moment, he theorizes that they were a regrouped section of the routed Amen division. He interprets the artistic representations to suggest that a high officer under Ramses hurried south to bring up the Ptah division, third force in the line of march, and it arrived in time to turn the tide of battle. Breasted also theorizes that Egyptian losses were heavier even than those of the Hittites. He attributes to "scribal flattery" the claim made in the "Poem" that Muwatallish humbly sought a truce on the morning after the battle.

Breasted's 1904 study remains a fundamental point of reference on this topic.

Gardiner, Alan H. *The Kadesh Inscriptions of Ramesses II.* Oxford: The University Press, for the Griffith Institute, 1960.

This publication by a distinguished Egyptologist offers a full translation of the various hieroglyphic records concerning Kadesh and a reassessment of their interdependence, considerably differing from the views of Breasted advanced more than fifty years earlier.

After a brief historical introduction, Gardiner arranges the translations in approximately the same order as Breasted. Following each translation is a line-by-line commentary, consisting mainly of philological notes for specialists. However, any serious student will find in Gardiner's translation and concluding discussions a valuable summary of a half century of scholarly publications in several languages, which have clarified obscurities in Breasted's texts and have added

insights from new sources such as Hittite inscriptions.

Gardiner attempts to show cooperative authorship for all the inscriptions, arguing that the so-called "Poem" would better be called a "literary record" intended to supplement the "pictorial record" of sculptural reliefs. He proposes that only Ramses himself could have inspired the elaborated records in such numerous versions; hence Gardiner believes that a few sculptors and scribes worked in close collaboration, putting into verbal form only such elements as could not be portrayed graphically. Thus many battle incidents were presented only in pictures, with brief legends or titles to identify figures and explain the actions.

In parallel columns Gardiner illustrates how the diverse inscriptions dovetail into each other, without as much inconsistency as earlier scholars assumed had resulted from unrelated efforts by different scribes and sculptors. Neither hieroglyphics nor sculptures were ever intended to be complete in themselves, and the double record illuminates "emotional and conceptual" aspects of the battle in ways which neither words nor sculpture could convey by themselves.

Hence, Gardiner argues, Ramses and his advisers "invented an entirely new technique of narration, one that recalls Greek drama or a modern film except that these latter are audible and dynamic. . . ." The Kadesh records are almost unique in Egyptian literature, paralleled only by a few captioned scenes carved earlier by Hatshepsut and some later sculptures placed by Ramses III. Since the scribes of Ramses II lacked experience in this double-media historiography, Gardiner considers their product to be "slipshod and repetitious."

In his detailed conclusions about the battle, Gardiner accepts the proposals of Eduard Meyer and A. H. Burne in the *Journal of Egyptian Archaeology*, 7, 191ff. that the "recruits from Amor" were troops arriving opportunely from detached assignment in the land of Amor.—*Roger B. McShane*

Additional Recommended Reading

Breasted, J. H. "The Age of Ramses II," in *The Cambridge Ancient History*. Vol. II, ch. 7. Cambridge: The University Press, 1924. Another clear summary of Breasted's viewpoints.
_____. *Ancient Records of Egypt*. New York: Russell and Russell, 1906, republished 1962. A study providing translations of Egyptian and Hittite records relating to the Battle of Kadesh.
The Cambridge Ancient History. Revised ed. Vol. II. Cambridge: The University Press, 1965. R. O. Faulkner in chapter 23 gives the Egyptian viewpoint, while A. Goetze in chapter 24 offers the Hittite perspective and a survey of the cuneiform records relating to the Battle of Kadesh.
Ceram, C. W. "The Battle of Kadesh," in *The Secret of the Hittites*. Ch. 9. New York: Alfred A. Knopf, Inc., 1963. A dramatic reconstruction of the event.
Gardiner, Alan H. *Egypt of the Pharaohs*. Ch. 10. New York: Oxford University Press, 1966. A discussion of the Battle of Kadesh and related inscriptions is included in this work.
Richard, James B., ed. *Ancient Near Eastern Texts Relating to the Old Testament*. Princeton: Princeton University Press, 1955. A well-known work giving ancient texts in translation.

ESTABLISHMENT OF THE UNITED KINGDOM

Type of event: Political: transformation of a tribal confederacy into a monarchy
Time: c. 1000 B.C.
Locale: Palestine

Principal personages:
SAMUEL, Hebrew visionary of Ramah appearing c. 1070, sponsor
  of Saul
SAUL, Benjamite peasant, first King of Israel c. 1020-c. 1000
DAVID, Judean peasant, leader of mercenary troops, King first of
  Judah c. 1000, and later of Israel also c. 993-c. 961
ABNER, military commander of Saul's troops
JOAB, military commander of David's troops
ISHBAAL, fourth son and successor of Saul as King over Israel
  c. 1000-c. 993

Summary of Event

The settlement of the Philistines along the southern coast of Palestine at the beginning of the eleventh century B.C. presented the Hebrew tribes occupying the central and southern hills with a challenge that could not be met through the military institutions of Israel's loose tribal confederacy. Coming from Crete, whence they had been displaced along with many other Aegean peoples in the turbulent era following the Dorian invasion, the Philistines brought with them the first iron tools and weapons known in Palestine. They organized themselves into five strong city-states and soon began to thrust inland into Hebrew territory. For two centuries the Hebrew tribes had successfully put together armies of peasantry led by temporary charismatic leaders, or "judges," to meet crises of invasion or threat from Canaanite city-states, but in a battle fought about 1050 B.C. the Hebrews were decisively defeated and the Ark of the Covenant itself was captured, after which the Philistines established garrisons in the central hill country.

With Israel pressed by the Philistines on the West, the Ammonites east of the Jordan seized the opportunity to regain territories

previously lost to the Hebrew tribe of Gilead to their north and laid siege to the Gileadite city of Jabesh. At this point Saul emerged as a charismatic military leader of combined tribal forces that routed the Ammonites and relieved the siege of Jabesh. On their return across the Jordan, the Israelite militia elected Saul king, and for the next several years he maintained a standing army and engaged Philistine troops in battle with varying degrees of success.

The Hebrew tradition regarding the emergence of the monarchy in this crisis is contained in the first book of Samuel; it is a composite narrative woven together from two sources, each of which has its own distinct and antithetical account of events and their evaluation. One source gives the account presented above, that Saul emerged as a political leader with a standing army following his successful leadership of the campaign against the Ammonites. The other source presents Saul as a figure subordinate to Samuel, who is portrayed as the last judge and the first prophet. Samuel, according to this account, commissioned Saul as a prince and anointed him as king over Israel after strongly protesting Israel's demand for a king in order to be "like the nations" and after warning of the dangers to be expected by Israel from the institution of dynastic monarchy. Upon Saul's failure to fulfill to the letter Samuel's instructions to conduct a holy war against the Amalekites in the south, Samuel proclaimed Saul's rejection by Yahweh and anointed David to be king in his stead. Saul did, however, continue in actuality to exercise rule over Israel in spite of the action of Samuel in "deposing" him in favor of David.

The traditions regarding the emergence of Saul's successor, David, are partly legendary. As a young man he was a member of Saul's court, a close friend of Saul's son Jonathan, and was given Saul's daughter Michal as wife. His popularity aroused Saul's jealousy and eventually he fled to the south, where he organized a guerrilla band and ingratiated himself with Hebrew tribesmen of Judah by warring on Amalekites and other groups that had long harassed them. At the same time, he took service with the Philistine Achish, King of Gath, as a mercenary leader of his warrior band. The fortunes of Saul continued to fall as a consequence of his alienation of the priesthood of Yahweh and his own mentally disturbed condition. He was finally decisively defeated and met his death in battle with the Philistines at Mount Gilboa. Saul's surviving son, Ishbaal, was taken by Abner,

his commander, to Mahanaim, east of the Jordan, and nominally made king. David in the meantime was elected king of Judah by tribal elders at Hebron. In the ensuing period of intrigue, Abner and Ishbaal were both assassinated, and in a second assembly at Hebron elders of the northern tribes made David king over Israel. All the Hebrew tribes were thus now bound to David in a united monarchy over Israel and Judah.

David now consolidated his hold upon the kingdom by decisive victories over the Philistines, Ammonites, Aramaeans, Moabites, and Edomites; by bringing the Canaanite city-states of Palestine under his own power; and by conquering the centrally-situated Jebusite city of Jerusalem, which he made the capital of his kingdom. There he established a centralized political administration and gave his state a solid legitimacy by bringing the Ark of the Covenant to Jerusalem and establishing the cult of Yahweh as an official institution. The measure of his success in state-building is the oracle of Nathan the prophet, as recorded in II Samuel 7, wherein Yahweh guaranteed the perpetuity of David's dynasty. For the brief period of less than a century of rule by David and his son Solomon, Israel enjoyed political unity, a considerable empire with international prestige, a flourishing economy, and a culture expressing the high spirits of successful nationalism.

Pertinent Literature

Alt, Albrecht. "The Formation of the Israelite State in Palestine," in *Essays on Old Testament History and Religion.* Pp. 223-309. Garden City, New York: Doubleday & Company, Inc., 1967.

In this study of the constitutional development of the monarchies of Saul, David, and Solomon, Albrecht Alt concentrates on the impact of Philistine and Canaanite military institutions on the earlier charismatic military leadership of the Hebrew tribal confederacy. The Philistines, professional soldiers ruled by city-state kings grouped in a league situated on the southwestern Palestinian littoral, had succeeded by 1250 in establishing a feudal hegemony over central Palestine. Their intention was to dominate Palestine as a ruling military class exacting tribute from Hebrew and Canaanite farmers and herdsmen. The Hebrew tribes, widely dispersed throughout the mountainous hinterland, had no common political organization and were united only by common loyalty to Yahweh, but their military defensive operations were conducted independently of tribal political organization by charismatic leaders, each appointed by Yahweh as "judge" in time of crisis.

Saul's rise to power was based initially on this traditional charisma, by which he united tribal conscripts for a successful campaign against Ammon, but at Gilgal the assembled militia proclaimed him, probably in solemn convenant, as "king," granting him continuing military authority based on the need for recurrent military conscription and continuity of command in the face of the magnitude of the Philistine crisis. Once established in this position, Saul relied not only on Israelite conscripts but also increasingly on a band of professional guerrilla-type warriors, a feature copied from Philistine military organization. No dynastic principle had been accepted by Israel, and the effort of Abner to secure the position of Saul's son, Ishbaal, to succeed his father after the disaster of Mount Gilboa failed for want of Yahweh's charismatic designation of Ishbaal as judge and Ishbaal's failure to be accepted by the conscript army of Israel as king.

David's rise to power was set in the context of Saul's professional soldiery, clearly the most effective response to the Philistine challenge. Finally, there was a repetition by David of the pattern of Saul's ascendancy. Perhaps by a fiction, David was declared endowed with Yahweh's charisma, and his success in war brought him acclamation as commander by the tribal elders, first of Judah and later of Israel. But David's military success came not through leadership of conscripts but rather through his own force of professional soldiers personally loyal to him. After the break with Saul, David's rise to power proceeded outside the territory and

political framework of the Israelite state. He was first a feudal prince over Ziklag as a vassal of the Philistine ruler of Gath, then acclaimed king over Judah at Hebron in solemn covenant. Judah was not a tribal state, Alt insists; it incorporated several distinct ethnic groups in southern Palestine.

The structure of David's regime was an amalgam of Hebraic and Canaanite types of monarchy bound together in the person of the king rather than organically. The covenant of Israel's elders with David was independent of the earlier covenant made by the elders of Judah. Jerusalem, a Canaanite city outside the Hebrew territories, was conquered and made a private royal domain of David as a king of a city-state. The Philistines were defeated but allowed to retain internal political control with their kings functioning as David's vassals. The Canaanite cities of the northwest plains were conquered and incorporated into the tribal territories of Israel on the basis of ancient territorial claims of the tribes, but they were not occupied by Hebrews, and provincial administrative boundaries were set to preserve the ethnic distinctions between Canaanite and Hebrew. Conquests east of the Jordan were made either vassal states subject to David on the pattern of the Philistine cities or else made royal domains of David on the pattern of Jerusalem.

Powerful tensions within David's empire were created by his unprecedented use of the conscript armies of Israel year after year for campaigns of conquest east of the Jordan River. In Israel's view, David exceeded his constitutional powers, and Alt believes that the internal crisis of the succession in David's reign was related to the burden of the military levy. The rebellion of Absalom was supported by Israel in the effort to replace David with a king more to Israel's liking, but it was put down by David's professional troops. The later rebellion of Sheba was an effort by Israel to withdraw from the personal union of the kingdom of Israel with that of Judah, and this effort was thwarted by the combined professional forces of David and the conscript army of Judah. Alt relates Solomon's avoidance of expansion of the empire to the idea of preventing further tension that might be created by use of the conscript armies for conquest. In the dynastic succession of Solomon to David's throne, the old concept of Yahweh's designation of commander by charisma is replaced by the new concept of Yahweh's covenant with the house of David, but this conception was accepted only by Judah, and at Solomon's death the whole imperial structure of Palestine, based as it was on the personal union of distinct political entities, fell apart and reverted to earlier conditions: the coexistence of several ethnic polities in Palestine.

Noth, Martin. *The History of Israel.* 2nd ed. New York: Harper & Row Publishers Incorporated, 1960.

Whereas Alt's account of the establishment of monarchy in Israel concentrates on development of constitutional forms, Noth focuses on the episodic and transitional character of Saul's rule and on the deliberately planned rise to power of David. Noting that monarchy came late in Israel's history in comparison with neighboring states, Noth argues that the anti-monarchic source in Samuel, though late in composition, must reflect the actual sentiments of many Israelites still loyal to the thought expressed by Gideon: Israel can have no king or dynasty because Yahweh alone rules over Israel. The conflict between the traditional concept of charismatic military leadership and continuous military and political authority is represented in both sources of Samuel by the conflict between Samuel and Saul. Samuel did encourage Saul to accept the charismatic role of judge in the crisis of the Ammonite siege of Jabesh but was unprepared for the acclamation of Saul as king by the militia at Gilgal, and he attempted to stop the development of Saul's power into a political role usurping religious functions. At any rate, Saul's success was short-lived. Two surprise victories over Philistine garrisons immediately following his acclamation as king did not establish the real authority of Israel over the Philistines, and in the decisive encounter at Mt. Gilboa the following spring, Saul and his army were disastrously overwhelmed by the Philistines. Noth thus accepts the indication of I Samuel 13:1 that Saul reigned for two years only, a figure thought by most scholars to be based on a corrupt text at that point.

In dealing with David's rise to power, Noth emphasizes the deliberate plan by which the young man of extraordinary political acumen ingratiated himself with the elders of Judah as a condottiere of a troop of professional soldiers, instigated his acclamation as king over Judah at Hebron, sought to secure a dynastic right to succeed Saul by marrying his daughter Michal, and profited from the murders of Abner and Ishbaal when a deputation of elders of Israel came to Hebron and acclaimed him king over Israel. Noth does not hold David responsible for the two murders. Thus, where Alt sees David's rise as engineered by the historical logic of events, specifically his role as commander of the only kind of army capable of meeting the Philistine military challenge, Noth sees a more deliberate scheme of planning, waiting, and seizing of opportunities presented to David in their proper course.

The struggle for the succession among David's sons is not so closely related by Noth as by Alt, who stresses Israelite dissatisfaction with David's imperial policies and exploitation of the conscript militia for trans-Jordanian conquest, but Noth does note that there must have been concern among the tribes as to whether David's policies perhaps exceeded Israel's authentic history, since Israel was only a portion of David's essentially personal empire. —*Carl W. Conrad*

Additional Recommended Reading

Bright, John. "From Tribal Confederacy to Dynastic State," in *A History of Israel*. Ch. 5. Philadelphia: Westminster Press, 1959. A detailed treatment with careful analysis of the sources.

De Vaux, Roland. "The Israelite Concept of the State," in *Ancient Israel*. Vol. 1: *Social Institutions*. Pt. II, ch. 4. New York: McGraw-Hill Book Company, 1965. A systematic presentation of the form and development of the monarchy in Israel.

Ehrlich, Ernst Ludwig. *A Concise History of Israel*. Chs. 7 & 8. New York: Harper & Row Publishers Incorporated, 1965. A concise evaluation of the reigns of Saul and David.

Hertzberg, Hans Wilhelm. *I & II Samuel: A Commentary*. Philadelphia: Westminster Press, 1965. A text and commentary dealing fully with source-analysis and historical evaluation of the chief historical document of the period.

ESTABLISHMENT OF THE KINGDOM OF ISRAEL

Type of event: Religious: division of Hebrew polity
Time: 922 B.C.
Locale: Palestine

Principal personages:
SOLOMON, King of the united nation 961-922
REHOBOAM, King of Judah 922-915
JEROBOAM, first King of Israel 922-901
SHEBA, a Benjamite
AHIJAH, a prophet

Summary of Event

The pressing problem of the Hebrews was to forge a group of independent tribes into a strong functioning nation in order to conquer Canaan and subdue the Philistines and their allies. Although there had been some feeling of unity among the Hebrew tribes which settled in Canaan, it took approximately two hundred years for a unified state to evolve. Even when once organized, it apparently never overcame the vested interests of groups and individuals for it managed to survive for less than a century.

At first the tribes acted together occasionally under the temporary leadership of a hero called a "judge" in the Bible. By 1000, it became evident that a more stable unity under a permanent king was desirable, and Saul was called upon to rule. His death at the hands of the Philistines on Mt. Gilboa allowed David, who had to some extent already usurped power under Saul, to be declared next leader of the united tribes. Apparently he won confirmation as king through a covenant with the tribes which left them some autonomy as well as the right to confirm his successors in office. Symptomatic of the lack of full acquiescence, especially on the part of the northern tribes, were the rebellions by David's son, Absalom, and by Sheba, a Benjamite. According to II Samuel 20:2 only "the men of Judah followed their king steadfastly."

Resentment against the monarchy increased, especially in the north during the reign of Solomon. Heavy exactions in money and men necessitated by his ambitious building programs became increasingly distasteful, as did his commercial alliance with Tyre involving repayment for supplies and services employed in the construction of the Temple. The tribal covenant entered into by David was virtually ignored; Judah was preferentially exempted from many of the onerous provisions demanded of the other tribes. More disturbing was Solomon's program of centralization which weakened the power of individual tribes by destroying their traditional boundaries through the creation of new administrative districts.

After Solomon's death, his son Rehoboam was immediately accepted as king by Judah. When Israel demurred, Rehoboam went to Shechem, the historic covenant center where Jacob had gone after his return from Haran and where the national assembly had been held in the time of Joshua. The assembled Israelites demanded that the oppressive rule imposed by Solomon be lightened, and they reminded Rehoboam that a king could not take the principle of hereditary monarchy for granted; nor did they intend to tolerate a second Solomon with a resplendent court resulting in extravagant demands for taxes and labor drafts.

When Rehoboam unfortunately heeded the advice of his luxury-minded young courtiers to ignore the demands of the northern Israelites, Jeroboam, a seditious leader of one of Solomon's labor battalions who had been forced to flee to Egypt for asylum, returned to take advantage of the new discontent. He was supported by the prophet Ahijah, who announced symbolically, by tearing a garment in ten pieces, that ten tribes would follow Jeroboam. Consequently, Jeroboam was proclaimed king at the Shechem assembly. He established his capital first at Shechem and then at Tirzah, placing sanctuaries at Dan and Bethel thus ending the united kingdom.

While the immediate cause of the breakup was the heavy-handed reign of the despotic Solomon which curtailed tribal freedoms and favored the south, the schism had deeper underlying causes. The hilly terrain encouraged sectional insularity. Each section had a different geography and therefore different economic orientation. The north, facing toward the plains, was agricultural and commercial; Judah, oriented toward the desert, was pastoral and nomadic. Moreover, the original separation of the northern or Jacob Hebrews and the southern or Abraham Hebrews was too deeply rooted to be wiped out in one or two generations. While Jeroboam and others had a personal interest in the breakup of the kingdom, the vital factor was the constant reassertion of tribal sympathies with all their religious implications. Whenever the northern Israelites established new religious centers, they implied the tacit rebellion of localism against the centralized regime in Jerusalem.

The northern branch of the Hebrew nation proved much stronger in population, economic resources, and cultural initiative. It possessed more fertile lands and its plain of Esdraelon controlled international highways. However, when great new empires arose in the vicinity, the more isolated and poorer Judah survived longer. Israel was destroyed by Assyria in 721, and became another "lost nation"; survival of Judaism was left to the weaker Judah.

Pertinent Literature

Lods, Adolphe. *Israel from Its Beginnings to the Middle of the Eighth Century.* Translated by S. H. Hooke. London: Routledge and Kegan Paul Ltd., 1932.

According to the Biblical account, the division of the Jewish nation involved a religious schism. It states that Jeroboam, fearing that the north would return to its allegiance to the "rightful" king, conceived the idea of making two golden calves, one at Bethel and the other at Dan, so that pilgrimages to Jerusalem would be unnecessary. Reputedly he also established other religious sanctuaries in high places, and appointed priests from outside the ranks of the Levites.

Lods shows that such an account is anachronistic. Jeroboam's supposed religious innovations would be disturbing only after the Josianic reforms in the late seventh century. Lods believes that passages in the Bible amply confirm the contention that the importations attributed to Jeroboam were actually old customs which had persisted in Israel after Judah had long abandoned or modified them. High sanctuaries devoted to local gods even in Judah were not condemned until the seventh century and non-Levite priests were still common in the time of David, since the priestly prerogatives of Levites were not established until the eighth century. The worship of golden calves was also well established in both south and north.

17

Any religious motivation to the split, Lods notes, would more likely have come from the desire to defend the traditional simplicity of Yahweh worship against the luxurious temple cult. The northerners were the religious conservatives; already the prophets Nathan and Ahijah were not enthusiastic about the Temple. The north rather than the south maintained itself as the true home of primitive Yahwism; the prophets Elijah, Elisha, Micaiah ben Imlah, Hosea, and even Amos, all came from Judah. Lods concludes that the split, then, was primarily political, with little if any of the religious motivation the Biblical account presents as primary.

Far from motivating the split, religion remained even after the schism a uniting force. Yahweh was still the one god of the two kingdoms; the Jews were still basically only one people, the people of Yahweh. Both parts, retaining the consciousness of belonging to a single religious nation, desired to reestablish unity but in different ways. The southern legitimists hoped for a return of the Israelite rebels to the authority of "David," while the northerners, and even some Judeans, felt that Judah should make the *rapprochement.*

Lods prefers to think that the difficulties stemmed from the persistent tribal consciousness which refused to be submerged in a larger state loyalty necessarily emerging out of the new conditions of a settled mode of life. Consolidation and centralization mitigated against ingrained ancient Bedouin individualism that was so strong in its opposition to a sophisticated commercial society.

Fleming, John Dick. *Israel's Golden Age: The Story of the United Kingdom.* Edinburgh: T. and T. Clark, 1907.

Fleming sees the period of the united Hebrew kingdom as the high point of ancient Jewish history, even though it soon decayed. During a single century the united kingdom solved many serious problems and precociously passed through all the successive stages of development: youth, manhood, and declining old age. Saul awakened the nation to a consciousness of its strength. Under David it reached its zenith of power and entered upon a course of vigorous development. During the reign of Solomon the first signs of decadence appeared; advances in expansion of trade, increase in wealth and luxury, and other refinements of civilization were dimming the great goals of the nation. The unity imposed upon the Jews was purchased dearly at the price of absolute, disciplined tyranny. Pompous religious ceremonial betraying a secularizing spirit obscured Israel's distinctive, yet simple, spiritual mission and character.

Jeroboam adroitly marshaled the attitude of general disaffection with the monarchy. As an overseer of the work on the fortifications for Jerusalem he had a good opportunity to learn the temper of Solomon's subjects and apparently sympathized with their complaints, encouraging a spirit of sedition. His action forced him into exile in Egypt. After Solomon's death Jeroboam returned to lead the rebellion. The division of the kingdom, according to Fleming, was fatal to the nation's prosperity and disastrous in other respects. The elements of inner discord, which had been conciliated or suppressed while the kingdom was united, now revived and prevented further growth. The nation wore itself out in fifty years, never again to rise to its former glory. Religious life also suffered irreparably. Rather than advancing along the line David chartered for it, the state reverted to the conditions of previous anarchic periods. Contrary to the view of Lods, Fleming sees a revival of heathenism and an increase in idolatry, particularly in the north.

—Joseph R. Rosenbloom

Additional Recommended Reading

Albright, W. F. *The Biblical Period from Abraham to Ezra.* New York: Harper & Row Publishers Incorporated, 1963. A concise, detailed account of a controversial period of Jewish history.

Bright, J. *Early Israel in Recent History Writing.* London: Student Christian Movement Press, 1956. A critical history in terms of modern scholarship.

Johnson, Paul. *A History of the Jews.* New York: Harper & Row, 1987. A lively, insightful account of Jewish history from its origins to the present that emphasizes the unique characteristics of Jewish history and the Jewish impact on the world.

Noth, Martin. *The History of Israel.* Translated by Stanley Goodman. New York: Harper & Row Publishers Incorporated, 1958. An excellent general history.

Orlinsky, Harry. *Ancient Israel.* Ithaca: Cornell University Press, 1964. A brief history of the period.

Robinson, H. Wheeler. *The History of Israel.* London: Duckworth, 1957. A sound general account of Hebrew history.

Robinson, Theodore H. *The Decline and Fall of the Hebrew Kingdoms.* Oxford: The University Press, 1926. A detailed account based directly on accounts of the Biblical prophets.

FOUNDING OF SYRACUSE

Type of event: Political: settlement of an overseas colony
Time: c. 733 B.C.
Locale: Southeastern coast of Sicily

Principal personage:
ARCHIAS, Corinthian nobleman, founder of Syracuse

Summary of Event

Greece has always been a poor country economically. Deposits of minerals are not extensive, and the soil itself is thin and stony. Much of the land is mountainous, so that only a quarter of its surface has ever been arable. At the dawn of Greek history, Homer observed that Hellas was married to poverty. As time went on and the population of Greece grew, many states found themselves unable to support their citizens. The result was an acute need for more land, and since it could be found only by emigration overseas, colonization began around 750 B.C. and continued for approximately five centuries. Overpopulation was always a major cause.

One of the first states to send out colonies was Corinth, even though she was, by Greek standards, proverbially wealthy. Her position on the isthmus placed her astride both the land route between the Peloponnesus and central Greece, and the short overland connection between the Corinthian and Saronic Gulfs. She charged tolls on both routes, but the revenue received was insufficient to pay for imported food. Therefore, about 733 B.C., Corinth decided to dispatch two expeditions overseas. Archias, a member of the noble family of the Bacchiadae, was selected to be the founder of the colony which was to settle on the east coast of the fertile island of Sicily. If the Corinthians followed the procedure that we know was used later, they consulted the god Apollo at Delphi to receive his sanction for the venture and perhaps some useful advice.

Unfortunately, we know nothing of the story of the voyage to Sicily or of the early years of the new colony. We can say that the risks the Corinthians faced were about equal to those encountered by European settlers in America in the seventeenth century. While the Atlantic Ocean is more dangerous than the Mediterranean Sea, the Europeans had larger and stronger ships than the Greeks, compasses for steering, and fairly good ideas on how to navigate by sun and stars. They also had firearms to defend themselves against counterattacks by the original occupants of the land, while the Greeks had essentially the same weapons as the people they dispossessed. We do know, however, that Archias and his Corinthian force succeeded, and that within a generation or two Syracuse became a large and flourishing state. As a colony, it was not governed by Corinth, but was fully autonomous. Corinth and Syracuse always enjoyed the close and amicable relations typical of the relationship between a Greek metropolis and her offshoots, for war between colony and mother city was felt to be a particularly shameful thing. There were exceptions, of course, as in the case of Corcyra, also founded by Corinth about 733; we know of two wars fought between her and Corinth before the end of the fifth century, and there are indications that there may have been others.

Syracuse became so mighty and populous that it was forced to send out its own colonies to other parts of Sicily; and the mother city and her daughter states came to play an important role in the life and history of Sicily. At the beginning of the fourth century B.C., Syracuse was powerful enough under the tyrant Dionysius to attempt with temporary success to impose her hegemony on Sicily and southern Italy. The city became a brilliant center of Greek civilization and played a role of exceptional historical importance, for it was through it more than any other state that Hellenic culture was transmitted to Rome from Greece and from Hellenistic Alexandria.

After 650 B.C. a second motive for colonization supplemented the drive to acquire more land for agriculture; some colonies were founded for commercial reasons. For example, shortly before 600, Naucratis was established in Egypt by Miletus, Aegina, Samos, and some smaller states as depots for badly needed exports of grain from Egypt to

Greece. In the west Massilia founded Emporium, whose name, "Trading Station," shows the intention of the founding city. Massilia, the modern Marseilles, also propagated Greek civilization up the valley of the Rhone into southern Gaul.

Corinth was not the only city to colonize extensively. Mention should also be made of Eretria, located on the island of Euboea, which settled many places on the northern coast of the Aegean, and the Miletus, an Ionian city with colonies especially numerous along the Black Sea coast. All this activity was of great significance, since Hellenism was spread from its original homeland into many parts of the Mediterranean. The Black Sea gradually became a Hellenic lake, and virtually all Sicily and the coastal regions of southern Italy were Hellenized by the descendents of the original Greek settlers of the western Mediterranean.

Pertinent Literature

Dunbabin, T. J. *The Western Greeks.* Oxford: The Clarendon Press, 1948.

One of the most fertile areas of Greek colonization was to the west of Hellas in Sicily and southern Italy. This region saw the establishment of many famous and powerful Greek states. Dunbabin's book covers the history of these western foundations from the time they were first sent out in the mid-eighth century, to 480 B.C. when Gelon of Syracuse defeated an attempt by the Carthaginians to extend their sway over the island and thus inaugurated the golden age of Hellenism in Sicily.

The early history of Greek Sicily is only partly known; literary evidence of the Greek invasion of the west is unfortunately scanty, so that one is forced to rely heavily upon the results of excavation. While pottery and other artifacts abound, their significance is difficult to establish. Sicily had been known to the inhabitants of Greece since early times,

as is proved by finds of Mycenean pottery in the island. It is with the eighth century that extensive amounts of Hellenic pottery begin to be found there. These deposits show that the Greeks had taken increased interest in Sicily at least a generation before the first wave of settlers set out about 750. Dunbabin thinks that the Greeks desired trade with the West, and that this was from the beginning one of the powerful motives leading to the foundation of the western colonies, although he agrees that land hunger was also a driving force. In regard to Syracuse, he points out that the city was built on the finest harbor on the eastern coast, and from this undoubted fact he concludes that commercial motives must have lain behind the choice of site. This conclusion may be right, but reasons for the geographical situation of the city are open to more than this one interpretation. Syracuse was originally built on a small island, later connected to the mainland by a short causeway; the intention of Archias may actually have been to settle in a place which could easily be defended against the native population in the hinterland.

The pre-Hellenic inhabitants of Sicily were the Sicels, or Sicans. From the time of their first contact with the Greeks they began slowly to exchange their native ways for Greek, so that by about the mid-fifth century B.C., the Sicels were almost completely assimilated into Hellenic culture. Hellenization proceeded in a number of ways. As Greek power gradually penetrated inland, Sicel communities were sometimes enslaved wholesale, up-rooted, and forced to work in a Greek environment. Gentler means, however, were also used; some Greek states made alliances with the more primitive Sicels and a few even permitted intermarriage. In these circumstances, the Sicels slowly changed themselves into Greeks by adopting the language and culture of the superior invaders. The island came to be thoroughly Hellenized except for the western tip, which for a time was under Cartha-

ginian influence. The Hellenization of southern Italy, however, proceeded much more slowly and less completely than that of Sicily, and although Greek civilization was known to mountain peoples such as the Samnites, they retained a good deal of their native Italian culture. Hellenism took hold best along the southern and western coasts at places like Taras (Tarentum) and Locri.

Colonies of the Dorian states of the Peloponnesus originally dominated the West, but later Ionian and Athenian influence began to be felt. This influence was all to the good for the development of the higher and finer aspects of Hellenism, for the level of civilization in the first colonies, as might be expected, lagged behind developments in Greece itself. While the western Greeks produced the remarkable law-givers Zaleucus of Locri and Charondas of Catana, it was not until the fifth century that Sicily and Italy came into their own and gave birth to such important figures as the philosopher Empedocles of Acragas and the rhetorician Gorgias of Leontini.

Graham, A. J. *Colony and Mother City in Ancient Greece.* Manchester: Manchester University Press, 1964.

One of the simple, old misconceptions of the status of colonial states in the Greek world was that each one became a completely free and sovereign new city. Graham's book shows that such independence was far from common and that any one of a number of different relationships between colony and metropolis might actually exist.

The foundation of a colony was almost always an official act of the founding state, and it sometimes occurred, therefore, that the mother city laid down conditions governing the life of the new colony. The metropolis provided the official Founder, *Oecist*, who was charged with the hazardous task of leading the settlers to the new site. The *Oecist*

was usually accorded the honors due a hero, a sort of semidivine being, and he was invariably worshiped after his death. The settlers took fire from the public hearth of the old city as a visible and material sign of the very definite religious links between the old city and the new. The colonists departed under the terms of an official act. Unfortunately, there are only a few examples of such foundation decrees extant, and all come from the fifth century or later, after the first great wave of colonists had emigrated. But these few surviving fragments help to illustrate some of the stipulations a metropolis might lay down.

Graham points out that the precise relations established depended upon a number of things. Primarily, there was the motive or temper of the founding city. Megara, for example, seems to have kept no control whatsoever over her colonies, and there is little evidence of her maintaining close relations with them. On the other hand, Miletus, a great trading state, founded many important colonies in the northern Aegean and Black Seas. She did not directly control them, but she did maintain close connections. Citizenship was mutual; that is, a Milesian who moved to Olbia could become legally a citizen of Olbia if he wished, and the Olbian a citizen of Miletus. Thasos, herself a colony of Paros, exercised real control over her foundations along the mineral-rich north shore of the Aegean. Here a second factor came into play: Thasos was quite close to her settlements, much closer than Miletus was to hers, so that the difficulties created by sheer distance were lacking.

Of all the important colonizing states of the early period, Corinth kept the closest control over her new colonies. She seems to have been determined to use them to help control the sea routes through the Gulf of Corinth in order to protect her imports of grain and other vital raw stuffs. The places settled by the Corinthian tyrants between 650 and 550, places such as Ambracia and Leu-cas, were subject to definite obligations. They were not only to perform certain religious duties and to use money nearly identical with that of the mother city, but they were also bound to have the same friends and enemies as Corinth and to be her allies in war. Graham, therefore, writes of Corinth and her colonial empire.

Athens did not take part in the early colonizing movement. By the fifth century, however, when she was faced with a rapidly expanding population, she sent out many settlements of a new kind. The old, independent colony of the archaic period, called *apoecia* in Greek, almost always had the status of a separate state, even if it was subject in one or more ways to the home government. The Athenians also developed a new legal concept which kept the settlers Athenian citizens still subject to the laws and the policies of the Assembly at Athens. It is likely that this kind of colony, called *cleruchy*, was intended to be an Athenian imperial outpost which might help the mother city to control the empire she had created in the Aegean. Since the colonists remained Athenians subject to Athens' will, the mother city was in no way deprived of military manpower or her ability to exercise her strength in strategic fashion. —*Samuel K. Eddy*

Additional Recommended Reading

Hadas, Moses. *Hellenistic Culture: Fusion and Diffusion.* New York: Columbia University Press, 1957. A study of the interaction between Hellenism and native Oriental cultures in the Hellenistic period, the last great age of Greek colonization.

Huxley, G. L. *The Early Ionians.* London: Faber and Faber, 1966. A description not only of the settlement of Ionian colonies but also of the contributions made by Ionians to Greek culture.

Roebuck, Carl A. *Ionian Trade and Colonization.* New York: Archaeological Institute of America, 1959. A useful account of Ionian colonization and its relationship to trade.

Rostovtzeff, M. I. *Iranians and Greeks in South Russia.* Oxford: The Clarendon Press, 1922. This classic work studies the contacts between Scyths and Greeks in the Black Sea region.

ISSUANCE OF DRACO'S CODE

Type of event: Legal: enactment of a general code of laws
Time: 621/620 B.C.
Locale: Athens

Principal personages:
DRACO, semimythical lawgiver
XENOPHANES (or ATHENOPHANES), who had Draco's homicide law
written on a stele in front of the Royal Portico

Summary of Event

According to ancient traditions, Draco was a Greek legislator who drew up the first code of law for the Athenians during the archonship of Aristaechmus in 621/620 B.C. Though Draco and his laws are mentioned over fifty times in various sources, the evidence is so conflicting that it is difficult to determine the nature and extent of his legislation. It has even been denied by such competent scholars as Beloch, De Sanctis, and Aymard that there ever was a human lawgiver with this name, the Greek *drakon* referring instead to a "serpent god" that the Athenians credited with drawing up their first legal code. However, Draco was also a common personal name. Prodicus was aware of the difficulty surrounding the word *drakon*, and his famous pun reported in Aristotle's *Rhetoric* scarcely makes sense if the Athenians believed that their lawgiver was a snake: "They are not the laws of a man but of a 'snake,' so severe are they."

Other scholars have maintained that much of the evidence regarding Draco's legislation is the product of fourth century research and merely proves, if anything, that he drew up some laws regarding homicide. Such narrow interpretation of his activities, however, does not really agree with all the evidence available. Aristotle obviously attributed laws other than those on homicide to Draco. He states in his *Constitution of Athens*, for instance, that after Solon had drawn up a constitution

and enacted new laws, "the ordinances of Draco ceased to be used, with the exception of those pertaining to murder [i.e. homicide]." Writers as early as Xenophon and Lysias refer to Draconian laws which were no longer in force. In 403, Tisamenus enacted a decree providing for the enforcement of the laws of Solon and of Draco as in earlier times. Various sources indicate that the legislation of Draco appeared to cover, in addition to homicide, such crimes as theft, vagrancy, adultery, the corruption of youth, neglect of the gods, and violation of the oath taken by jurors. Like other early lawgivers, Draco probably did not so much initiate new legislation as reduce customary law to an orderly and usable form in writing. He may also have drawn upon the decisions of earlier magistrates as recorded by the thesmothetes, or judges. According to Aristotle's *Politics*, there was nothing unusual enough to mention about Draco's laws "except the greatness and severity of their penalties." Indeed, the severity of these laws had become legendary; Plutarch in his life of Solon reports that Draco's laws, except those relating to homicide, were repealed by Solon because they prescribed punishments regarded as too severe. Idleness or stealing a cabbage or an apple were capital offenses as serious as sacrilege or murder, and it was held that his laws were written not in ink but in blood. When Draco was asked why he assigned the death penalty for

24

most offenses, he is reputed to have replied: "Small ones deserve that, and I have no higher for the greater crimes."

Such severity should not cause surprise. Most early codes of law were harsh in assigning severe penalties for petty crimes, as attested by early Hebrew law, Zaleucus' code, and the Twelve Tables of Rome. Not until the time of the Enlightenment was there concern to make the punishment fit the crime, and in England some severe and unreasonable penalties prescribed in Elizabethan times remained in force through the nineteenth century. Consequently, Draco's harshness, considering the times, can be overexaggerated. Death was not the only penalty inflicted on violators, lesser infringements drawing fines, disfranchisement, or exile. In the case of homicide, his legislation appears enlightened in that it drew careful distinction between willful murder and accidental or justifiable manslaughter. Evidence for such a view comes not only from the legal procedures which were established in his day but also from a copy of his homicide law which was erected in front of the Royal Portico in 409/408 by a decree of the Council and People initiated by Xenophanes, or Athenophanes.

Moreover, Draco's laws marked definite advances. By designating crimes, fixing penalties, and establishing rules of procedure, he made it easier for the poor and the weak to obtain justice. His laws on homicide so effectively put an end to the blood feuds which had plagued Athens that other primitive communities adopted Athenian laws generally.

In this context it is well to recall Fustel de Coulanges' *Ancient City* which grew up gradually out of fused independent tribes that, in turn, had grown out of phratral or combinations of related families. The ancient city developed out of a gradual federation of groups, and it never was an "assembly of individuals." Draco's code represents the time when the coalescing city was forced to curtail the sovereignty of the tribe and family and to interfere first of all, for the sake of peace, in its prerogative of the blood feud. In the case of intentional homicide old tribal rights were still honored, but in the case of self-defense the new city saw a reasonable place to begin its encroachments on tribal rights. In the case of involuntary homicide, probably often occurring between persons of different groups and unknown to each other, the city again saw wisdom in restricting old tribal blood feuds. Consequently, Draco's code should be interesting not only for a history of Athenian jurisprudence but also as an index of the growing jurisdiction of the city of Athens itself. That the "state" did not concern itself with murder in Homer's day is quite likely inasmuch as the "city" in that era had not developed out of tribal associations but still represented the bailiwick of a noble family.

Pertinent Literature

Adcock, F. E. "Draco," in *The Cambridge Ancient History.* Vol. IV. New York: The Macmillan Company, 1930.

This classic article represents, more or less, the traditional view of the story of Draco. The issuance of the code is pictured as an attempt, in the confusion over the sacrilege of murdering Cylon's followers, to standardize the practice of judges.

Since Solon's legislation overshadowed Draco's it is difficult to disentangle the latter's contribution to the later code. However, Adcock rightly sees that Draco's legislation on homicide was prompted by the problem of the blood feud. This popular pastime was rooted in the conviction that a murdered man's spirit cried for revenge and adversely affected the fertility of the soil until it secured satisfaction. So vital was this revenge that along with his father's possessions a son also inherited the obligation to punish the murderers of his father.

Adcock states that in Homeric society the state had no direct interest in murder; it remained a "diplomatic incident between families." In Greece proper, however, he thinks that the Delphian shrine taught after the eighth century that a killing defiled not only the perpetrator but also his city as well until it was purified. The state had to anathematize even an unknown killer to clear the land of guilt, and eventually it had to take an interest in a man claiming innocence, because the killing of a guiltless man in a blood feud obviously left the guilty party still at large to blight the land. Thus the Areopagus provided a sanctuary where those claiming innocence could be heard.

Adcock believes that it was at this point, for some inexplainable reason, that a moral judgment was first made regarding murder. If a would-be killer were himself killed in the assault, he would be to all intents and purposes his own murderer so that his spirit could have no just claim for vengeance. So arose the moral concept of justifiable homicide which Draco's code respects. Draco, however, went on to designate unintentional homicide, which was judged at the sanctuary of Pallas. The kinsmen of the dead man were required to leave such a person alone to go into exile until he was pardoned by the family or the dead man's phratry. This arrangement, claims Adcock, represents a "compromise between the anger of the dead man, the guilt of blood, and moral ideas of a more enlightened time."

Draco allows the family to prosecute for homicide or in the absence of a relative, the phratry of the deceased. The board of fifty-one "jurors" mentioned in connection with the code seems, in Adcock's opinion, to constitute a new Draconian court. He believes that these "jurors," former priests of sanctuary tribunals, were secularized and even organized as itinerant justices to adjudicate the cases of suppliants.

In short, Draco's murder laws represent to Adcock a more enlightened morality on one hand and "a more active intervention by the state on the other." Draco's code became a permanent part of Athenian jurisprudence, and Plato in his *Laws* incorporated Draco's statutes into his model state.

Hignett, C. *A History of the Athenian Constitution to the End of the Fifth Century* B.C. Oxford: The Clarendon Press, 1952.

In an appendix to this history of the Athenian constitution, Hignett discusses Draco's code and the ephetai or "jurors," placing special emphasis on his law pertaining to homicide. He starts with the historical fact that in the fourth century there were five separate courts dealing with cases of homicide, one of a sacral and four of a civil character. These latter four dealt with different types of homicide. The Areopagus handled cases of deliberate murder; the Palladian court tried those accused of involuntary homicide; the Delphinion court had cognizance of those responsible for accidental or justifiable manslaughter; and, finally, the court at Phreatto passed judgment on those who had been exiled for involuntary homicide and were later accused of willful murder. In a trial at Phreatto the defendant had to make his defense from a boat moored near the land in the harbor of Piraeus since he could not set foot on Attic soil.

The fifty-one ephetai mentioned by Pollux and in the inscription of 409/408 containing a copy of Draco's homicide law are generally assumed to have been jurors in the last three courts. In order to determine who these people were, Hignett examines what is known of Draco and his legislation.

In trying to ascertain the originality of Draco's murder legislation, it is relevant to ask first whether he drew up a full code of laws. Ancient writers maintain that Draco did indeed draw up a comprehensive code, the whole of which was repealed by Solon with the exception of the laws on homicide. The decree of Tisamenos, for example, ordained that Athenians should continue to use the *thesmoi* or ordinances of Draco, and the *nomoi* or laws of Solon. Since the Athenians of the fourth century ascribed their homicide laws to Draco and their other early laws to Solon, it is obvious that at least the former went back to pre-Solonian times. There is therefore no reason for not admitting the tradition that the homicide regulations were drafted by Draco. According to Atthidographers he drew them up during the archonship of Aristaechumus (621/620 B.C.). It seems likely that he was not one of the thesmothetes that year but the recipient of special legislative powers.

This idea does not carry with it the conclusion that Draco drew up a general code of laws, an honor generally ascribed to Solon. Texts adduced to prove Draco's authorship of a general code are inconclusive: "The fourth-century tradition that Draco promulgated a general code of great severity" might simply reflect "a popular memory of the severe pun-ishments inflicted by the magistrates in the pre-Solonian period."

Even though Draco is accepted as a historical figure who first codified the rules of procedure in cases of homicide, the question remains whether he drafted into his homicide laws elements from an earlier age. This incorporation would appear to be likely if one regards the ephetai as jurors in three of the criminal courts. They cannot be identified with the old council of the Areopagus which probably tried all homicide cases in an early stage of the aristocratic period. Since the ephetai tried cases of lesser importance than those still reserved for the Areopagus in later centuries, "it is possible that the ephetai were originally appointed to relieve the Areopagus, which as a council had other duties as well, of some of the burden of jurisdiction." Such delegation of authority probably took place before Draco formulated his homicide laws, since the copy made in 409/408 presupposes the existence of the ephetai and, apparently, the different sites of their courts. Upon such considerations the originality of Draco is diminished insofar as he is merely reorganizing existing discrimination in kinds of murders already attended to by different courts.

There remains the question of how much Draco's provisions were modified after his lifetime. Buried in Solon's code as Draco's laws are, it is impossible to tell.

—*M. Joseph Costelloe*

Additional Recommended Reading

Bonner, Robert J., and Gertrude Smith. *The Administration of Justice from Homer to Aristotle.* Chicago: University of Chicago Press, 1930-1938. 2 vols. A comprehensive study of Greek courts, with frequent references to Draco's legislation.

Greenidge, A. H. J. *A Handbook of Greek Constitutional History.* New York: The Macmillan Company, 1896. A clear presentation of the many problems connected with Greek laws, including those of Draco, and constitutions.

Jones, J. Walter. *The Law and Legal Theory of the Greeks. An Introduction.* Oxford: The Clarendon Press, 1956. A study somewhat skeptical about the code of laws commonly ascribed to Draco.

Linforth, Ivan M. *Solon the Athenian.* Berkeley: University of California Press, 1949. A study involving Draco in the background of the Solonian code.

Stroud, Ronald Sidney. *The Law of Drakon on Homicide.* University of California, Berkeley, Ph.D., 1965. Ann Arbor: University Microfilms, Inc. This doctoral dissertation favors the acceptance of much of the ancient data.

Tod, Marcus N. *A Selection of Greek Historical Inscriptions to the End of the Fifth Century B.C.* Oxford: The Clarendon Press, 1946. A reproduction of the Greek text of, and brief commentary on, the marble stele erected in 409/408 containing the text of Draco's law on homicide.

FALL OF BABYLON

Type of event: Military: capture of the Chaldean capital by the Persians
Time: October, 539 B.C.
Locale: Babylon, south of modern Baghdad

Principal personages:
NOBONIDUS, last independent King of Babylon 556-539
NEBUCHADREZZAR, King of Babylon 605-561
CYRUS II (CYRUS THE GREAT), Achemenian King of Persia 559-
c. 529
BELSHAZZAR, son of Nabonidus

Summary of Event

Babylon, centrally located in the Tigris-Euphrates valley, had been the capital city of Semitic kings who ruled most of the Fertile Crescent from 1900 to 1600 B.C. Best known of these rulers was Hammurabi. During the following millenium Babylon remained a vital economic and cultural center, acknowledged as a sacred city by the Assyrians and others. After the fall of Nineveh in 612, Babylon became the capital of a new dynasty of "Chaldean" rulers, beginning with Nabopolassar who had shared with the Medes in the overthrow of Assyria. The next Chaldean king, Nebuchadrezzar, known through the Hebrew Bible as the conqueror of Jerusalem, controlled the entire Fertile Crescent and Phoenicia, even going so far as to invade Egypt. He enlarged and beautified many cities as his part in a religious revival. Even by modern standards Babylon became a huge city covering five hundred acres with paved streets, more than a thousand temples, elaborate gateways, and sumptuous palaces. For a Median princess whom he married, the King created the famous Hanging Gardens. He designed formidable defenses including a triple circle of walls around Babylon itself and earthworks connecting the two rivers in a wider fortification which enclosed many other cities.

After Nebuchadrezzar, a short period of

disorder ended in 556 when an official not directly of royal descent was crowned king. Nabu-na'id, or Nabonidus to Greek historians, was over sixty years old at the time, a pious man from a priestly family who devoted much energy to religious affairs. In an attempt to make the moon-god, Sin, the supreme diety over his kingdom, he had huge temples erected for him as well as for other gods. Fascination with the past led him to dig for ancient foundation stones and to collect historical records. During much of his reign he was absent from Babylon on expeditions to Arabia and Syria, leaving affairs at home in charge of his son Bel-shar-usur, the Belshazzar of the Bible.

When Nabonidus sought to rebuild a temple of Sin in Harran, the strategic center of northern Mesopotamia then held by the Medes, he sought military aid from Cyrus, the ruler of Persia. Cyrus used Babylonian support to overcome the Medes, and then he marched westward to capture large areas of territory formerly subject to Nebuchadrezzar. By 546 his Persian troops dominated western Asia Minor and Greek cities along the eastern Mediterranean coast. Cyrus then marched eastward into India. Only Babylon remained unconquered.

In 540 the elderly Nabonidus returned to Babylon to defend his kingdom. Lacking sol-

29

diers to maintain all the fortifications developed by Nebuchadrezzar, he concentrated on a smaller area. Belshazzar was put in charge of troops guarding a defense rectangle including the cities of Opis, Sippar, Cutha, and Borsippa, which were considered essential to the defense of Babylon. Inscriptions record efforts during a four-month period to bring into Babylon the gods of other more distant cities, making these unprotected cities culti-cally dependent.

By propaganda Cyrus had gained the admiration or respect of certain residents in Babylonia. His later reputation for religious tolerance and mercy is known of through the Greek historian Herodotus and through Hebrew prophets who saw Cyrus as a savior of the oppressed. Some historians believe there was resentment in Babylonian cities against Nabonidus' religious programs or as a result of economic difficulties. Perhaps it was a desire to reconcile native Babylonians that led Nabonidus, at the beginning of 539, to participate at Babylon, for the first time in eleven years, in the New Year festival, an old rite involving the triumph of Marduk over forces of evil; it also purified and reinstated the king.

Also in 539 Cyrus came. With overwhelming numerical superiority and with the support of a "fifth column" within some Babylo-nian cities, the Persian army quickly breached the Chaldean defenses. Early in October, Cyrus attacked the city of Opis, aided by a turncoat Babylonian governor. There was rioting within the defensive perimeter, and a battle was fought in which Belshazzar was killed. Within a few more days, remaining key cities were seized or they surrendered without siege, and Nabonidus fled from Babylon.

Herodotus enlivens his account of Babylon's capture with a story that Cyrus diverted the Euphrates river into an old floodway, allowing his army to enter the city through a nearly dry river bed. The other cuneiform record simply states that "the army of Cyrus entered Babylon without a battle" to receive the acclaim of many citizens.

While the fall of the Chaldean dynasty ended the political leadership of Babylon, it did not cause the decline of the city as an economic and cultural center. Cyrus granted the area considerable autonomy and made Babylon his winter headquarters. A century later Herodotus described it as still "surpassing in splendor any city in the known world." Indeed, one result of Cyrus' victory was the economic unification of Mesopotamia with the Iranian plateau, a move which was important for later Parthian and Moslem cultures.

Pertinent Literature

Saggs, H. W. F. *The Greatness That Was Babylon.* New York: Hawthorn Books, Inc., 1962.

This work by a professor of the University of London is one of the best recent accounts in English summarizing the Mesopotamian civilizations as a whole from their prehistoric origins down to the fall of Babylon. Written for the general reader, it lacks documentation but it is a careful work of scholarship, introducing in simple terms much of the textual and archaeological evidence, and correlating into the story various aspects of life such as economics which were neglected in most older publications.

Saggs presents not only a broad understanding of the diverse cultures in this cradle of civilization but also an unusual thesis concerning the fall of the city of Babylon at the hands of Cyrus. Many earlier scholars tended to blame the conquest of Babylonia on the weakness of Nabonidus, his preoccupation with building temples, and his antiquarian interest in archaeological research. In sharp contrast, Saggs considers that Nabonidus was "a statesman of high ability" who recognized the serious problems facing his kingdom and who took vigorous action to remedy economic and cultural difficulties. It was precisely in order to set up some unifying symbol for his many diverse subject peoples that the King honored the moon-god Sin, since the old Babylonian deity Marduk had little appeal to Arabians and Arameans. It was to deal with famine and inflation that Nabonidus was absent from Babylon for so long. He spent the time not in mystical religious retreat, as many earlier historians believed, but in concluding a military expedition to Syria and Arabia, to secure trade routes replacing those now dominated by the Medes and Persians in the East and Northeast.

The final reason for the collapse of Babylon, according to Saggs, was neither ineptitude nor inaction by Nabonidus but "the presence within the city of a 'fifth column'" of discontented citizens who still regarded a Chaldean ruler as a foreigner alien to Babylon. Resenting the religious campaign which had subordinated Marduk to Sin and blaming Nabonidus for their economic difficulties, these Babylonians led by priests of Marduk enthusiastically welcomed Cyrus. The generosity with which Cyrus treated Babylon is considered by Saggs as evidence for this view. Cyrus restored the gods of the Akkadian cities to their traditional places, and in no way was the city of Babylon itself damaged.

Saggs recognizes in the conquest of Babylon not merely the fall of an unpopular dynasty but also evidence for new forces which had sprung up from cultural influences that weakened the old system of city-states. For example, alphabetic Aramaic had begun to replace the more complex Akkadian cuneiform even before 539, reducing writing from over six hundred signs to a script which utilized twenty-two letters. Furthermore, the earlier overthrow of Assyrian rule had left the Near East fragmented; Chaldean rulers had been forced to maintain a costly standing army even when Babylonian commerce had been disrupted. Saggs relates his studies of Mesopotamian social and economic developments to these political changes.

Wohil, Howard. "A Note on the Fall of Babylon," in *Journal of the Ancient Near Eastern Society of Columbia University.* Vol. 1, no. 2 (Spring, 1969), 28-38.

This article reviews in a clear and scholarly fashion historical evidence about the fall of Babylon in 539, and proposes a fresh theory about the defense strategy of Nabonidus. Since he uses the same sources which have been used by scholars since the publication in 1891 of a "Nabonidus-Cyrus Chronicle," Wohil considers it necessary to begin by surveying such sources. The Nabonidus-Cyrus Chronicle is a narrative probably drawn from records of the temple of Marduk in Babylon. Two Akkadian inscriptions, the "Cyrus Cylinder" and the "Verse Account," are of less value, in Wohil's opinion, partly because he regards them as pieces of Persian propaganda which malign Nabonidus as a weak religious fanatic and justify rule by Cyrus. He regards Greek and Hebrew sources composed much later as even less trustworthy.

Wohil is sympathetic to Nabonidus and does not indict him for weakness or disinterest. His defeat, according to the author, was caused not so much by treachery, although that was not absent, but by the difficulties involved in defending Babylon in 540-539, apart from the fact that he was compelled to use seminomadic mercenaries commanded by Babylonian nobles some of whom were of doubtful loyalty. Analyzing the defenses developed by Nebuchadrezzar,

Wohil provides an excellent map which demonstrates how Nabonidus was forced to limit the area he could defend around Babylon. Opposing the view of Olmstead and others that the movement of foreign gods into Babylon was a foolish fetish on the part of Nabonidus which supposedly turned the citizenry against him, Wohil notes that the four cities within the narrowed defense perimeter which Nabonidus set up did not send their deities to Babylon. Rather, it was only from the cities outside the area which Nabonidus despaired of defending and which was to be abandoned to Cyrus, that he gathered in the gods along with their chief priests into Babylon. The simple fact is that when Cyrus captured Opis,

Wohil reasons, the integrity of Nabonidus' defenses broke down, leaving the other cities, including Babylon, vulnerable.

Wohil accepts the tale of Herodotus that Cyrus drained the Tigris River as a scheme to capture Opis, but he offers no evaluation of the other story by Herodotus about the Persians diverting the Euphrates River in order to enter Babylon. Even Wohil's logical study leaves some mystery about the quick surrender of that city.

In his footnotes, the author provides a fine bibliography of scholarship during the past eighty years relating to the fall of Babylon. —*Roger B. McShane*

Additional Recommended Reading

Dougherty, Raymond P. *Nabonidus and Belshazzar.* (Yale Oriental series, Researches 15.) New Haven: Yale University Press, 1929. Translations of the cuneiform sources with commentaries may be found in the works cited above.

Herodotus. *The Persian Wars.* Book I, 178-191. Translated by G. Rawlinson. New York: Random House, 1942. An ancient source on Babylon and its capture. Many other translations are available.

Olmstead, Albert T. E. *History of the Persian Empire.* Pp. 34-58. Chicago: University of Chicago Press, 1948. An account of the capture of Babylon which emphasizes the resentment of the priests against Nabonidus.

Pritchard, James B. *Ancient Near Eastern Texts Relating to the Old Testament.* Princeton: Princeton University Press, 1950, 1955. A scholarly work including Babylonian texts.

Rogers, Robert W. *A History of Babylonia and Assyria.* 6th ed. Vol. II. New York and Cincinnati: Abingdon Press, 1915. A study of the neo-Babylonian Kingdom, blaming its fall on the weakness of Nabonidus.

Roux, Georges. *Ancient Iraq.* Cleveland: World Publishing Company, 1964 and 1965. A popular survey of Mesopotamian empires, with a brief account of Cyrus's conquests.

RETURN FROM THE CAPTIVITY

Type of event: Politico-religious: repatriation of the Jews
Time: c. 538-c. 450 B.C.
Locale: Palestine

Principal personages:
CYRUS THE GREAT, King of Persia 559-c. 529
ZERUBBABEL, descendant of King David; governor of Judah,
    rebuilder of the temple between 520 and 516
HAGGAI, a prophet
ZECHARIAH, a prophet
NEHEMIAH, Governor of Palestine c. 445
SANBALLAT, Samaritan leader c. 445
EZRA, Jewish scribe c. 425

Summary of Event

The four centuries of Jewish history from 586 until 166 comprised a period of physical weakness but of religious growth and strength. The very destruction of the Temple and the nation encouraged Second Isaiah to reach such a lofty concept as the universality of God.

The return from the Babylonian exile was made possible by an edict of Cyrus the Great in 538 which gave evidence of his appreciation for local autonomy and for the cultural and religious integrity of his peoples. The books of Chronicles record that 42,360 Jews with their servants returned under the combined leadership of the prince Zerubbabel and the high priest Joshua. The numbers appear to be exaggerated when compared to those suggested by the prophets Haggai and Zechariah, who imply that the community was weak and struggling. In order to develop a new central shrine, a second Temple was built and completed, probably by 516. Though not as large or grandiose as that of Solomon, it stood as a symbol of triumph and hope to a revived Judaism until Jerusalem was destroyed by the Romans in A.D. 70.

The returned exiles, however, had their problems. First of all, Zerubbabel, a legiti-mate descendant of David, plotted to reestablish the old dynasty. Taking advantage of the death of Cyrus' son Cambyses with consequent turmoil and open rebellion in the Persian Empire, he established himself as King in Jerusalem, but was either executed or deported.

Once the exuberance of the return had passed, the Jews were faced with the harsh realities of the situation. Palestine was agriculturally poor and also isolated from trade routes. On to this mixed scene of joy and despair appeared first Nehemiah and then Ezra, presumably in that order since Nehemiah seems to set the stage for Ezra. Nehemiah, a cupbearer to the Persian King Artaxerxes, requested permission to go to Jerusalem as governor to help his coreligionists struggling to adjust to Palestine. The Temple had been rebuilt but it had been as quickly defiled, the Sabbath was regularly desecrated with commercial activities, and the city's defenses were in disrepair. Intensive work enabled Nehemiah to rebuild the city's walls and consequently to guarantee the integrity of the Jewish cult by isolating his people from their neighbors including even the Samaritans, despite the fact that under the leadership of

Sanballat they had sought some political and religious rapprochement with the Jews. Disregarding considerable intermarriage between the two groups, Nehemiah preferred to exclude them as a mixed people, even going to the length of trying to separate couples who had intermarried. To thwart religious syncretism and to maintain a pure Yahwism, Nehemiah would unify only those Jews who, because of their experiences in the Exile, were highly motivated religiously.

Hoping to solidify Nehemiah's program, Ezra, a scribe, established the law of the Pentateuch as the politico-religious constitution of the Jews. This official promulgation of the Law, tantamount to its canonization as the first part of the Hebrew Scriptures, was the first important effort since Josiah's Deuteronomic reform to establish the Jewish community on the basis of the written word of God. Ezra's dispensation fixed the basis for Judaism so effectively that normative Judaism continued to develop as a legalistic and exclusive community for the next thousand years.

The only vindication for the parochialism of both Nehemiah and Ezra, so far removed from the universalism of Amos or Second Isaiah, is its desire to enable Biblical faith to prosper in a protected environment. A new type of optimistic prophecy encouraged men such as Haggai, Zechariah, Malachi, Third Isaiah and Joel, who labored in turn by emphasizing the Temple, institutional reform, and the cult to provide a religious structure which could replace the crumbled political order. Concern for social justice and for a universal worship of God took second place.

The Jews maintained their peaceful isolation during virtually the whole Persian period, not even participating in the sole rebellion of the Syro-Palestinian provinces, that of the Phoenician cities in 351. Except for the abortive aspirations of Zerubbabel, the Jews devoted themselves to internal affairs, mainly the purification of Judaism and the maintenance of the Law as the undisputed cornerstone of the community. The solidity and depth of this reformed Judaism was soon to be tested by the impact of Hellenism which came with the Greek conquests of Alexander the Great in the fourth century.

Pertinent Literature

Welch, Adam C. *Poste-Exilic Judaism.* Edinburgh: William Blackwood and Sons Ltd., 1935.

Welch interprets the entire post-exilic development of Judaism as a defensive and conservative effort, in the face of threatening conditions of the period, to maintain Jewish identity and purity of worship. He outlines the characteristics of the new policy of retrenchment as they were determined by the ideals and convictions of the men who guided this movement. Among these Nehemiah was only nominally important. Admittedly a picturesque personality and a figure of some importance as a Persian official, he merely supported the programs already in progress and conceived of and directed by lesser known figures.

The program itself emphasized a studied hostility on the part of Jews toward alien life in general and justified their reaction against the outside world as a means to restore their own peculiar life and renew the conditions of the past. This conservative course based on institutionalized religion was decisive in determining the future. Jewish leaders rejected the extreme proposals of Ezekiel including the restoration of the kingdom with a descendant of Jehoiachim on the throne, allotting equal portions of land to the twelve tribes to unify them, and placing the Temple and the priests outside the capital. He would have new laws for priestly temple service as well as new royal obligations to the cult. The new leaders chose instead to make a descendant of Zadok high priest, and reinstated an ancient Levitical law.

Yet because conditions were different, some changes in the cult had to be made. The injunction of appearing in Jerusalem three times each year was quietly dropped because of the widespread Jewish dispersion. An offering sent to the Temple would suffice. The Temple with an elaborate priesthood and liturgy became a symbol of unity for a people bent solely on enriching their relationship with God.

While all those developments gave a *raison d'être* to the life of the scattered nation, they still offered little opportunity for personal involvement. Welch sees this gap between corporate and individual life bridged by the development of an elaborate scheme of penitential atonement, an arrangement which tied the individual Jew both to God and the Temple through sacrifices as means of justification. In this intensified ritual system sin itself became chiefly ceremonial defilement rather than moral transgression as in the Mosaic and prophetic systems. But this religion of outward forms and signs succeeded in enabling the Jews to sense quickly in a visible way any invading influences from their heathen surroundings. Sabbath observance and circumcision naturally assumed new importance in distinguishing Jews from the polyglot population of the Palestine to which the exiles returned. While such stressing of the outward signs of nationality caused the faith to lose some of its prophetic universalism, the times called for a Judaism more interested in preserving itself than in enlightening the world.

Noth, Martin. *The History of Israel.* Translated by Stanley Godman. Pp. 229-354. New York: Harper and Row Publishers Incorporated, 1958.

Noth's general view of the Jewish nation colors his entire historical interpretation and particularly the period covered in this section. He sees Israel as a unique phenomenon in the midst of other historical nations. The secret of Israel's distinction is the mystery of God's involvement, a result of which is Israel's estrangement in the world of its own time, its existence as an entity separated from the world in which it lives. For Noth, therefore, certain happenings in the history of Israel are without parallel. The idea of Israel transcends the idea of nationhood which ended in 586 B.C. The terms "Judaism" and "Israel" came to be synonymous after the national period ceased.

The beginning of this development came in the Persian period when some of the Jews returned from captivity. Unlike most conquerors who introduced their own official religions, at least in their provincial capitals, the Persians accepted the traditions and characteristics of their subject peoples even to the extent of actively supporting them. The Persian policy of toleration thus allowed the new Israel to come into being and flourish. Cyrus not only allowed the Jews to return to Palestine, but he and his successors also financed some of their projects, released valuable articles which had been taken by Nebuchadrezzar, and made outstanding Jewish government officials available to the struggling community.

Noth indicates that even with these encouragements, the Jews found the process of rebuilding their community a difficult one. Funds were in short supply, agricultural conditions were poor, and the process of changing the primarily political nature of Judaism into a religious one was difficult. Israel was now to be a religious community centered about a shrine in Jerusalem, a temple state.

Two personalities, more than any others known to us, accomplished most of this.

Nehemiah built the wall, cleansed religious practice of many abuses, and improved the general welfare of the people. He excluded non-Jewish and mixed peoples from the Temple, thereby furthering the policy of strict social and religious isolation which Noth sees as characteristic of the history of Israel after the loss of its political independence. The necessary welding together of the new Israel comprising the Jews of Palestine as well as those of the Diaspora was the task of Ezra. This was done through a renewal of the ancient covenant as practiced among the Jews in Babylonia where ritual observance was stricter than in Palestine. The Pentateuch would bring stability to the Jews of Palestine as it had to those in Babylon.

The Temple was no longer simply a royal shrine but a center for public worship for Jews in Jerusalem and the religious center regardless of where they lived. This period is also seen as crucial by Noth since the Pentateuch not only acquired definitive form during it but also became a holy book binding together the whole community wherever it was located. —*Joseph R. Rosenbloom*

Additional Recommended Reading

Bevan, Edwyn Robert. *Jerusalem Under the High Priests.* London: E. Arnold, 1920. A history of the role of the priesthood in ancient Israel.

Browne, L. E. *From Babylon to Bethlehem.* Cambridge: Heffer, 1951. A general account of postexilic Jewish history leading to Christianity.

Graetz, H. *History of the Jews.* Vol. I, pp. 354-411. Philadelphia: Jewish Publication Society, 1891. A standard comprehensive account of Jewish history.

Johnson, Paul. *A History of the Jews.* New York: Harper & Row, 1987. A lively, insightful account of Jewish history from its origins to the present that emphasizes the unique characteristics of Jewish history and the Jewish impact on the world.

Meyers, Jacob M. *Chronicles.* New York: Doubleday & Company, Inc., 1966. 2 vols. A study of the Biblical history of Israel written during the postexilic period.

_____. *Ezra and Nehemiah.* New York: Doubleday & Company, Inc., 1965. A detailed analysis of the major Biblical historical sources of this period.

Robinson, T. H., and W. O. E. Oesterley. *A History of Israel.* Vol. II. Oxford: The University Press, 1932. An excellent history of the period.

INSTITUTION OF THE PLEBEIAN TRIBUNATE

Type of event: Constitutional: recognition of the rights of the lower orders of society
Time: 494/493 B.C.
Locale: Rome

Principal personages:
MANIUS VALERIUS, dictator in 494
MENENIUS AGRIPPA, ambassador of the senate to the dissident
plebeians
SICINIUS, leader of the plebeian revolt
GAIUS LICINIUS and
LUCIUS ALBINUS, first tribunes to be chosen by the plebeians

Summary of Event

Because of the lack of contemporary sources, and because evidence was at times deliberately suppressed and falsified for purposes of family aggrandizement or for purposes of moral or artistic edification, much early Roman history lies shrouded in obscurity and myth. Despite conflicting details, however, there seems to be a hard core of fact relating to the institution of the plebeian tribunate as described by Dionysius of Halicarnassus and Livy. A secession of the plebs, prompted by their abuse at the hands of patricians, was followed by the election of officers to represent plebeians and defend their rights; ultimately an oath was sworn by the plebeians to regard as inviolable the persons of their new tribunes. Conflicting accounts exist about the place of secession, whether on the Aventine hill or the Sacred Mount; about the number of tribunes elected, whether two, four, or five; about the manner of their election; and about the oath taken making them sacrosanct.

According to Livy, trouble broke Appius Claudius and Publius Servilius; the plebeians complained that while they were fighting in the army to preserve Roman independence, they were being enslaved at home by patrician creditors. Their feelings were particularly exasperated by the pitiful sight of a

former soldier who, having lost his home and his crops to the enemy, had to borrow money in order to pay his taxes. To induce plebeians to take up arms against a Volscian army, Servilius was forced to order that no Roman citizen should be held in chains or in prison to prevent him from enlisting, that no one should seize or sell a soldier's property while he was in service, and that no one should harass his children or grandchildren. But continued pressure on debtors caused the plebs to become violent; they began to assemble at night on the Aventine and Esquiline, and they refused to fight against the invading Sabines. An edict by the dictator Manius Valerius giving greater protection to plebeians from their creditors made it possible to muster an army; but in the absence of permanent adjustments, the plebs took the advice of a certain Sicinius and withdrew to the Sacred Mount three miles from the city across the Anio River. This secession caused panic in the city among the patricians who were at one and the same time afraid of hostile foreign invaders and also of those plebeians who remained behind. According to Livy, the senate compromised with a constitutional innovation.

This new agreement, a milestone in the struggle between the orders, created an exclusive plebeian office to protect "the people" from the aristocratic consuls. The "tribunes of the people" at first had only a negative function because they could do no more than "forbid" overt acts inimical to a plebeian at the instant of its perpetration. Moreover, aid had to be initiated by a complaining plebeian, so a tribune could not absent himself from the city for a whole night nor shut his doors at any time. The person of the tribune was declared sacrosanct by a *lex sacrata*; anyone who interfered with a tribune doing his duty became an outlaw, liable to be killed by plebeians.

At first there were two tribunes, or four or five according to some sources, but the number grew to ten. This strange negative office, creating a set of parallel officials working at cross-purposes with the old magistrates of the state, was intended partly to satisfy plebeian unrest and partly to keep plebeians from becoming regular magistrates which would have usurped the prerogative of the nobility. In 471 a law transferred the election of tribunes from the assembly of the *curiae* to that of the *comitia tributa*, an event and date which Eduard Meyer and some other authorities associate with the actual creation of the plebeian tribunate itself. Eventually the veto of a plebeian tribune permitted him to negate the passage of any legislation prejudicial to plebeian concerns. So it was only natural that tribunes began to sit in the senate to make known their objection to laws before they were actually passed, or to suggest legislation and even to call together the senate. The tribunes were also able to veto acts of the consuls and other magistrates except dictators. In 287, plebiscites of their *comitia tributa* were given the same force as laws passed by the senate or the *comitia centuriata*.

Because of its invaluable power of veto, the office of plebeian tribune came to be sought after avidly. Even patricians had themselves adopted by plebeians in order to become eligible. It is ironic that this weak, plebeian, negative, makeshift office became so powerful that the Emperor Augustus used the authority of the plebeian tribunate to rule Rome in preference to consular *imperium* because of the unique right of the former to initiate or veto legislation.

Pertinent Literature

Greenidge, A. H. J. *Roman Public Life.* London: Macmillan & Company, 1922.

A. H. J. Greenidge was the author of a number of excellent works on problems of Roman law and constitution. Among these is his *Roman Public Life*; though first published in 1901, it remains a standard item in any bibliography on the subject.

Greenidge's exposition of the power of the tribunate is largely concerned with the constitutional aspects of this strange office which in some ways set up a state within a state. He notes that from the beginning the tribunate involved a dual authority: a negative control over the whole people represented in the person of their magistrates, all of whom at this stage in Roman history were aristocrats, and a positive authority within the plebeian or nonnoble community of Rome. Evidence of their power is seen in the right of veto and the right to elicit "plebiscites," *scita plebei* or *plebiscita*, from the plebeian *concilium* or "assembly." The tribunate was established in order to counteract the consular *imperium*, and any plebeian who felt that he had been injured by the order of a magistrate could ask for a tribune's help or *auxilium*. If granted, the tribune's response took the form of a veto of the offensive decree. Since this power of intercession had to be exercised by the tribune in person, he was expected to be available at all times for on-the-spot action.

This negative control which the tribunes exercised over Roman magistrates would have been meaningless without means of enforcement. Such enforcement could have been arranged for through judicial prosecution before the regular courts of the community, but such dependence upon agencies outside an officer himself was not consonant with the Roman idea of magistracy. Every magistrate, by virtue of being a magistrate, had to have to a greater or less degree the power to enforce his own decrees. This power, known as *coercitio*, belonged to the tribunes as a logical consequence of their right of veto. The sanctity of their persons, guaranteed by the plebs, made resistance impossible; and where necessary they could use almost any means—arrest, imprisonment, fines, scourgings, and even executions—in their defense of the plebs. In time, the exercise of summary jurisdiction over citizens in matters involving severe penalties became subject to the right of appeal on the part of the accused. When an appeal was made, the tribune brought the case before the plebeian assembly.

This right of dealing with the plebs, a necessary consequence of the tribune's *auxilium*, was extended so that the tribunes could propose measures of concern to the plebeians for debate in the assembly. Eventually in 287, such *plebiscita* were raised to the level of laws and made binding not only upon plebeians but upon patricians as well.

The community of the plebs was modeled upon that of the larger community of the *populus*. Two aediles were assigned to the tribunes in imitation of the two quaestors who assisted the consuls. But since the plebs was not strictly the community of the *populus*, nor even in the beginning a legalized corporation within the city, the tribunes were therefore not magistrates in the constitutional sense of the term. They enjoyed no use of *imperium*, no right to perform *auspicia*, and did not even earn the distinction of wearing *insignia* of office. Their power rested upon a religious sanction, upon the oath which the plebeians took to eliminate anyone who attacked their tribunes. This oath prompts Greenidge to say: "Perhaps Rome is the only state that has definitely invested the demagogue or 'champion of the people' with a halo of sanctity."

Taylor, L. R. "Forerunners of the Gracchi," in *Journal of Roman Studies.* Vol. LII, 1962, pp. 19-27.

While Cicero called the tribunate an office born in sedition to create sedition, L. R. Taylor sees it only gradually transformed into an instrument of revolution, and then more as a symptom than a cause of decline. There were two periods when this office was especially active: from the beginning until the passing of the *lex Hortensia* in 287; and from the tribunate of Tiberius Gracchus in 133 until Caesar's dictatorship, a period when the tribunate was especially revolutionary and violent.

The author is interested primarily in the interim period when it is generally held that the tribunate was placidly cooperative with the senate. Indeed, after the acceptance of plebeians into the consulship there was a period of cooperation even though the tribune Gaius Flaminius and his followers between 232 and 216 generally bypassed the senate in order to appeal directly to the people. The war with Hannibal naturally encouraged unity. But in 171, centurions who were disgruntled with the conditions of recall into service during the Macedonian Wars appealed to the tribunes to help them defy the levy. To the author it was the year 151 which inaugurated the "period of defiance of the will of the senate" leading directly to the rise of the Gracchi. Trouble broke out when forces were needed for new wars in Spain. The common soldiers, anticipating little booty and a long engagement, appealed to the tribunes. In obstructing the levy of troops the tribunes were, indeed, following a tradition established when the first tribunes seceded to the Sacred Mount to avoid a levy. In the fracas, the tribunes illegally seized the consuls and put them in prison, a new departure establishing "a precedent which was to be followed several times in the next century." In the eighteen years following this event and preceding the tribunate of Tiberius Gracchus, twenty-three episodes are recorded involving relatively unknown tribunes, which show serious strife between them and the magistrates and the senatorial majority. Tribunitian legislation proposed in defiance of senatorial authority must have been frequent judging from the *lex Aelia* and the *lex Fufia*, passed about the year 150, which tried to curb troublesome legislation and the "fury of the tribunes" by regulating the manner and time of proposing bills. The main items of contention were terms concerning soldiers' enlistments and agrarian laws. When in 149 a tribunitian bill vainly called for an investigation of a treacherous attack on the Lusitanians, the tribune L. Calpurnius Piso sponsored the law which established a permanent court to try magistrates accused of extortion from allies and provincials. Further tribunitian laws interfered in the distribution of provinces and appointments to major commands. Tribunes presented the *lex Gabinia* in 139 and the *lex*

Cassia in 137, which, though never passed, threatened patrician political monopolies by demanding a secret ballot in judicial assemblies. Continued strife came out of the long Spanish wars when tribunes supported battle-tired veterans demanding release from service. In 140 a tribune even tried to prevent the departure of a consul for Spain. In 138 two tribunes, one of whom was regarded by Cicero as the foulest of men, demanded that the consuls release veterans from service. When the consuls refused to act, they were, in the manner of 138, led off to prison. Continuing troubles in Spain, over which Scipio was put in charge supported by the tribunes, and the slave war in Sicily with possible repercussions in Italy, form the background for the election of Tiberius Gracchus to the tribunate in 133.

Taylor considers tribunitian defiance of the authority of the senate, especially in military matters, a sign of decay in the mixed Roman constitution which Polybius saw distributed evenly among the magistrates, the senate, and the people. Between 155 and 134 the tribunes were men of small stature who helped to deepen the growing factionalism in the ruling classes by carrying out the designs of ambitious individuals. While, indeed, the imprisonment of the two consuls in 138 was the only revolutionary act during this period, the continual interference of tribunes in levies, army discipline, and the relations of subject peoples makes them true forerunners of the Gracchi and the later demagogues of the great age of revolution which was to follow.

—M. Joseph Costelloe

Additional Recommended Reading

Heitland, W. E. *The Roman Republic.* Cambridge: The University Press, 1923. 3 vols. A classic general study first published in 1909 but still valuable.

Jolowicz, H. F. *Historical Introduction to the Study of Roman Law.* 2d ed. Cambridge: The University Press, 1952. The author sees the tribunate, although an integral part of the Roman constitution, as an instrument of party strife.

Jones, H. Stuart. "Plebeian Institutions," in *Cambridge Ancient History.* Vol. VII, pp. 450-

456. New York: The Macmillan Company, 1928. A view holding traditional accounts of the plebeian tribunate to be later efforts to read some legality into the office.

Lewis, Naphtali, and Meyer Reinhold. *Roman Civilization.* Vol. I: *The Republic.* New York: Columbia University Press, 1951. Translations of passages from Dionysius of Halicarnassus, Valerius Maximus, and Plutarch describe the creation of the tribunate together with its powers and duties.

Lintott, A. W. *Violence in Republican Rome.* London: Oxford University Press, 1968. A view of the tribunate as a formalization of the conflict between the oligarchic and democratic elements in Roman society.

Wolff, Hans Julius. *Roman Law: An Historical Introduction.* Norman: University of Oklahoma Press, 1951. A thesis that the democratic character of the tribunate disappeared in the later Republic so that it became the willing tool of the senatorial aristocracy.

THE NAVAL LAW OF THEMISTOCLES

Type of event: Political: enactment of defense measures
Time: c. 483 B.C.
Locale: Athens

Principal personages:
THEMISTOCLES, son of Neocles, archon and general
ARISTIDES, son of Lysimachus, Athenian statesman
PERICLES, son of Xanthippus, Athenian statesman and general

Summary of Event

About 488 B.C., war broke out between Athens and the island state of Aegina over commercial rivalry. For some time each side was content to raid the other's shipping, but in about 485, Athens determined to bring the conflict to a decisive finish. Building her navy up to a strength of seventy ships, approximating her rival's well-manned fleet, Athens boldly invaded the island state. The attempt, however, proved abortive.

About 484 B.C., fresh and rich veins of silver-bearing ore were discovered near Laurium in southern Attica. What to do with the sudden new wealth that poured into the state's treasury from these mines became a major political issue. Under Aristides' leadership, conservatives called for distributing the surplus money among the citizens; Themistocles had other ideas, based on his conviction that security of Athens' trade and safety of her vital imports of food, timber, and industrial metals depended upon her control of the sea. As archon in 493 he had already begun giving this conviction tangible form by successfully pressing for construction of a new and better harbor at Piraeus. He now proposed to use the state's new income to build an invincible navy, and moved the passage of a naval law providing for a fleet of two hundred warships. Aegina, with no silver mines under her direct control, could scarcely hope to compete with such an armada. The assembly voted the proposal into

law and incidentally, though not without encouragement from the faction supporting Themistocles, ostracized Aristides.

Between 483 and 480 the ships were built, and when, in the latter year, the Persians invaded Greece, relations were hastily patched up with Aegina and Aristides was recalled. In the naval campaigns against Xerxes, the Athenian ships were the mainstay of the united Greek fleet. Operations steadily reduced Persian naval power, and the Athenian navy emerged from the war as the most powerful fleet in Greek waters. By 460 Athens was able to turn her attention to Aegina again, and after the Aeginetan fleet had been destroyed in a great battle, she successfully invaded the island. In 457, after a siege, Aegina surrendered to Athens and agreed to pay tribute.

Historically, the creation of a new military institution has frequently carried with it unforeseen social and political consequences. This condition now occurred at Athens because of her huge new navy. The crew of a single trireme consisted of almost two hundred men, including a captain, six subordinate officers, some half-dozen sailors, and 170 oarsmen. The rowers were freemen recruited from the class of *thetes*, the poorest and up until this time the least important politically of the four census groups. But now, as maritime power became a major factor in the total strength of the state, the Athenians

42

realized that their continued supremacy depended as much on the lowly oar-pulling *thetes* as it did on the middle-class infantry. Statesmen such as Ephialtes and Pericles began marshaling the voting strength of the *thetes* in the Assembly and made them conscious of their political power as a class. Since the sailors resided for the most part in the port of Piraeus or in the city of Athens, they found it easier to attend meetings of the assembly than did the rural population, and they gradually came to dominate action in that body. Thus, for example, Pericles was able to secure the ostracism of the aristocratic statesmen Cimon and Thucydides (son of Melesias), whose followings came mostly from rural areas.

Over the next several decades, the power of the urban democrats led to enactment of reforms suggested by Ephialtes and Pericles. The upperclass *aeroeopagus* was stripped of all its powers except that of trying cases of murder. *Zeugitae*, or middle-class farmers, were admitted to the archonships. Athenian citizenship was restricted to persons both of whose parents were native born. Instituting state pay for service on the Council or juries made it possible for *thetes* of the lowest class to take a direct part in government, thereby rendering a more democratic, popular tone to the Assembly and courts. The result was what many ancient commentators called "radical democracy."

The furthering of democracy was accompanied by development of a theory of seapower. Athens' fleet made her mistress of the maritime trade routes in the Aegean Sea, and she could therefore manipulate to a considerable degree the flow of important commodities such as grain, timber, and metal. By supervising movement and importation of these materials, Athens could control the power of the Aegean states. Such use of seapower, propounded in modern times in the doctrine of the American Admiral Mahan that "he who rules the sea rules the land," was to be exploited to its fullest by Pericles in the years immediately preceding the Peloponnesian War. As part of his program to make Athens invulnerable, Themistocles supervised the erection of massive walls which transformed Piraeus and Athens into a single impregnable fortress. Recognizing the relative weakness of Athens' land army, and that in time of war an efficient hostile army would have little trouble devastating the Attic countryside, Themistocles reasoned that Athens' citizenry could find shelter inside the walls and could survive on food brought in on merchant ships convoyed and protected by the foremost navy of Greece, the fleet begun by Themistocles.

Pertinent Literature

Frisch, Hartvig. *The Constitution of the Athenians.* Copenhagen: Nordisk Vorlag, 1942.

Athens is generally associated with ancient democracy and enlightened idealism. It comes, therefore, as something of a surprise to realize that most Athenian writers whose work has survived show a strong antidemocratic point of view. One such was the pamphleteer who wrote *The Constitution of the Athenians.* Frisch has produced an English translation together with an admirable commentary, full notes, and discussion. The name of the author of the pamphlet is unknown. Since the manuscript has come down to us in the corpus of Xenophon's work, he is sometimes called Pseudo-Xenophon, but more often the Old Oligarch. The exact date at which he wrote is also unknown. Frisch ably argues a case for 432 B.C. some months in advance of the outbreak of the Peloponnesian War, and a date about 430 B.C. is probably correct. An oligarch he certainly was, a man possibly of noble birth and certainly of the upper class. He was horrified to see the lowest born citizens rising to prominence, holding office, making a stir in the courts, and voicing their uneducated opinions in the Assembly. While he disliked democracy, he nonetheless realized that the sailors had greatly increased the power of Athens, and he gave the *thetes* full credit for having done so. If it was power for themselves they had wanted, power they had received, and they now managed it well in their interest.

In the chapter titled "Sea-Power and Defensive Theory," Frisch shows that the Athenians well understood the naval and military strategy developed by Themistocles and Pericles. The defense works included ringwalls around Athens and Piraeus, and three Long Walls, each stretching about five miles to connect the two cities. The whole complex was an impregnable stronghold; given the military technique of the fifth century, Athens could not be successfully carried by storm. It held powerful weapons in its own hands. No Greek state was entirely self-sufficient. If one was rich in a commodity such as iron, it was poor in another such as grain. Athens, by controlling the exchange of goods by sea, controlled the power of many

of the Greek states, since no state could import what it required without permission from Athens, whose citizens could secure all their needs from overseas. In the naval sphere Athenian strategy was offensive: to raid the enemy by landing troops from the fleet in his territory. On the mainland front its strategy was defensive, based on holding the fortifications. Pitched battles would not be fought against powerful armies. Only small states might be attacked. The Old Oligarch complained that such strategy made the role of the middle and upper classes in the army secondary to that of the lowest classes operating the fleet.

The Old Oligarch ends his tract with an interesting section on the possibility of overthrowing the democratic regime in favor of a more narrowly based government. He says that such an action, to be successful, would have to have many men supporting it, and that the antidemocratic forces were too few to accomplish it in the face of the numerous *thetes*. His extreme, if cynical, dislike of democracy shows the unfortunate factionalism which had arisen in Athens, the unhappy result of the creation of that "radical democracy" which had grown out of the dockyards and fleet.

Singer, Charles, ed. *A History of Technology*. Vol. 2: *The Mediterranean Civilization and the Middle Ages*. Oxford: The Clarendon Press, 1956.

The Naval Law of Themistocles was a political act of the Athenian Assembly. It was, however, one thing to vote for a fleet of two hundred warships, and another matter of technique and hard work to have them built. Most books on Greek history have little or nothing to say about ancient technology, but Singer and his colleagues have produced a book on the technical knowledge of the ancient world which covers such subjects as shipbuilding, metallurgy, mining, and so on, explaining the methods necessary for the actual procurement of Themistocles' ships.

The construction of the ships would not have been possible without silver money to pay the shipwrights and to purchase timber. Athens had one of the few sources of silver in the Aegean region, and C. N. Bromehead explains in the chapter on "Mining and Quarrying" in *A History of Technology*, how it was exploited. Silver-bearing lead sulphide ore (galena) had been discovered at Laurium in Mycenean times, but Athenian mining did not begin until the sixth century, as we know from the archaeological investigation of the ancient pits. The finding of the most valuable deposits of ore was made about 484 B.C. by a man named Callias, who must have been a persistent and imaginative man, for the rich veins of galena lie under two layers of limestone which are themselves some distance underground. Eventually, over two thousand vertical shafts were dug to reach the ore, the deepest descending nearly four hundred feet. Forced ventilation was provided by means of baffles which caught surface winds and deflected air down the shafts. Fires could also be built at the bottoms of some shafts to force the air in the mines up and out, thus creating down drafts in adjacent shafts and along the connecting galleries which were being worked. The miners used small oil lamps set in niches for light, and iron chisels, hammers, and picks for digging. By the end of the first century A.D. when the mines were exhausted the Athenian miners had excavated more than two million tons of material a shovelful at a time, and from their smelting operations they left behind enormous slag heaps which extracted less than sixty ounces of pure silver per ton of ore.

T. C. Lethbridge's chapter on "Shipbuilding" is a brief survey of the evolution of Greek and Roman designs and methods. The standard warship before Themistocles' generation had been the penteconter, a ship driven by fifty oars. Towards the end of the sixth century the need for more speed suggested an increase in oarpower. But wooden ships could not be lengthened indefinitely because they tended to warp. The solution was to lengthen the ship only slightly and to superimpose two additional banks of oarsmen above the original one so that 170 men could be employed. The invention of this kind of warship, the trireme, is attributed to Aminocles of Corinth. A trireme was about 120 feet long, with a beam of fourteen feet and a draft of three. It displaced about eighty tons. Two hundred ships would require, allowing for the inevitable wastage of wood-working, well over sixteen thousand tons of timber. Tall trees were required for keels and masts, and the best came to Athens from Macedonia and the north shore of the Aegean. The Athenians' organization for the transport of this mass of lumber must itself have been impressive. Triremes were built from a keel and latitudinal framing, with the hull planking sawed with considerable skill to fit the curving lines of the ship's body. The few fragments of Greek ships which have been found show that the standard of their carpentry and joinery was high. —*Samuel K. Eddy*

Additional Recommended Reading

Cary, Max. "Callias o Laccoplutos," in *Classical Review.* Vol. 50 (1936), p. 55. The title of this article, which is written in English, means "Callias the Pit-Wealthy"; it contains what little information is available about a remarkable man.

Havelock, Eric A. *The Liberal Temper in Greek Politics.* New Haven: Yale University Press, 1957. A treatise discussing the democratic views of Greek liberals.

Morrison, J. S. "Notes on Certain Greek Nautical Terms," in *Classical Quarterly.* Vol. 41 (1947), pp. 122-135. A short study describing the trireme and its equipment.

Perrin, Bernadotte. *Plutarch's Themistocles and Aristides.* New York: Charles Scribner's Sons, 1901. There are no adequate biographies of Themistocles or of Aristides; Plutarch's ancient versions are here translated, and the reader is helped with introductions and copious notes.

PERSIAN INVASION OF GREECE

Type of event: Military: occupation of northern Greece
Time: 480-479 B.C.
Locale: Greece, the Aegean Sea, and western Asia Minor

Principal personages:
XERXES, King of the Kings of the Persian Empire 486-465
LEONIDAS, King of Sparta 487-480
THEMISTOCLES, Athenian general
EURYBIADES, Spartan admiral, commander in chief of the Greek
    fleet 481-480
ADIMANTUS, Corinthian general 480
PAUSANIAS, nephew of Leonidas and Regent of Sparta 480-c. 470

Summary of Event

Cyrus the Great, founder of the Persian empire, subjected the Greek states of western Asia Minor, or Ionia, to Persia. The Ionians resented the loss of their sovereignty, and in 499, they rebelled against Cyrus' successor, Darius I. Their action was supported by two states in Old Hellas, Eretria and Athens. At first the Ionian revolt went well, but Darius soon gathered overwhelming forces and reimposed Persian authority by 493 B.C. He then determined to invade Old Greece, to punish the states which had assisted the Ionian cities, and to end a vexatious frontier problem. His first attack in 492 miscarried when much of the Persian fleet was wrecked in a storm, and his second attempt in 490 failed when his army was driven into the sea at Marathon in Attica. He therefore planned a third invasion on a lavish scale. Darius, however, died in 486, and it fell to his son Xerxes to complete the preparation of his empire's forces.

The great invasion finally began in the spring of 480. An enormous host of more than one hundred thousand soldiers was supported by a fleet of six hundred warships. The Greeks could not fail to learn about the assembling of such masses, and in the winter of 481-480 representatives of the larger states

met at Corinth to discuss resistance. The Delphic Oracle had to be persuaded to modify its initial prophecy of doom to one of doubtful outcome, and it was with some trepidation that a decision was taken to fight under Spartan leadership. Appeals to other Greek states to join the patriotic cities were rejected by some of the more important ones, notably anti-Spartan Argos. Ultimately, only thirty-one states fought on the Greek side. There were actually more Greek states on the side of Xerxes, although these served under compulsion.

The Greeks decided to delay the Persians' advance by holding the narrow pass at Thermopylae with eight thousand men and the adjacent strait between Thermopylae and the island of Euboea with their fleet. It was not until August that the Persians came up against these fortified positions. Three days passed as Xerxes vainly sent his best troops against the well-armored Peloponnesian infantry fighting under King Leonidas of Sparta. Simultaneously, a series of inconclusive but costly naval engagements were fought off Cape Artemisium on Euboea; the Persians had earlier lost about two hundred warships in a storm. Xerxes, however, turned the position at Thermopylae by marching around it

46

through the mountains. Most of the Greeks escaped encirclement in time, but Leonidas with his bodyguard of three hundred Spartans and the seven-hundred-man army of Tespiae were cut off and could only die resisting bravely to the end.

With the position on land lost, the Greek fleet retreated and took station on the island of Salamis off the western coast of Attica. The population of Athens had already been evacuated to the Peloponnesus. There was more wavering among the Greeks at Salamis, some even considering defection, but at last honor prevailed, and, led by Eurybiades of Sparta, Themistocles of Athens, and Adimantus of Corinth, the Greek sailors prepared to fight. The Persians, fearing that the Greek fleet might escape westward, decided upon an immediate attack, and late in September the Battle of Salamis was fought in the narrow strait between the island and the mainland. The Persians had about 350 ships, the Greeks probably 310, of which the majority were Athenian. The conflict lasted most of the day, and by sunset the Greeks were victorious. With the campaigning season nearly over, Xerxes withdrew from devastated Attica and left half his army to winter in Boeotia. The rest of the army and the shattered fleet retired with the King to Asia.

The war was resumed the following spring. After a second Persian devastation of Attica, a hard-fought land battle took place at Plataea, a small state between Athens and Boeotia. Under the command of the Spartan Regent Pausanias, the Greeks gained the victory, and the Spartan infantry showed once more their undoubted excellence. The Persian army was forced into rapid retreat.

While this campaign was being fought in Greece, the Hellenic fleet had crossed the Aegean to seek out the remnants of Xerxes' navy. Off the island of Mycale the Greeks completed its destruction. Thus, the great force which Xerxes had led against the Hellenes was either destroyed or forced back into Asia, and, as the poet Simonides wrote, "Hellas put on the crown of freedom."

These victories did not end the war with Persia, but they did end Persian efforts to invade Greece. The liberation of Ionia now became the goal of the Greek states and by 477 most of it had been freed. As a result of these campaigns Athens became one of the most important military powers of Greece.

The successful repulsion of the horde of Xerxes had an effect that is hard to document. It seems that the spiritual euphoria resulting from their naval and military successes added to the Greeks' awareness of their specifically Hellenic virtues and imparted a special keenness to succeeding generations. We see this in the drama of Aeschylus of Athens and in the poetry of Pindar of Thebes.

Pertinent Literature

Herodotus. *The Histories.* Translated from the Greek by A. de Sélincourt. Baltimore: Penguin Books, 1954.

Herodotus, the historian of the Persian Wars, was born about 485 B.C. at Halicarnassus, a city on the coast of Asia Minor where Greek and Carian freely mingled. He apparently came from a prominent family, for he was forced to flee the city at a time of political turmoil. He was, therefore, a man accustomed to looking at the world as a member of its ruling class. After his exile he traveled extensively, visiting Egypt, the Levant, Mesopotamia, the Black Sea regions, Greece itself, and, finally, southern Italy. All this gave him an awareness of the diversity of humanity and an opportunity to gain knowledge from veterans of the Persian Wars, probably from both sides.

Herodotus wrote his account of what was then the greatest event in Greek experience in order that "the memory of the past may not be blotted out from among men by time, and that great and marvelous deeds done by Greeks and foreigners against each other may not lack renown." By this he shows himself to have two strong qualities. First, he was keenly excited by the manly and virtuous deeds of famous men; his book abounds in biographical detail: Polycritus of Aegina, he tells us, fought best in the Battle of Salamis. Second, he was as deeply interested in the history of Asia as in that of Greece. In fact, his impartiality towards the Persians earned him the epithet: "barbarophile."

In his first five books Herodotus describes, often with amusing and charming digressions on their culture and ethnography, the countries that took part in the war. At the end of Book 5 he begins the main narrative of the campaigns and proceeds with it to the end of Book 9, where the Persians are in full retreat. Herodotus then makes a Persian nobleman give his own moral on Xerxes' defeat: the Persians, by conquering the rich plains of the Near East, had grown luxurious and soft, so that they could be beaten by the poor but tough hill peoples of Greece.

To Herodotus this denouement took place in a world in which gods and men mingled and interacted. Men were responsible for what they did, and by their actions they might win fair fame and glory. But they might also earn blame, guilt, and defeat, for the gods were guardians of the cosmic order. Xerxes, arrogantly aspiring to conquer Greece, committed the fault of *hybris*, that is, of overstepping the bounds of his rightful position as King of Asia. The gods therefore afflicted him with *ate*, blind infatuation, and in this state he crazily and recklessly invaded Greece. He even ordered the waters of the Hellespont lashed for disobedience to himself. In this condition he inevitably and deservedly suffered his *nemesis:* defeat on the battlegrounds of Greece.

As a historian Herodotus had certain limitations. He had for the most part only oral traditions of varying reliability to draw on, but he was not uncritical of them. His remarks on the book written by Hecataeus of Miletus show this, as does his often-used phrase, "They say this, but I do not believe it." Yet, he naïvely calculated the strength of the Persian forces at over five million men, a clearly impossible figure, and he became a biased partisan of Athens. In his account of the Battle of Salamis he tells outrageously untrue stories of the Corinthian General Adimantus. The best that can be said of Herodotus here is that he also admits he had heard the stories were false.

In spite of his limitations Herodotus deserves our respect, for his work showed a great advance in Greek historical thought. His predecessors had been content with short and simple chronicles. Herodotus was the first Greek to write narrative history in which a mass of individual facts was collected and set forth within a unifying, interpretive context.

Hignett, C. H. *Xerxes' Invasion of Greece.* Oxford: The Clarendon Press, 1963.

C. H. Hignett's book is the product of some forty years of research and reflection on the problems connected with the reconstruction of the history of the Persian invasion. Its principal thesis is that the only reliable source of knowledge of the war is Herodotus. Hignett, in a valuable introduction, reviews what is known of the books of ancient writers other than Herodotus, and is able to demonstrate that their work was, on the whole, shorter, more jejune, and less accurate than the history of the great Halicarnassian. For example, an important secondary account is the *Hellenica* of Ephorus of Cymae, a universal history from remote times down to the fourth century B.C. Ephorus tells us that Leonidas' Spartans one night actually raided the camp of the Great King and very nearly laid hands on Xerxes himself. This story is highly improbable on the face of it, since the Greeks had chosen to fight at Thermopylae because they could fight defensively behind fortifications in a narrow place and thus nullify the effect of the Persians' vast numbers. Why, then, should they risk disaster by striking straight into the middle of the Persian camp? Herodotus says nothing of this adventurous incident, and Hignett regards it as romantic invention. In consequence, the modern scholar must use the work of the other ancient historians only with the greatest care and skepticism.

Hignett is also penetrating in his criticism of Herodotus' own account. Herodotus says that at some time before the Battle of Thermopylae the Spartans received an oracle from Delphi that one of their kings must die in the war or the state itself would fall. Herodotus, a pious man, was likely to believe Delphic prophecies. Leonidas, we are to believe, during the retreat from Thermopylae, remained behind when the Persians had turned his position and bravely died to save the state. This, Hignett thinks, is Spartan propaganda, probably invented to explain away the disaster of the death of one of its kings. Since the whole Thespian army died along with Leonidas' three hundred Spartans, and since it is inconceivable that the Thespians would have allowed the whole flower of their manhood to perish merely to help fulfill a prophecy of doubtful authenticity which was to them irrelevant, the story must be an invention. Hignett then goes on to speculate on why Leonidas did not withdraw from the pass in time, and concludes that unless fresh evidence comes to hand we can never know.

This book is not easy reading, since much of it is taken up with technical, critical analyses concerning the credibility of parts of Herodotus' narrative. Moreover, narratives of battles are interrupted by discussions about the topography of the battlefields, and Hignett admits that he has little direct familiarity with them. Despite such defects, together with a few details of chronology in which he differs from general scholarly opinion, Hignett's book is the most careful treatment of the campaigns of 480 and 479 B.C.

—*Samuel K. Eddy*

Additional Recommended Reading

Burn, A. R. *Persia and the Greeks.* New York: St. Martin's Press, 1962. A narrative covering events from the sixth century to Xerxes' defeats in 479.

How, W. W., and J. A. Wells. *A Commentary on Herodotus.* Oxford: The Clarendon Press, 1912. 2 vols. An obsolescent work but one still useful for bringing together passages in ancient literature which supplement and explain Herodotus.

Olmstead, A. T. *A History of the Persian Empire.* Chicago: University of Chicago Press, 1948. A somewhat uncritical account of the wars from the Persian viewpoint by a distinguished Orientalist.

CREATION OF THE ATHENIAN EMPIRE

Type of event: Political: establishment of a large political unit
Time: 470-448 B.C.
Locale: The Aegean Sea

Principal personages:
ARISTIDES, son of Lysimachus, Athenian statesman
CIMON, son of Miltiades, Athenian general and statesman
PERICLES, son of Xanthippus, Athenian general and statesman
THUCYDIDES, son of Melesias, Athenian statesman

Summary of Event

After the Persian invasion of Greece had been repulsed in the spring of 477 B.C., delegates from the liberated Greek cities of Ionia and Athens assembled and agreed to combine forces in a league whose stated aims were to protect the Aegean area from fresh Persian offensives and to ravage Xerxes' territory. The headquarters of this confederacy was located on the sacred island of Delos, and it came to be called the Delian League. In the beginning an assembly of representatives determined policy, with each state, large or small, exercising one vote. Each member contributed either ships or money; the respective assessments of ships and money were the work of Aristides of Athens, whose determinations were so fair that he was afterwards called "The Just." The money was kept on Delos under the supervision of a board of Athenians called Hellenic Treasurers. Fleet and army were both commanded by Athenians since Athens was the largest and most powerful of the allied states and Athenians had won great prestige in defeating the Persians.

At first all went well. The league fleet maintained the security of the Aegean and even successfully attacked the Persian-held island of Cyprus. Such victories led some members of the confederacy to regard the Persian menace as broken, and about 470 B.C. Naxos, tired of onerous naval service, unilaterally seceded. The Athenians, supported by a majority of the allies, felt that the withdrawal of Naxos might portend the dissolution of the league to Persia's advantage. Naxos was therefore besieged and reduced to obedience. This act set an important precedent. Moreover, the league's assessment of the situation was shown to be correct the next year when the reconstituted Persian navy sailed towards the Aegean but was defeated in the Battle of Eurymedon by the league fleet led by Athens' excellent general Cimon.

Because providing ships year after year was a hardship for some members, Athens, upon the suggestion of Cimon, introduced the policy of allowing any state to convert its obligation of furnishing ships to one of paying money. Gradually most did so, until by 445 only seven states of a regular membership of some 150 still contributed triremes. At the time the change must have seemed statesmanlike, but it actually cloaked a great danger to the league. As time went on only the Athenians and the few other states with fleets were capable of serious naval action; the ships of the money-paying cities decayed and their crews lacked practice. The Athenians, meanwhile, not only increased the size of their navy but also introduced improved models of triremes and new naval tactics, so that by the 440's their navy was a virtually invincible force.

50

In 460 B.C., the Delian confederates attacked the Persians in Egypt, but the offensive ended with the annihilation of a league fleet in 454. For a time it seemed that the Persian naval forces might again invade the Aegean. To meet the immediate danger this threat posed to the league's accumulated treasure on the unfortified island of Delos it was agreed to move the fund to the heavily guarded Acropolis at Athens. When peace was made with Persia in 448, however, the money was not moved back. Athens assumed sole control of this enormous sum of five thousand talents and insisted that the annual sums thereafter be paid to her. Over the next decades this money was used to maintain Athens' navy, to build the remarkable series of buildings erected on the Acropolis, and to finance future wars. Meetings of the league's assembly stopped; the league had become an Athenian empire.

Some members of the league strongly objected to this new regime and rebelled against it, but their naval weakness made them easy to suppress. Rebellious states were compelled to accept democratic, pro-Athenian governments; other states had their legal and commercial relations with Athens subjected to regulation. A few were forced to accept Athenian garrisons or to cede territory for Athenian settlers. The man mainly responsible for this program was Pericles. He was filled with the vision of an idealized Athens, not only as a supreme military power but also as a model of political organization and advanced culture. "Our state," he once said, "is the education of Hellas." His more extreme acts of imperialism were condemned by conservatives such as the statesman Thucydides, son of Melesias, but by the 440's some thousands of Athenians received wages for various services from the annual payments of the allies. As a result the masses backed Pericles, and Thucydides was ostracized. "It may have been wrong to acquire the empire," said Pericles, "but it would certainly be dangerous to let it go." Thus, while necessity had dictated the punishment of Naxos, greed and fear compelled the Athenians to keep their grip on their former allies. Athens, in her own eyes "the Hellas of Hellas," was the tyrant-city in the eyes of other Greeks. Certain members of the former league appealed to Sparta for help, and, when the Peloponnesian War broke out in 431, most Greeks supported Sparta in the hope of seeing Athenian power destroyed.

All this was unfortunate because Athens was, in other ways, the most humane and liberal state in Greece. She was democratic. She tolerated free speech to a remarkable degree. She provided work for her poor and treated her slaves with relative humanity. From all parts of the Hellenic world artists, poets, and philosophers streamed in to visit her, so that she became the intellectual and moral beacon of the Aegean world, a true city of light. But her crass subjection of allies turned much of the world against her and may have prevented the Delian League from becoming an instrument for the gradual and voluntary unification of the innumerable small, quarrelsome, and warlike Greek states.

Pertinent Literature

Tod, Marcus N., E. M. Walker, and F. E. Adcock. *The Cambridge Ancient History.* Vol. V, pp. 1-112; 165-192. Cambridge: The University Press, 1927.

It must be made clear, before discussing this book, that there is no one work that gives an adequate account of Athens' conversion from leader of a voluntary confederation to the ruler of an empire. The reason is that the evidence is hard to interpret. The literary evidence for the period 477-439 B.C. is of uneven quantity and uncertain quality. We have an excellent, nearly contemporary authority in the Athenian historian Thucydides. His subject, however, was the war of 431-404 B.C., and he felt that he did not have to detail events of the preceding fifty years when the empire was being formed. There is also the history of Diodorus Siculus, who lived in the time of Julius Caesar. His account, based on the *Hellenica* of Ephorus, who wrote in the fourth century, covers the whole of the fifth century. Ephorus, however, was uncritical, and unfortunately his narrative is often inaccurate; moreover, Diodorus, an unskillful man, debased the work still more. Plutarch, the famous biographer and ultra-moralist of the early second century, was somewhat more careful than either Ephorus or Diodorus, and he records valuable details concerning Aristides, Cimon, and Pericles in his *Parallel Lives.* His most trustworthy passages are those based on the work of Thucydides, but sections derived from other fifth century writers, such as Ion of Chios, are regarded with some suspicion by modern scholars and, as a result, valuable time and effort has had to be expended on source criticism to the detriment of historical narrative.

Apart from the ancient writers, there is a considerable amount of epigraphic evidence in the form of inscriptions recording decrees of the Athenian Assembly, some of which have only recently been found. Here too, however, there are problems. The series of inscriptions which indirectly record the amounts of tribute paid by each allied state after 454, for example, received definitive publication only in 1948, and since then the accuracy of the publication has been questioned. Other inscriptions, usually mutilated but more or less restorable, contain the texts of various treaties between the subject allies and Athens. The dates assigned to many of these inscriptions have lately been challenged by

Harold Mattingly among others. Many of the objections have been answered by Benjamin D. Meritt, but the controversy has tended to create doubt and hesitation rather than stimulate constructive reevaluation.

Given the necessity for meticulous criticism of ancient literary sources and for careful restoration of inscriptions, then, historians have often overspecialized, in the process losing sight of the whole problem. Admittedly, for example, Athenian imperialism was decisively affected by purely internal events at Athens, such as the quarrel between Pericles and the statesman Thucydides over democratic reform, but while we have an excellent book on the constitutional history of Athens, with some remarks on foreign affairs, and an excellent book on the financial and imperial policies of Athens, with some remarks on internal affairs, the overall result is that we do not have a single book combining both subjects which is up-to-date and takes economic history into account. Writers are reluctant to deal with the biographies of the men of this period because they are uncertain about Plutarch's trustworthiness. Thus, no one book adequately covers all facets of the creation of the Athenian empire.

Now to return to the literature cited above.

Tod, Walker, and Adcock contributed five chapters to the fifth volume of *The Cambridge Ancient History* which appeared in 1927. Tod, a famous epigrapher, wrote on the economic history of the fifth century, which explains with little detail one reason for Athens' early successes, namely her wealth. The Rev. E. M. Walker contributed three chapters on the creation of the Delian League, interstate relations, and the democratic reforms of Pericles. Professor Adcock wrote on the years from 445 to 431 and of Athens' relations with her subject allies.

Though written before the important studies of B. D. Meritt and other scholars on the texts of the Athenian inscriptions were completed, these chapters are not entirely obsolete. Each man was an expert. Walker was, perhaps, the least skilled of the three men because he wrote under the influence of perverse conceptions such as the claim that Athens insisted upon the establishment of democratic constitutions everywhere in her empire. We are certain today that such was not the case. Athens was imperialistic but not ideologically fanatic. Volume V of *The Cambridge Ancient History* does combine some economic history of the fifth century with the internal and external history of Athens and her allies.

Meritt, B. D., H. T. Wade-Gery, and M. F. McGregor. *The Athenian Tribute Lists.* Vol. III. The American School of Classical Studies at Athens. Princeton: Princeton University Press, 1950.

No student of Greek history should ignore this important book. B. D. Meritt is a veteran epigrapher of great reputation who has worked to reconstitute and interpret the chipped and mutilated surfaces of the Athenian inscriptions. With his no less distinguished colleagues, he undertook the publication of the surviving fragments of the Athenian tribute-quota lists, and the first volume of this work appeared in 1939. Volume II, a republication of the old fragments along with a few new ones, appeared in 1948. Finally, Volume III was published in 1950. It is divided into three sections. Part I is a critical and highly technical discussion of the contents of the lists themselves. Part II is a learned analysis of various problems connected with the literary sources, including a consideration of textual problems in Thucydides and a carefully reasoned outline of the chronology of the period from 477 to 431 B.C. Part III is a history of the Delian League from its inception until the fall of Athens in 404.

It is a detailed account which necessarily concentrates on Athens. Little is said about the Athenian allies, and even less about Sparta and her allies. It is based on more and better evidence than was available to Walker and Adcock. Considerable attention is given to the financial history of Athens. On this point we are in a tantalizing position. With part of the evidence for the administration of Athens' money in our hands, we can partially reconstruct a detailed picture of the economic resources available to the Athenian government at various stages between 454 and 420 B.C. But in going into this matter, Meritt and his colleagues overreach themselves. They appear to think that the epigraphical record combined with literary evidence gives us virtually a complete picture of Athenian finance, that, as A. W. Gomme said, these fragmentary stones are like the pieces of a puzzle which fit side by side. But in fact they do not; there are important gaps in the surviving inscriptions, and the three authors have gone too far in filling them in by what amounts to guesswork. Still, *The Athenian Tribute Lists* is a useful book, indispensable for the study of Athens' change from *hegemon* to master of the Aegean.

—*Samuel K. Eddy*

Additional Recommended Reading

Andreades, A. M. *A History of Greek Public Finance.* Translated from the Greek by C. N. Brown. Rev. ed. Cambridge: Harvard University Press, 1933. An older survey of what is known of the financial institutions and practices of the Greek states.

Barron, John P. "Religious Propaganda of the Delian League," in *Journal of Hellenic Studies.*

Vol. 84 (1964), pp. 35-48. A study of Athens' attempt to distill an opiate for the masses in the subject states.

Bradeen, Donald W. "The Popularity of the Athenian Empire," in *Historia.* Vol. IX (1960), pp. 257-269. An answer to Ste. Croix' article.

Green, Peter. *Alexander to Actium: The Historical Evolution of the Hellenistic Age.* Berkeley: University of California Press, 1990. A monumental history of the Hellenistic world that offers a comprehensive overview of the age, including its political, social, artistic, and literary features.

Laidlaw, W. A. *A History of Delos.* Oxford: Basil Blackwell, 1933. A narrative of the island's history including a survey of its impressive archaeological remains.

Laistner, M. L. W. *A History of the Greek World from 479 to 323 B.C.* London: Methuen, 1936. An older but competent survey of Greek history which includes the history of the transformation of the Delian League.

Mattingly, Harold B. "The Growth of Athenian Imperialism," in *Historia.* Vol. XII (1963), pp. 257-273. One of the author's more recent articles revising the accepted dating of Athenian inscriptions.

Meritt, B. D., and H. T. Wade-Gery. "The Dating of Documents to the Mid-Fifth Century," in *Journal of Hellenic Studies.* Vol. 83 (1963), pp. 100-117. An answer to Mattingly's approach and methods.

Ste. Croix, G. E. M. de. "The Character of the Athenian Empire," in *Historia.* Vol. III (1954), pp. 1-41. This work argues that most Greeks in the Empire did not hate Athens by 431 B.C.

FORMULATION OF THE "TWELVE TABLES" OF ROMAN LAW

Type of event: Legal: enactment of a code of laws
Time: 451-449 B.C.
Locale: Rome

Principal personages:
APPIUS CLAUDIUS,
TITUS GENUCIUS,
PUBLIUS SESTIUS,
LUCIUS VETURIUS,
GAIUS JULIUS,
AULUS MANLIUS,
PUBLIUS SULPICIUS,
PUBLIUS CURIATIUS,
TITUS ROMILIUS, and
SPURIUS POSTUMIUS, decemvirs in 451 B.C.

APPIUS CLAUDIUS,
MARCUS CORNELIUS MALUGINENSIS,
MARCUS SERGIUS,
LUCIUS MINUCIUS,
QUINTUS FABIUS VIBULANUS,
QUINTUS POETELIUS,
TITUS ANTONIUS MERENDA,
CAESO DUILLIUS,
SPURIUS OPPIUS CORNICEN, and
MANIUS RABULEUS, decemvirs in 450 B.C.

Summary of Event

The formulation of the Twelve Tables of Roman Law, as recorded by Livy and Dionysius of Halicarnassus, was one of the most significant events in the "struggle of the orders" between patricians and plebeians in Rome during the fifth century B.C. In 462, according to the traditional date of the *fasti*, Gaius Terentilius Harsa, a tribune of the plebs, made a spirited attack on the authority of the consuls, saying that their unregulated and unlimited power brought down all the terrors and penalties of the law upon the plebs. Harsa suggested that five men should be appointed to compose a code of laws which would put a check upon the patricians who as judges were interpreters of the unwritten customary law and who as priests determined the validity of the complex legal procedures. His proposal was rejected, as was another in 454 when the tribunes suggested that a commission composed of both patricians and plebeians should draw up the code.

In 452 the tribunes insisted that the work of codification should begin. To expedite the task it was decided that the ordinary magistracies should be suspended and that, instead, *decemviri legibus scribundis*, "ten men for writing the laws," should be chosen to rule the state the following year without

55

being subject to appeal. After some debate, the plebeians agreed to surrender their demand to be represented on the board along with the patricians, but they did so with the understanding that their sacral laws would not be abrogated.

The ten elected decemvirs set about framing the laws and set them up on ten tables in the Forum. After amending them according to suggestions received, they presented their work to the *comitia centuriata* for formal ratification. It soon became apparent that two more tables would have to be added to make the corpus complete, and so decemvirs were again elected by the *comitia centuriata* after considerable canvassing. Appius Claudius, who had been chairman of the first decemvirate was reelected with nine new colleagues.

The second decemvirate is traditionally pictured as drafting the two additional tables amidst a reign of terror. For some unknown reason they began to act like tyrants by oppressing the plebeians, and only a secession of the plebs forced them out of office at the expiration of their commission.

Legendary though much of this account of the formulation of the Twelve Tables may be, there is little doubt about the antiquity of the ancient code which Livy, with some exaggeration, describes as "the source of all public and private law" for Rome.

While the original text of the Twelve Tables is said to have been lost in the sack of Rome by the Gauls about 390 B.C., copies remained so that Cicero reported in his *De legibus* that boys still had to memorize them in his day. Provisions of the code were never repealed although many lapsed through neglect and irrelevancy. Some one hundred and forty fragments or paraphrases show that the code was genuinely Roman in content and largely a codification of already existing custom. The code had only two constitutional provisions: one forbidding *privilegia*, and the other forbidding trial of a citizen on a capital charge by any assembly except the *comitia*

centuriata. Assembly at night was forbidden. Dealing with private, public, and sacral law, the code concerned itself, among other matters, with the guardianship and status of women and property, the guardianship of lunatics and prodigals, division of inheritances, and rights concerning land. The laws were absolute imperatives and protected property above life; an insolvent debtor, for instance, could be fettered for sixty days and then executed or put up for sale, and many believed that the code allowed dismemberment of a debtor's body to satisfy several creditors. One was permitted to kill a thief only if he came at night or actually used a weapon. Dreadfully deformed children were to be killed. Blood revenge was recognized if satisfaction was denied in other ways. The father, as absolute head of the family could sell, with certain safeguards, his sons into slavery. Although marriage rites were simple, intermarriage between plebeian and patrician was forbidden. Penalties were harsh, death being meted out in five different ways including burning at the stake and casting from the Tarpeian rock. Bribery, libel, sorcery, cutting other people's crops, and even theft were capital offenses. Besides the death penalty other forms of punishment recognized were being fined, fettered, or flogged; retaliation in kind; civil disgrace; banishment; and slavery. Fines for injuring persons were graduated according to the value traditionally ascribed to individuals. Plebeians gained through a law allowing a thirty-day interval to discharge a debt before the infliction of penalty. Interest was fixed, probably at eight and one third percent, and "not according to the free choice of the wealthy."

Apart from obvious legal significance, the Twelve Tables are of great interest to philologists because of the archaic language used and to historians because the ordinances provide the best information available on the economic and social conditions of Rome during the fifth century.

Pertinent Literature

Pais, Ettore. *Ancient Italy.* Translated by C. Densmore Curtis. Chicago: University of Chicago Press, 1908.

Pais has been in the forefront of discussion concerning the relationship of the Twelve Tables of Roman law to Athenian and other Greek law. The subject was brought up by the ancients themselves who unanimously believed that the Roman Law was modeled upon Athenian legislation. Tradition had it that three commissioners were sent from Rome to study the laws of Athens before beginning work on the Roman code. Since only short, matter-of-fact fragments of the Twelve Tables exist, the question is made so difficult that Pais feels he can give no conclusive answers. Mommsen, the great authority on Roman law, accepted the Greek origin of the laws of the Twelve Tables, but Pais believes that he should have drawn his conclusions from a wider study than mere consideration of linguistics.

Pais points out that three contradictory stories exist explaining how Rome received knowledge of Greek jurisprudence: one records that such information came in the form of an embassy from Greece; another gives credit to a Greek philosopher who came to Rome; and a third postulates a Roman embassy sent to Greece on a mission of inquiry. He also points out that the general character of Greek law is different from the specific character of the Twelve Tables, and that the latter differs sharply in the matter of strict agnation. There is no evidence of direct borrowings from very early Greek law and yet the Roman fragments indicate a tradition of legal procedure, especially in the case of retaliation, more ancient than any used in contemporary Greek cities, especially Athens. Clearly the laws of Solon are not transported bodily to Rome, although portions of the funerary laws may be related to Solon's enactments. Furthermore, Pais suggests that

there was no need for Rome to go to Athens to survey her code, since the Twelve Tables emanated, he believes, from the time of the censor Appius Claudius (not the decemvir) between 312 and 304. Thus Rome had plenty of time to learn about Greek law from the new Athenian colony of Thurii founded in 446. It seems relevant, too, that even Magna Graecia itself did not await the spread of Athenian influence before building its own codes such as that made by the famous Zeleucus for Locri, or that by the still-more-famous Charondas for the Chalcidian cities of Italy.

Pais favors Tacitus' thesis that the code came from all cities who could offer model laws. Dionysius of Halicarnassus seems to reflect the same view in remarking that an embassy was sent not only to Athens but to many Greek cities of Italy. Pais is partial to the influence of Thurii where an Attic code was put into effect in 446 after being compiled under a commission by the sage Protagoras of Abdera. This code, in turn, was a composite of items from Locri, the Chalcidian cities, cities of the Peloponnesus, and Crete, as well as Athens. Given out under the venerable name of Charondas it spread from Thurii to Athens, thence to Sicily and apparently to Cappadocia in Asia Minor. Zeleucus of Locri, too, was said to have incorporated the laws of many codes, especially those of Lycurgus, Solon, and Minor. If in compiling a code for cosmopolitan Thurii, where Dorian, Ionian, and Athenian cultures met, Protagoras leaned heavily on the code of Locri, it is easy to see why Zeleucus in some traditions is regarded as the lawgiver of Thurii. Pais asks whether this code which spread to Athens could possibly have moved to Naples and from there to Latium. He believes that a study of the code of Charondas, as does the one from Thurii, reveals that the Romans adopted certain legislation, such as laws relating to the obligation to and care of orphans, which was not in harmony with their national character.

Whatever the case, it is clear that Magna Graecia is foremost in legal codification and that these compilations represent, in virtually all cases, the experiences of more than one city.

Finally Pais tries to argue for a composite influence of Magna Graecia, especially Thurii, on Roman law by showing that much of Roman religion and attitudes toward education stem from Italian Greece rather than Athens proper.

Jolowicz, H. F. *Historical Introduction to the Study of Roman Law.* Cambridge: The University Press, 1952.

Until the end of the nineteenth century the Twelve Tables were generally accepted as authentic. In his *Storia di Roma*, published in 1898, Pais sowed considerable doubt not only about the details surrounding the story of the Tables, such as the palpably legendary account of Virginia, but also concerning the entire historical tradition of the code itself. He believes that the fifth century decemvirate is historically indefensible and holds that this fictious board was a variant of the *decemviri stlitibus judicandis* known to have been established about the same time to decide cases involving the status of a freeman. This interpretation would make Appius Claudius the decemvir a "legendary double" for Appius Claudius the blind, who was censor in 312. The Tables, most likely the result of several legislative acts according to this view, grew up gradually over many years and received their final form in the fourth century. Only in that century, Pais thinks, was pontifical authority sufficiently blunted to allow law to be so secularized.

The whole episode, he holds, is clarified if one sees some relationships between the Twelve Tables and the so-called *Jus Flavianum* exacted when Gnaeus Flavius was aedile in 304. Flavius, a secretary to Appius Claudius the censor, is reputed to have stolen and published a collection of laws made by his master which revealed on what days a legal action could be taken. This populariza-

tion of law and the opening of the pontificate to plebeians by the Ogulnian Law of 300 convince Pais that the fourth century fits the whole situation better than the mid-fifth. Consequently the decemvirate should be discarded and the event placed in the late fourth century.

Many other matters contribute to his doubts. In general, he makes it clear that reliable information for Roman history is simply not available before the burning of Rome about 390. More specifically, the provisions of the Twelve Tables are too divergent; some are barbaric and others reveal a sophistication in which Greek influence seems at work. Traditions concerning the decemviri are unbelievable. The last two tables are said to be unfair because they forbade intermarriage between the orders yet they were not repealed in 449 by Valerius and Horatius, who were clearly sympathetic to the plebs.

Lambert, a French writer of the early 1920's, is even more iconoclastic than Pais. He considers that the so-called Twelve Tables code is actually a collection of antiquarian materials made in the first half of the second century probably by a Sextus Aelius. As such it was never an actual legislative instrument.

H. F. Jolowicz points out that scholars were generally unconvinced by the work of Pais and Lambert. While admitting that interpolations were made easy by the absence of a standard text of the code, they considered it inconceivable that Romans of the first century should be misled about an episode as recent as these authors would make it. As Jolowicz puts it, both Sextus Aelius' and Gnaeus Flavius' times lay in the full view of history. Moreover, tradition so firmly held the Twelve Tables to be an organic whole that it affected the entire subsequent history of Roman jurisprudence. Furthermore, considering how archaic the laws are, far too much so for 200 or 300 B.C., it would have been virtually impossible for the Roman Law to grow into the sophisticated system it became by the time of Cicero if the Twelve Tables were as late as these scholars assert.

It is now generally accepted that the Twelve Tables were an enacted code of laws and that, as a law of peasant proprietors suited to a day of little commerce, they fit the period around 450. Modern scholars assume that details surrounding adoption of the code are fictitious or glamorized. As a product of the fifth century the code remains a tribute to the precocious Roman mind in that it so early separated law from religion and that it devotes itself almost exclusively to private law. Apparently it never introduced any constitutional change; otherwise, it would be difficult to explain how the old constitution could have been so easily restored when the decemvirate was abolished.

—M. Joseph Costelloe

Additional Recommended Reading

Coleman-Norton, P. R. *The Twelve Tables Prefaced, Arranged, Translated, Annotated.* Princeton: Princeton University Press, 1952. A work extremely helpful in explaining the significance of individual laws.

Frank, Tenney. *An Economic Survey of Ancient Rome.* Vol. I. Baltimore: The Johns Hopkins Press, 1933. This survey deals with the laws of the Twelve Tables in relation to the economic history of Rome.

Warmington, E. H., ed. *Remains of Old Latin.* Newly edited and translated by E. H. Warmington. Vol. III: *Lucilius; The Twelve Tables.* Cambridge: Harvard University Press, 1938. This volume in the Loeb Classical Library contains the Latin text, an English translation, and the contexts in which individual laws are cited.

Wolff, Hans Julius. *Roman Law. An Historical Introduction.* Norman: University of Oklahoma Press, 1951. Wolff notes that codifications of Roman law in the fifth century B.C. and the sixth century A.D. stand at the beginning and end of the Law of the Roman state.

ENACTMENT OF THE CANULEIAN LAW

Type of event: Legal: issuance of social legislation
Time: 445 B.C.
Locale: Rome

Principal personage:
GAIUS CANULEIUS, plebeian tribune in 445 B.C.

Summary of Event

During the last decade of the sixth century B.C., the political community already established at Rome started on the long road of political development that led to the Republican constitution of the first century B.C. The traditional system of kingship was overthrown and replaced by two annually-elected magistrates equipped with broad executive powers. Legislative initiative and a general intangible but effective substance of political power was vested in the senate, a self-sustaining body of elder counselors. Although both these organs of government appeared to be republican in character, they were unable to forestall civil strife at Rome and, in fact, they reflected the basic discrepancy in Roman society that engendered that strife. This dichotomy was the so-called "struggle of the orders," a patterned class conflict which was contested on almost all levels of communal life.

The two classes engaged in the struggle were known as patricians and plebeians. After 509, the traditional date for the beginning of the Roman Republic, the plebeians held an inferior position within the Roman state. They were excluded from holding political office and from the senate, since such honors were reserved for the patricians. Furthermore the plebeians were barred from the official religious bodies of the state and, by one of the laws in the Twelve Tables, from intermarriage with the patricians. The cause and significance of these prohibitions can be found in the underlying social structure of Rome.

The predominant social unit was the *gens* or clan, which was composed of a group of families linked by a common name and the veneration of a common male ancestor. The origin of the *gens* structure has been keenly disputed, but there is general agreement today that it was an outgrowth of the economic progress within the early agrarian society of Rome. Increased wealth caused a split into upper and lower classes that hardened into richer and poorer families. Members of the richer and more powerful clans called themselves patricians, perhaps because of their exclusive hold on the senate, whose original members were termed *patres*, or fathers. This nobility of wealth eventually became a nobility of blood which claimed for itself the fullness of citizenship and total dominance in all aspects of political life. For the fifth century B.C. there is evidence for the existence of fifty such patrician clans, entrenched in power and maintained by privilege.

Opposed to the patricians were the plebeians. There is also some debate as to their origin but they were probably not racially distinct from the patricians. In general they were the poorer elements of Roman society who had not shared in the economic advances of the early years of Roman history. This original core was augmented by workers and peasants who had been either attracted to Rome by its commercial growth or engulfed by the spread of Roman conquest. Together these various strands formed the *plebs*, or multitude. It must be understood that the plebeians were not a servile class; they always possessed a number of political and civil rights. Furthermore the plebeians also had a *gens* structure within which individual plebeian clans gradually increased in size and wealth. Gradually they became discontented with their second-class status: throughout the first half of the fifth century they repeatedly demanded, and obtained, greater equity within the state. They acquired their own officials, the tribunes of the *plebs*, to act as their protectors and leaders. In 449, a special commission completed the first written codification of law at Rome, the famous Twelve Tables, which made knowledge of the law accessible to everyone so that it was no longer the private province of the patricians. These gains were not obtained without patrician resistance, as evidenced by the inclusion in the Twelve Tables of the ban on intermarriage, a blatant reminder that the plebeians did not enjoy total equality.

In this regard it is misleading to say that marriage between the two groups was interdicted. The Roman Law recognized various forms of marriage, the simplest being the mere living together of a man and woman. If such an arrangement persisted uninterruptedly for one year, the two parties were considered legally married, except in the case of patricians and plebeians. A plebeian woman could share the house of a patrician man for the required period without her, or the children of such a union, becoming patrician, results which normally followed in a legal marriage. The decisive factor in this bizarre arrangement was a religious one. The only valid marriage ceremony for patricians was the solemn, religious one called *confarreatio*. For a valid marriage between the two groups, therefore, the plebeians would have to be permitted entrance into the tenaciously guarded domain of patrician religion.

This impasse was circumvented in 445 by Gaius Canuleius, a tribune of the people, who proposed a law rescinding the ban on intermarriage. The law did not eliminate the exclusion of plebeians from the ceremony of *confarreatio*; instead it recognized cohabitation and another secular form of marriage as legally binding so that the wife and her children gained patrician status. It seems probable that the patricians at first rejected even this compromise which left their religion intact. The plebeians countered with their most effective weapon, a mass withdrawal from the communal life of the city. This drastic measure compelled the patricians to accept the law. With its enactment, the plebeians shed another vestige of their inferior status. Civil strife between the two classes persisted, but for the plebeians the Canuleian law came to stand as one of their more gratifying victories.

Pertinent Literature

Mommsen, Theodore. *The History of Rome.* New York: Charles Scribner and Sons, 1900.

Although Mommsen's original work in German is more than one hundred years old, it wears its age extremely well. Clearly wrong in many of his conclusions and occasionally haphazard in his use of evidence, Mommsen's nonetheless remains one of the most comprehensive and in many respects the most stimulating account of the Republic of Rome. For the very early period of the Republic, Mommsen did not hesitate to reconstruct a cohesive and detailed account of the struggles between the patricians and plebeians.

This reconstruction requires as its basic hypothesis that the plebeians were originally a client class. In the Rome of the kings, to be a citizen meant to be a member of a *gens.* Membership in a *gens* was determined solely by patrilinear descent, and as a result citizens were termed *patricii,* or those who could lay claim to a legitimate father. Anyone not in this position was either a slave or a client. Whereas a slave was a mere chattel, a client, although deprived of all legally established rights, enjoyed a sort of protected freedom as a result of his special relation to a patrician patron. While the patron possessed complete control over his client, *dominium,* the Roman Law provided that once this control was allowed to lapse through disuse, it could never revert to the original patron or his heirs.

This class of independent clients was augmented through the territorial expansion of the Roman kings. While the aristocratic families of conquered areas were admitted into the circle of patricians, the majority of the conquered peoples were incorporated as clients, often under the patronage of the king himself. Protected from abuse, they combined with the independent clients by marriage and other legal relationships that soon formed a new *gens* framework. The normal birth increase of this group was accelerated by the citizens' traditional tolerance of foreigners. Its size became even more pronounced since the patricians, as the exclusive holders of citizenship, were alone capable of fighting and dying in Rome's wars of expansion.

Out of this background emerged the ple-beians, numerous and deprived of civil rights. Mommsen found the first adjustment of this situation in the constitutional reforms of the sixth king of Rome, Servius Tullius, traditionally 578-535 B.C. He established the *comitiae curiatae,* which organized the populace of Rome along military capabilities and admitted into its ranks the wealthier plebeians. The Servian reforms also imposed on this group of plebeians the duty of tax payments, but in return did not provide them with any secure political rights. This anomalous situation only increased plebeian clamor for political equity, which was not satisfied by the grudging concessions made by the patricians during the early decades of the Republic. The wealthier plebeians were admitted into the senate, but only as silent members, allowed neither to vote nor to advise. For Mommsen, the eventual loss of all patrician privileges resulted from their failure to admit the wealthier plebeians to full equality of rights. Through their narrow-minded self-esteem, they clung to the obsolete arrangement of a previous generation and contributed significantly to the growing factionalism which was only eradicated by passage of a whole array of new laws. Much of this reconstruction is tenuous at best and at worst totally wrong, as the next suggested reading makes clear. Yet Mommsen's work contains, along with a wealth of information, a consistent analysis of many of the political attitudes that dominated Rome's later development.

Jones, H. Stuart. "The Primitive Institutions of Rome," in *Cambridge Ancient History,* Vol. VII, ch. 13. Cambridge: The University Press, 1954.

The Canuleian Law presents a number of distinct historical problems. Information about it is meager and many of its aspects are highly problematical. In this situation by far the best guide is H. Stuart Jones. In any evaluation of the early political developments of Rome, a sober eye must be focused on the nature of the evidence since much of it is either legendary or the product of later Roman historians who attempted to explain customs and ceremonies whose original significance had long since faded from historical memory. With these strictures in mind, at least some negative judgments can be made about the primitive status of patricians and plebeians.

It has been argued by Mommsen and other ancient historians that the leading men of the patrician *gentes*, the so-called *patres familiarum*, were the chief organizers of the overthrow of the Etruscan-dominated monarchy, and that they afterwards monopolized the running of the newly-fashioned republican government. Proponents of this view point to the plebeian name of the third king of Rome, Marcius, and to the plebeian names of three of the seven hills of Rome as evidence that the plebeians were in the ascendancy in the city and were supported by the Etruscan kings to offset and isolate the power of the patricians. This situation was reversed in the patrician dominance of the early Republic when new tribes incorporated into the state were designated by the names of existing patrician *gentes*.

This theory, however attractive, runs counter to other, reliable ancient traditions. It is reported of the early kings that when they spread Roman dominion over nearby cities, they incorporated the members of those cities into the citizen population of Rome and bestowed patrician standing on the more powerful families. A clear indication of the early power of the patricians is that the kingship at Rome was not a hereditary title that automatically passed from the father to his eldest son. Instead, the *patres* had the duty of ratifying the selection of the new king. Furthermore the patrician claim of being the sole repository of the knowledge of divine and human law, and especially of maintaining correct relations with the gods, would have been scarcely tenable if they owed this position to a violent usurpation of primacy. In his refutation of this theory, Jones advances positive conclusions. The plebeians were an essential ingredient of pre-Republican Rome, equipped with their own *gens* structure and with a limited amount of political rights.

These conclusions rule out the explanation of the plebeians as originally a client class, totally dependent on the patricians, especially in the light of ancient accounts that the patricians and their clients often united in elections to stifle the opposition of the plebeians. The client system does represent, however, one of the main causes of the rapid growth of the plebeians. As the limited number of patrician families suffered the inevitable decline to which every exclusive caste is liable, clients who had thereby lost their patrician patronage joined the ranks of the plebeians and added their own grievances to the list of plebeian complaints. The rapidly increasing number of plebeians and the persistent demand made on Rome for a more efficient military organization made the removal of plebeian discontent imperative. The Canuleian law eliminated one of the more obvious causes of unrest by permitting free interchange between plebeians and patricians and eventually producing the patricio-plebeian nobility of the later Republic that led Rome to internal stability and foreign supremacy.—*George M. Pepe*

Additional Recommended Reading

De Coulanges, Fustel. *The Ancient City.* Boston: Lothrop, Lee and Shepard Co., 1901. Also in paperback by Doubleday. A provocative and speculative account of the origins of Roman society.

Last, Hugh. "The Servian Reforms," in *Journal of Roman Studies.* XXXV (1945), 30-48. An attempt to demonstrate that plebeians and patricians used to intermarry, and that the ban was an innovation which indicates an increasing split, not present earlier, between the two groups.

Nilsson, M. P. "The Introduction of Hoplite Tactics at Rome: Its Date and Its Consequences,"

in *Journal of Roman Studies.* XIX (1929), 1-11. A suggestion that the new military formation, in which plebeians fought side-by-side with patricians, required that plebeians be
accorded equality in political and social life as well as on the battlefield.

Rose, H. J. "Patricians and Plebeians at Rome," in *Journal of Roman Studies.* XII (1922),
106-133. An argument that the distinction between the two groups developed out of the
value attached to private ownership of landed property.

THUCYDIDES WRITES THE *HISTORY OF THE PELOPONNESIAN WAR*

Type of event: Military: an account of contemporary history
Time: 433-c. 403 B.C.
Locale: Athens and other parts of Greece

Principal personage:
THUCYDIDES, son of Olorus, Athenian general and historian

Summary of Event

The Peloponnesian War broke out in March, 431 B.C., with a sudden night attack by Thebes upon Plataea, a small Greek state allied to Athens. More serious fighting began in May, when Sparta and her Peloponnesian allies invaded and laid waste the northwestern districts of Attica. At the same time an Athenian fleet landed troops in the Peloponnesus to ravage parts of it. The hostilities thus begun lasted for twenty-seven years, with some intervals of peace, and only ended with the complete overthrow of Athens and her empire. The war was the greatest event in Greek history in the fifth century, surpassing in importance even the Persian wars because it left Greece transformed. The war was responsible for political revolutions, the forcible transfer of some entire populations, and the wholesale slaughter of others. The invasion of Sicily by Athens brought in the western Greeks so that almost the whole Hellenic world and part of the non-Hellenic were involved. The material destruction caused was reparable; the moral havoc was not.

When the fighting commenced, Thucydides began to write a history of the war which was to be, as he put it, a "possession for all time." His account was primarily a description of the results of Athens' imperialist policy, which he regarded as the fundamental cause of the war and its prime driving force. The restless activity of Athens and her desire to dominate more and more states caused Sparta to attack her in self-defense to avoid her becoming so rich and powerful that she controlled the whole Greek world. Imperialist motives kept the war going especially when Athens became involved in the invasion of Sicily. To Thucydides this greed for power was a fundamental characteristic of some men. Granted the consistency of human nature from one generation to the next, imperialist states would rise again, and the "possession for all time" was intended to be a case study of the virulence of such a disease.

Thucydides tells us that he began to collect information on the events of the war as soon as it began, which probably means 433 B.C. when Athens sent out warships to engage the Corinthians if the latter continued their war with the Athenian ally Corcyra. Until 424 the historian lived in his native Athens, and he must have culled most of his information from Athenian sources; he was then a general, but the Assembly judged that he failed to carry out Athens' policy efficiently, and he was exiled. He lost his commission but gained the opportunity to study the war from a non-Athenian point of view, and the details he gives of the activity of some of Athens' enemies, soldiers such as Aristeus of Corinth and Brasidas of Sparta, show that he was able to supplement extensively his knowledge of the war outside Athens.

Thucydides was not completely impartial, but he did attempt, with some success, to be objective. He soon realized that inconsistencies among the reports of the eyewitnesses of an event could be resolved only by the most careful collection and sifting of evidence. Such continuous questioning led him occasionally to make revisions in earlier parts of his narrative, so that there are a few passages in conflict with others. The reason that they survive is that Thucydides died while his work was incomplete; he never had the opportunity to give it the final revision and polish which no doubt he intended.

He was an accurate writer. He gives the text of a treaty made by Athens and Argos in 420 B.C. Fortunately, the stone recording the alliance has been found, and in a document which amounts to about a page and a half of English, the official Athenian version and its reproduction by the historian differ in only a few unimportant words, and some of the differences may be due to faulty transmission of the text, for Thucydides was not in Athens to read it and may never have visited Argos. The objectivity of the writer is consequently beyond dispute and is seen best, perhaps, in his treatment of Cleon, the man who did the

most to secure his exile. While Thucydides might have wished to misrepresent Cleon's role at Athens, he contented himself with one introductory remark on Cleon, calling him "the most violent of the citizens," and then proceeded with his narrative.

The *History of the Peloponnesian War* contains many speeches of the principal protagonists such as Archidamus of Sparta and Pericles of Athens. The insertion of these extended remarks was a clever artistic device in an age which prized highly the art of public speaking, and the speeches add a sense of immediacy to the narrative. There is, however, considerable modern controversy concerning their accuracy.

Thucydides' precision, detachment, and passionate desire to tell the truth captured the imagination of the next generation of Greek historians, and no less than three writers of the fourth century, Cratippus, Theopompus, and Xenophon, paid him the enormous compliment of beginning their histories of Greece from the point in 411 B.C. where the unfinished text of Thucydides abruptly ends.

Pertinent Literature

Gomme, A. W. *A Historical Commentary on Thucydides.* Oxford: The Clarendon Press, 1945-56. 3 vols.

A. W. Gomme, formerly Lecturer in Classics at the University of Glasgow, has written a commentary on Thucydides which is an ornament of British scholarship, indispensable for a well-rounded study of Thucydides, the Peloponnesian War, and the history of Greece in the fifth century. Unfortunately Gomme, like Thucydides, did not live to complete his work; the third volume ends at Book V, chapter 24 of Thucydides in the year 421 B.C.

Gomme opens with an essay of eighty-eight pages on some necessary preliminary considerations, and in it he lays down princi-

ples for the use of Thucydides' work by modern historians. There is an important section on those aspects of Greek life about which Thucydides assumes his readers will know and of which he says little. These aspects include economic conditions, the political constitutions of the Greek states, and the military and naval techniques. Thucydides, of course, knew much about these matters; for example, his book shows that he understood the extraordinary value that economic strength and accumulated capital had for the military power of a state. But he does not go into the details of economic life because he could assume that his readers knew of them, much as a modern historian of, say, the foreign policy of President Kennedy might assume that his readers had a basic understanding of the Constitution of the United States. It is unfortunate that Thucydides did not say more on these subjects. He certainly had the knowledge, and critics who say that he was blind in these areas are incorrect.

Having made this point, Gomme continues with an extremely valuable assessment of surviving histories of Greek writers other than Thucydides. He disposes of the incompetent Diodorus Siculus (who based his books on the scarcely more competent Ephorus of Cymae) in short order, and passes on to the more important Plutarch, biographer and essayist of A.D. 100. Gomme knew Plutarch's work intimately, and obviously admired him as a charming, honest, and sensible man, but he shows that Plutarch did not have the same deep understanding of the realities of Greek political life of the fifth century which even Ephorus had. Plutarch could not be expected to have such insight for he lived six centuries later in an age of monarchs.

Gomme expended considerable effort on the problems raised by Thucydides' use of speeches, and he has satisfactorily answered them. Thucydides claimed that his versions of the speeches were either as close to the actual words used as he could make them, or that they recounted the things that had to be said on specific occasions. This curious language led several modern scholars to attack the accuracy of the speeches on the ground that they were Thucydidean inventions, pure literary creations. Gomme counterattacked this view and showed that the speeches, if we are to think Thucydides an honest historian, must be approximations to what was actually said. The speeches are certainly not exact transcriptions of the orators' words, for Spartans did not speak Doric nor eastern Greeks Aeolic or Ionic. All the speakers are recorded in Thucydidean style; but there is no reason to think that because of this fact the accounts are anything but paraphrases of the original speeches.

The rest of Gomme's work is given over to a close, detailed, and precise commentary on the text of Thucydides, often taken sentence by sentence, occasionally word by word. To be fully appreciated, Gomme's well-reasoned remarks must be read. A knowledge of Greek is essential here and there. He has made important contributions not only to the restoration of corrupt manuscript readings, but, above all, to our understanding of the history of the late fifth century. His comments reveal a scholar of enormous erudition, well read in European languages, careful, judicious, and incisive. In him the greatest historian of ancient times found a worthy commentator.

Adcock, F. E. *Thucydides and His History.* Cambridge: The University Press, 1963.

Sir Frank Adcock's slim volume on Thucydides is the best short introduction to the man and his work which we have in English, and ably presents a summary of previous scholarship on these subjects, to which he himself has been a notable contributor.

The author begins with a brief account of Thucydides' life and environment. Thucydides was born before 455 B.C. at Athens, and thus grew up in a milieu touched by the first rationalists of European history, the Sophists. It was also the time when the medical school of Hippocrates of Cos was making studies of disease based on empirical methods. Much of this rational, empirical attitude is apparent in Thucydides' idea of history. The gods do not intervene in human affairs, as Herodotus had thought, but instead man is the sole agency of cause. The history is written not so much to show why the war occurred as to show how the course of the war unfolded. In this, Thucydides resembles Hippocrates, who was less concerned with the origins of disease than with the effects of illness on the patient. Thucydides, however, was more than a cold observer; he was a political man with a concern for the interests of the city-state. The affairs and well-being of the individual citizen had to be subordinated to the good of all, that is, to the good of the state. The ability of a statesman to realize practical results seems to have impressed him as much as considerations of good and evil, although that is not to say that Thucydides had a light approach to morals. He was, on the whole, antidemocratic, distrusting the decisions of popular assemblies as subject to ignorance and mob psychology.

Sir Frank raises a number of interesting side issues. He goes into the matter of the speeches and backs up Gomme's interpretation. He thinks that the obvious lies told in some speeches are sure evidence that the general accuracy of what was really said is maintained. As a veteran of Athenian public life Thucydides was, of course, aware that some Greek statesmen took as their model the Homeric "Odysseus of many wiles." There is a fascinating page on the official secrecy of the Greek governments, of which there was certainly less then than exists today, although Sparta was an exception to this general rule. Adcock is also good on Thucydides' methods of composition, and his argument that the historian wrote as the war proceeded is entirely convincing. He shows conclusively that Thucydides did not merely accumulate material during the war and then compose the history after the end of hostilities. His conjecture that Thucydides was drowned at sea about 403 B.C. while returning to Athens from exile cannot be proved, as Sir Frank knows, but it is certainly plausible and accounts for the broken ending of the history in 411 B.C. On the other hand, some scholars believe that Thucydides was murdered, perhaps in Thrace.

There is one quality in this book, however, which is unfortunate, and that is Adcock's prejudice. In discussing the responsibility for the outbreak of the war he asserts that Athens was in the right and the Peloponnesians were the aggressors. This contradicts what Thucydides himself says. It is true that the Spartans crossed the Attic frontier before a single Athenian marine landed in the Peloponnesus, but Thucydides says that Sparta was compelled to attack by reason of Athens' forward policy and tireless efforts to gain new allies. Athens was guilty of indirect aggression at Corcyra in 433 and at Potidaea in 432 before the Peloponnesians struck in 431. Adcock even seems to adopt Athens' own evaluation of her imperial position and lack of war-guilt. On the origin of the Peloponnesian War, he says, in tortuous language, "The defence of the Athenian empire, because it was deserved not so much morally as by its very existence, raised it (the empire) above challenge, like the Statue of Athena Promachos on the Acropolis, inspired by wisdom like the Athena of legend embodied in the Athena of the Parthenon." This is a curious doctrine of phil-Atticism. —*Samuel K. Eddy*

Additional Recommended Reading

Brunt, P. A. "Thucydides and Alcibiades," in *Revue des études grecques.* Vol. 65 (1952), 59-96. Written in English, this article demonstrates Thucydides' methods of obtaining information from participants in the war, in this case from the Athenian Alcibiades.

De Romilly, Jacqueline. *Thucydides and Athenian Imperialism.* Translated from the French by Philip Trody. New York: Barnes and Noble, Inc., 1947, reissued 1964. A thesis that imperialism is the unifying theme of Thucydides' work.

Thucydides Writes the History of the Peloponnesian War

Finley, M. I. *Thucydides.* Ann Arbor: University of Michigan Press, 1963, and in paperback. An analysis of Thucydidean thought and methods.

Thucydides. *The Peloponnesian War.* Translated from the Greek by Rex Warner. Baltimore, Maryland: Penguin Books, Inc., 1954. An accurate and readable translation of the ancient historian's masterpiece.

ATHENIAN INVASION OF SICILY

Type of event: Military: launching of naval attack
Time: June, 415-September, 413 B.C.
Locale: Syracuse

Principal personages

NICIAS, conservative Athenian statesman and general
ALCIBIADES, radical Athenian politician and general
DEMOSTHENES, Athenian general
HERMOCRATES, Syracusan statesman and general
GYLIPPUS, Spartan soldier
GONGYLUS, fifth century Corinthian naval officer

Summary of Event

In 421 B.C., the first phase of the Peloponnesian War ended. As soon as Athens had regained her strength, she began under the leadership of Alcibiades, young and brilliant but sinister, to attempt a decisive victory over Sparta and her Peloponnesian allies. In early 415, this leader proposed attacking Sicily, using the pretext of assisting an ally of Athens there and of stopping the supply of Sicilian grain to the Peloponnesians. Victory over the latter could be secured, Alcibiades contended, if Athens captured the vital Sicilian source of food and recruited mercenaries. The Sicilian Greeks, he went on erroneously, were a mongrel people, unskilled at war, and they would be easy prey. This program of aggression was opposed by the cautious Nicias without success. In June, 415, the Athenians sent out a fleet hitherto unrivaled in Greek history for its magnificence. There were 134 warships, of which thirty-four came from Athens' allies, who were thus dragged into a war which was not of their making. The embarked army numbered 6,500 men, of whom only a third were Athenian.

The expedition sailed under the command of Alcibiades and Nicias. Shortly before it did so, however, certain religious statues in Athens were mutilated by unknown persons. After the fleet had sailed, a formal indict-

ment for this sacrilege was made against Alcibiades, and he was ordered home for trial. Fearing that he would be unjustly condemned, Alcibiades defected to Sparta and in revenge urged an attack against Athens.

His desertion did not stop the Athenians' effort in Sicily under the hesitant Nicias. His offensive soon became an attack on the chief Sicilian state of Syracuse, a colony of Corinth. Nicias procrastinated and the campaigning season of 415 ended with Syracuse scarcely damaged. The Athenians were forced to withdraw into winter quarters.

The Syracusans, efficiently led by Hermocrates, meanwhile managed to dispatch envoys past the Athenian fleet to beg the mother city, Corinth, for help; Corinth, in turn, appealed to Sparta. The Peloponnesian response was good, the Spartans sending one contingent under Gylippus and the Corinthians another under Gongylus.

In 414, a few more Athenian troops arrived in Sicily, and Nicias pressed the siege of Syracuse, a strong, walled city built on a peninsula which separated a large bay, the Grand Harbor, from the sea. The Athenians seized part of the Grand Harbor, fortified it, and blockaded the city by sea, hoping by building a wall across the landward end of the peninsula to invest Syracuse completely and force her surrender through lack of food. With each Athenian victory the wall advanced. Syracuse despaired. Blockaded by sea, she now looked on helplessly as her land routes too were choked off. There seemed no other course but to capitulate. Then, just in time to keep Syracuse from negotiating, Gongylus slipped inside the city to report Gylippus' approach with relief forces. Gylippus' strategy was to extend a counterwall out of Syracuse at right angles to Nicias' five-foot wall to head off its completion. During the summer fierce combats raged around the ends of the two walls. By a narrow margin Gylippus carried his fortifications past Nicias' and thus frustrated the Athenian offensive. In the autumn, operations stalled and Nicias asked for reinforcements.

In the winter of 414-413, the Spartans, finally determined to renew the conflict in Old Hellas, attacked Athens, so that the latter was now fully engaged in two theaters. Athens nonetheless responded to Nicias' appeals, and seventy-three additional triremes (fifty-one Athenian) along with five thousand hoplites (twelve hundred Athenian) were dispatched under the command of Demosthenes. Before he could join Nicias, fresh naval forces reached Syracuse from the Peloponnesus and parts of Sicily. The Syracusans made a bid for victory, and in June and July, 413, they won a series of naval actions in the Grand Harbor. At this point Demosthenes arrived, reestablished Athenian naval supremacy, and dashed Syracusan hopes.

Demosthenes and Nicias next decided to capture Gylippus' counterwall in order to retrieve gains made in the campaign of the year before. The Athenian army went forward by night and came extremely close to success, but in the darkness it lost cohesion and was repulsed. Demosthenes promptly advised Nicias to begin immediate withdrawal by sea, but once more Nicias delayed, believing an eclipse of the moon an omen against evacuation. The Syracusans then resumed their naval offensive, and in September defeated the Athenian fleet in a great battle in the Grand Harbor, compelling Nicias to resort to the forlorn hope of escaping by land. Complete disaster followed. The Syracusan cavalry and light troops harried their enemy and wore them down under a hail of missiles until Nicias surrendered. The Syracusans executed both him and Demosthenes, and imprisoned their men in quarries for months. Those who did not die under these conditions were sold into slavery.

The defeat of Athens was complete. She had lost over two hundred triremes and nearly fifty thousand men, mostly soldiers and sailors of her allies. These appalling losses convinced many statesmen that Athens was finished. In the winter of 413-412, the allied states began to revolt and join Sparta. The Persians, too, entered the war against Athens, thus effecting the grand coalition which was to bring the proud city-state to her knees.

Pertinent Literature

Ferguson, W. S. "The Athenian Expedition to Sicily"; "The Oligarchic Movement in Athens"; and "The Fall of the Athenian Empire," in *The Cambridge Ancient History*. 5th impression. Vol. V, pp. 282-375. Cambridge: The University Press, 1958.

Our main sources of information on the Athenian invasion of Sicily are the sixth and seventh books of the history of the Athenian Thucydides, one of the literary monuments of antiquity. Thucydides' narrative is thought-ful, vivid, and dramatic. We sit in the assembly at Athens as Alcibiades and Nicias debate the merits of making the attack; we watch the first grand armada row out of Piraeus after libations have been poured to the gods; we storm the heights of Epipolae with Demosthenes' men.

Little can be added to this great account. Since only details can be gleaned from Plutarch's biographies of Alcibiades and Nicias and from the corpus of Greek inscriptions, the task of the modern historian, as Ferguson reminds us, is really little more than that of paraphrasing Thucydides and adding a few items from other authorities. Ferguson does so succinctly in less than forty pages. He points out the ignorance of both the Athenian and Syracusan popular assemblies concerning the size, resources, and intentions of the other. The Athenians grossly misjudged the numbers and fighting quality of the Syracusans, and the latter completely disregarded the reports, which Hermocrates believed, of the approach of Nicias' fleet in 415. Neither state had a professional staff of any kind to collect information about foreign powers for the benefit of policy-making bodies.

Thucydides' contention that the Athenians might have won if Nicias had acted more decisively is a point still being argued by historians. Thucydides' opinion has been accepted by some modern authorities, although there are others who feel that in the realm of grand strategy Thucydides' judgment was only that of a regimental commander with above-average competence. While no certain answer can be given, we can say that even if Athens had forced Syracuse to surrender in 415, she could not have held the state indefi-

nitely without committing part of her strength to garrison it, and that, given time, Syracuse and her allies could have raised much of the island against Athens and broken her hold. In this sense, as Thucydides knew, the expedition was a fatal blunder.

The effect of the destruction of the expedition on Athens herself, as Ferguson shows, was ruinous. Outraged oligarchs overthrew the democrats in 411. The conservatives, in turn, speedily showed their incompetence either to win the war by military victory or to end it by negotiation, and the resurgent democrats soon overthrew them. In the poisoned atmosphere at Athens men distrusted one another, and the single-minded effort which Athens should have mounted against her enemies was blunted.

Ferguson's third chapter recounts the last years of the Peloponnesian War. Athens was able to keep alive the long naval conflict, in Ionian waters, against Sparta and Persia until 405. Simultaneously, operations of the Peloponnesian and Boeotian armies in Attica slowly but systematically devastated the country. It is indeed remarkable that Athens, assailed by so many enemies, was able to hold off their superior numbers for so long. Finally, closely besieged, with her fleets sunk or captured, supported only by a single ally of the once great Delian League, she surrendered in 404, compelled to give up her imperial ambitions.

Adcock, F. E. *The Greek and Macedonian Art of War.* (Sather Classical Lectures, Vol. 30). Berkeley: The University of California Press, 1957.

The fighting in Sicily involved almost all forms of classical Greek warfare. This short volume of essays covers the development of the various modes of Greek warfare from the sixth to the second century B.C.

The main force of a city-state's army was made up of slow-moving, heavily armored infantrymen called "hoplites" who fought in

close order in formal ranks. This formation, called the phalanx, was usually made up of columns eight hoplites deep and as broad as the manpower of the state permitted. There was little tactical maneuvering and little use of reserves, so that a battle was decided in a short time by the spearmanship of the front ranks of hoplites or even by the sheer weight of their charge. In a country as mountainous as Greece, it is strange that such cumbersome soldiers in such an unwieldy formation predominated, and that fast-moving light infantry was slow to develop. But warfare was mainly a matter of attacking or defending crops, of bringing about or preventing starvation. Therefore, the development of mobile troops suitable for mountain fighting seemed irrelevant for warfare that went on in the plains where the food was grown. Light-armed troops, however, were known and were of some use to the Syracusans, especially during the final retreat of the Athenians.

The Greeks did not possess effective cavalry. The Syracusan horse were of greatest use not in the pitched battles between hoplites around the heads of the walls, but in harassing tactics. The Athenians had to feed themselves in part by living off the country, and the Syracusan cavalry often fell upon foraging parties. But against an unbroken phalanx Greek cavalry was useless.

The technique of the siege was almost always simple circumvallation and starvation of the enemy. Before the Peloponnesian War we know of no certain case of successful assault on a walled city. The Greeks knew that fortified places might be stormed, but until the fourth century they had no specialized equipment, such as catapults, to assist them in doing so. They therefore shrank from direct assaults since such tactics were always very expensive in men. For Nicias to have stormed Syracuse was unthinkable, and this fact explains the rival strategies of wall and counterwall.

Greek navies were made up of a nucleus of triremes. On long passages they could be propelled by sails, but in action they relied exclusively on oarpower. Such a ship was so packed with the two hundred men of its crew that it could not carry enough food or water to give it long range. Hence, Greek navies could scarcely operate more than one or two days' row, about thirty-five or seventy miles, from home base. Nicias therefore first had to make a base for his ships before he could begin work with his army. Battles between fleets had been decided in early times by the smothering fire of arrows and javelins and by boarding, but by the time of the Peloponnesian War complex fleet tactics employing ramming were well understood, as were defensive formations for coping with them. In the last battle in the Grand Harbor the Corinthians showed the Syracusans a variant form of ramming by hitting head on. Normally, this tactic would have resulted in the crippling of both lightly built triremes, but the Corinthians had incorporated a special strengthening in their prows; and with this innovation their ships survived while the enemy's were disabled. Thus, often the fortunes of war turn upon the employment of a new strategy.

—Samuel K. Eddy

Additional Recommended Reading

Benson, E. F. *The Life of Alcibiades*. London: E. Benn, 1928. The life of the most remarkable Greek of his time.

Brunt, P. A. "Thucydides and Alcibiades," in *Revue des études grecques*. Vol. 65 (1952), 59-96. This interesting and ingenious article in English deals with the relations between the two men and the historian's assessment of the General.

Meritt, Benjamin D. "The Alliance Between Athens and Egesta," in *Bulletin de correspondence hellénique*. Vol. 88 (1964), 413-415. A discussion in English of the text of the treaty with Egesta (Segesta), the city in Sicily which was allied with Athens.

Westlake, H. D. "Athenian Aims in Sicily, 427-424 B.C.," in *Historia*. Vol. IX (1960), 385-402. A disclosure of Athens' relations with Sicily before the invasion of 415.

MARCH OF THE TEN THOUSAND

Type of event: Military: invasion and retreat of an army
Time: 401 B.C.
Locale: Persian Empire

Principal personages:
CYRUS II, Persian satrap of western Asia Minor, brother of
    Artaxerxes
ARTAXERXES II, King of Persia 404-359
XENOPHON, chronicler of the march
CLEARCHUS, Spartan general in Cyrus' army
TISSAPHERNES, Persian commander at Cunaxa

Summary of Event

The epic March of the Ten Thousand took place against the background of Sparta's newly acquired hegemony in Greece after the disastrous Peloponnesian War (431-404 B.C.) and Persia's slowly declining strength in Asia Minor. Cyrus II, a Persian satrap in the area, was willing to foment dynastic troubles in the empire because of his ambition to seize the Persian throne from his recently crowned brother, Artaxerxes II Memnon. Cyrus was supported by the Ionian Greeks who, having been treated as pawns of military policy and treachery during the period of Sparta's domination, hoped for concessions from Cyrus. At the same time they hoped to weaken the Persian colossus by supporting dynastic division.

Cyrus apparently experienced little difficulty in recruiting a large mercenary army, of which some thirteen thousand were Greeks, mostly Spartans, more or less fresh from recent fighting at home. In the spring of 401, his army broke camp at Sardis and began what turned out to be one of the most famous marches in history. The army mutinied when it learned that it was to invade the very depths of the Persian empire and not merely to reduce some hill tribes to obedience in southern Asia Minor. Only the entreaties of Clearchus, who was Cyrus' leading general

from Sparta, promises of additional pay, and the arrival of timely reinforcements induced the mercenaries to continue the journey. The Persians, whether out of weakness or in pursuit of a policy of attrition against the Greeks, did not seriously challenge the passage of the army. Near the village of Cunaxa, not far north of the Persian city of Babylon, the dispute over the throne was decided in the summer of 401. Cyrus managed to defeat his brother's army, but his rashness in wishing to dispatch Artaxerxes personally induced him to ride into the heart of the battle where the King's picked guard was protecting him. Cyrus' impetuosity cost him his life as a javelin pierced him under the eye. His death left the expedition stranded deep in hostile country. The Greek leaders, refusing to surrender, naïvely tried to negotiate with Tissaphernes, the leading Persian military commander at Cunaxa, for safe passage of their troops out of Persia. Tissaphernes, as might be expected, responded by having many of them seized and put to death.

The ten thousand Greeks who survived, instead of following the western route by which they had come into Persia, decided to move northward up the Tigris valley. Upon learning of the fate of their negotiating generals, they elected new ones from their ranks to lead their forces home. One of those chosen was the Athenian Xenophon, who after his return to Greece leisurely recorded the whole dramatic episode in his famous *Anabasis*, characterized by a simple straightforward style that has since become the traditional primer for aspiring Greek scholars. On the march up the valley, the retreating army was constantly harassed by the forces of Tissaphernes who, however, never risked a pitched battle. Further north, when the Persians had been left behind, savage hillmen rolled masses of rock down upon the straggling units of the army as they struggled through narrow passes. Snow, cold, and hunger took their toll in the vast barren winter wasteland of Armenia. With great rejoicing, the Greeks finally reached Trapezus on the coast where they could again behold the familiar waves of the sea even though these were only the waters of the Black Sea which meant they were still far from home. Here they foraged for supplies, became involved in frays with local cities, and generally made a nuisance of themselves while resting for a month before setting out for home. The last part of the retreat from Trapezus to Chalcedon was somewhat anticlimactic, a journey undertaken by land and sea. Upon returning home some of

the "ten thousand," now reduced to six thousand, entered the service of Thracian chieftains or of Sparta, who was then in the process of preparing for a war with Persia.

The whole episode took on major significance. A direct consequence was war between Sparta and Persia between 400 and 387, Sparta having responded to urgings from Ionian cities trying to defend themselves against the strenuous efforts of Tissaphernes, who had been made satrap of Asia Minor and was commissioned to recapture them. After initial successes by the Greeks, Persian money stirred up trouble in Greece. So prolonged was the struggle and so weakening to the Greek cities involved, especially Athens, Thebes, Corinth, and Sparta itself, that in 387 Persia was able to dictate the King's Peace, which brought the Ionian cities once more under Persian control. This disaster, together with the open display of Persian weakness revealed during the March of the Ten Thousand—as well as initial Spartan victories in the war of 400-387, and the general exhaustion of Greece itself—encouraged first Philip of Macedon and later his son Alexander to undertake not only the conquest of Persia but the occupation of all Greece as well.

Pertinent Literature

Mahaffy, J. P. *The Progress of Hellenism in Alexander's Empire*. Chicago: University of Chicago Press, 1905.

The standard interpretation of the March of the Ten Thousand regards it as a foreshadowing of Alexander's conquest some sixty years later. Mahaffy, the well-known classics scholar of the early twentieth century, in the first of a series of lectures delivered at the University of Chicago, prefers to go further. He sees in Xenophon, the leader and chronicler of the retreat, a distinct "precursor" of the coming Hellenistic Age. Mahaffy views the coming era with mixed feelings, an age

when a new civility and novel slants in art and literature "could not but dilute the purity of Hellenic civilization."

The new age, rather than beginning with Alexander, was a "thing of older growth" dating from the time when Athens lost its central position "in politics as well as in letters." The dispersion of Greeks after the Peloponnesian War brought other peoples more and more into the Greek overall view of the world. The growing use of Greek mercenaries by Persians and Egyptians, as well as the friendliness of Cyrus toward the Ionian cities, point to a new cosmopolitanism. Intellectuals, too, were loosening "the bonds of city patriotism." Men such as Isocrates saw that being an Athenian "was not a matter of birth but of culture." If Socrates thought in wider terms, Xenophon in his own way betrayed the same inclinations in his lesser known works.

Indeed, to Mahaffy, Xenophon, the hero of the March of the Ten Thousand, represents almost "the first step in the transition from 'Hellenedom' to Hellenism." He sees indications of this outlook not only in Xenophon's eclectic Greek vocabulary and simple style foreshadowing the *lingua franca* of the Hellenistic world, but also in his adoption of foreign niceties such as hunting (a sport unknown to Greeks in the Classical Age), his fondness for using Persian examples whenever he speaks of gracious living, and his wide travels in the Persian Empire, Asia Minor, and Thrace while he was in the service of Cyrus and later of Agesilaus. Mahaffy apologizes for his failure to be ultra-modern in not deciding "to go West." One of the most significant indications that Xenophon was a precursor of attitudes yet to come, Mahaffy insists, is his mistrust of democracy as unworkable and antiquated. He supposedly realized that any government which "exposes its executive government to constant criticism" and to consequent changes of military plans is "wholly unfit to make foreign conquests and to rule an extended empire." Xenophon's admiration for the strict discipline of aristocratic Sparta is clearly evinced in his tract *On the Lacedaemonian Polity*. Here is

no "capricious tyrant" in the form of a popular assembly tending to misuse liberty. Even in his early career as a writer Xenophon in his *Hiero* regarded the "attaining to a tyranny as the very acme" of ambitious Greeks' desires. His most revealing endorsement of monarchy is to be found in his neglected work *On the Education of Cyrus*. While his *Oeconomicus* merely urges that a man with a "ruling soul" (in Socratic terms) necessarily should be put in charge of things, his work on Cyrus openly vindicates monarchy built on the Persian model and the tract is virtually a monarch's handbook. Xenophon greatly admired the loyalty and discipline of Persian nobles, whose devotion to Cyrus causes them to perform menial tasks for him without complaint, men who are "far greater gentlemen than the Greeks." Xenophon, according to Mahaffy, is practically saying that a Ptolemy or a Seleucus must come if a great empire is to be managed. Even if one dismisses the more unpleasant aspects of this book as "semisophistical argumentation," Xenophon basically subscribes to all of it as a man fully convinced of the necessity of monarchy for the coming age. That his *On the Education of Cyrus* accurately forecast the future seems obvious considering the fact that within a hundred years there was scarcely a Greek city that "was not directly or indirectly under the control of a king." Mahaffy wonders if Alexander managed to read it or whether Aristotle, as his conservative mentor, kept such a book from his pupil as being incompatible with the Hellenic mind. It is obvious that Mahaffy's lecture is strained and has serious limitations. It is, however, interesting and provocative.

Nussbaum, G. B. *The Ten Thousand. A Study in Social Organization and Action in Xenophon's Anabasis.* Leiden: E. J. Brill, 1967.

G. B. Nussbaum, a historian of ancient history at the University of Kiel, has added an important dimension to a full understanding of the March of the Ten Thousand. The central theme of Nussbaum's work is that the Ten Thousand constituted a bona-fide communal or political organization.

The real story of the *Anabasis*, the author observes, began with the death of Cyrus, the rebellious younger brother of Artaxerxes II, in the Battle of Cunaxa. Until then the ten thousand or so Greek mercenaries fighting under Cyrus had remained a self-contained military unit. After the battle, the Ten Thousand (whose number was roughly equal to the population of a Greek *polis*) reacted to their isolation by becoming a moving *polis* seeking to find its way home to the Greek world. Nussbaum holds that the political character of the army did not manifest itself until they reached the Black Sea, but thereafter their identity assumed greater importance than before because they were out of danger and able to consolidate their political feelings.

Nussbaum states that while the Army of the Ten Thousand naturally had three subdivisions—soldiers, captains, and generals—a fourth element, the "assembly," representing the army as a whole, welded the three groups together into a political community. Nussbaum's observations on the nature and functioning of the assembly are especially interesting.

The author holds that from the time the Ten Thousand entered the service of Cyrus, the assembly played an important role as the "one natural and proper vehicle for the governing activity in the community and especially for directive decisions." Xenophon, however, does not record in the *Anabasis* any assembly meetings between the Battle of Cunaxa and the army's arrival on the shores of the Black Sea, except the one held to consider a course of action following the kidnaping of the generals by the Persians. It was then that the soldiers chose new generals to lead them home, one of whom was Xenophon. During the final stage of the march from Trapezus on the Black Sea to western Asia Minor, however, the assembly met more frequently, according to Nussbaum, than indicated by the twenty assemblies described in Books V through VII of the *Anabasis*. The function of the assembly was, in most cases, to give backing and authority to the leaders in their plans of action.

Elsewhere in his book, Nussbaum paints an interesting contrast between the motivations of leadership shown by Clearchus and Xenophon. Clearchus is depicted as the typical military-minded Spartan to whom organization meant discipline and discipline meant fear. On the other hand, Xenophon, the cultivated Athenian, exercised a civil and political leadership based upon his men's consent and incentive. Even when it was justified, he was apparently reluctant to use compulsion, which in the army invariably meant physical punishment. Once the army was out of extreme danger, he avoided it entirely as he then considered the army as virtually a state above such treatment and the ordinary soldier as a citizen above such degradation. As a citizen, Xenophon himself tolerated criticism; once, to the shame of his soldiers, he descended from his mount to give orders when an infantryman complained about his issuing directions while comfortably seated on horseback. This incident vividly illustrates the difference between the totalitarian approach of Clearchus and the democratic concepts of Xenophon as to relations between the rulers and the ruled. Whether the extenuating circumstances of warfare demand at all times a rigid totalitarian approach, however, is a question social philosophers have long debated.—*Edward P. Keleher*

Additional Recommended Reading

Anderson, J. K. *Military Theory and Practice in the Age of Xenophon.* Berkeley: University of California Press, 1970. A study of Sparta's military techniques during her brief hegemony over Greece early in the fourth century.

Bury, J. B. *A History of Greece to the Death of Alexander the Great*. Revised by Russell Meiggs. 3rd ed. New York: St. Martin's Press, 1966. A good classic introduction to the story of the March of the Ten Thousand.

Cook, J. M. *Greeks in Ionia and the East*. London: Thames and Hudson, 1962. A study of the Greeks who lived under Persian rule.

Parke, H. W. *Greek Mercenary Soldiers. From the Earliest Times to the Battle of Ipsus*. Oxford: The Clarendon Press, 1933. Chapter V deals with the recruitment and organization of the Ten Thousand.

Xenophon. *Anabasis*. Translated by Carleton L. Brownson. Cambridge: Harvard University Press, 1921. Xenophon's own account of the epic march.

DEATH OF SOCRATES

Type of event: Political: state execution
Time: 399 B.C.
Locale: Athens

Principal personages:
SOCRATES, Athenian citizen and informal teacher
MELETUS AND ANYTUS, contemporary Athenian citizens who
  brought the indictment against Socrates
ARISTOPHANES, Athenian comic dramatist
CRITO, wealthy Athenian disciple of Socrates who sought
  acquittal, but later a means of escape, for the condemned
  Socrates
ALCIBIADES, talented Athenian citizen
CRITIAS, Athenian oligarchic leader of the Thirty Tyrants in 404
PLATO, Athenian disciple of Socrates who wrote the most vivid
  account of the trial, imprisonment, and death of Socrates in
  his *Apology*, *Crito* and *Phaedo*

Summary of Event

The conclusion and aftermath of the Peloponnesian War left Athenian democrats bitter and resentful. The empire had crumbled, the fleet and walls of Athens had been dismantled, and democracy had been restored only after a period of oppressive oligarchic rule and bloody civil war. In the person of Socrates there seemed to stand the symbol, if not the principal cause, of all the factors of intellectual and moral enervation which had destroyed from within the power of Athenian democracy to prosecute the war successfully and to sustain the integrity of its own governmental institutions. An indictment was therefore brought against Socrates in 399 by a religious fanatic, Meletus, supported by the politician Anytus and by the orator Lycon, on the charge of impiety. Socrates was officially charged with failing to worship the gods of the state, introducing new gods of his own, and corrupting the youth of Athens. Although his accusers demanded the death penalty, their intention seems to have been to drive Socrates into self-imposed exile, a sentence which they believed he himself would propose if found guilty.

Plato's *Apology* makes it clear that Socrates was identified in his accusers' minds with the natural philosophers and Sophists whose teachings had indeed contributed to the deterioration of the traditional Athenian religious and political values. The natural philosophers had promulgated doctrines of a world sustained by impersonal laws rather than by personal deities, and the Sophists had encouraged their young noble pupils to be skeptical of all forms of institutional authority. Most damaging of all in their teaching was the doctrine of political power based on the assumptions that every individual's natural inclination was toward self-aggrandizement, and that the law of the state was an artificial restriction upon the individual's self-realization.

It was the Sophists rather than Socrates who were responsible for these demoralizing ideas. Socrates himself scrupulously lived by the laws of Athens and fully participated in the formal religion of the state. He did, however, openly criticize the tendency of the democracy to entrust tasks of professional competence to amateurs chosen by popularity or,

79

worse still, by lot. Moreover, he freely associated with the young aristocrats who were the most conspicuous pupils of the Sophists. To the Athenian who did not know him intimately, Socrates must have appeared to be a typical Sophist, and it was as such that he was caricatured in the *Clouds* of Aristophanes in 423, a play which must have left an indelible impression on many Athenian minds. After the double humiliation of defeat and revolution in 404, people remembered Alcibiades, who had deserted to the enemy during the war and severely damaged the Athenian war effort, and Critias, who had been instrumental in the oligarchic revolutions of 411 and 404; they also recalled that these two men had been associates of Socrates in their youth, and so Socrates seemed an ideal scapegoat for the frustrated resentment of many Athenians. A majority of 280 out of 400 voted for condemnation at his trial.

The *Apology* of Plato presents a portrait of Socrates as an earnest moralist who, though no Sophist, was indeed a real threat to whatever aspects of the Athenian tradition could not be rationally grounded. Far from the atheist his accusers would have proved him, he believed in objective moral values and a transcendent deity of truth. Athenians who were personally confronted by him were faced with a relentless challenge to their pretense of certain knowledge in matters of religion and morals. Although he himself professed ignorance in these areas, he claimed a wisdom unique among men by virtue of his awareness of ignorance. Socrates stood on common ground with the Sophists in refusing to acknowledge any self-evident authority in traditional Greek theological and moral

ideals. Yet he differed from them in that his skepticism was methodological rather than radical; he believed that valid moral ideals could ultimately be grounded rationally, although the effort might be long and arduous. To this end he committed himself to a life of intellectual inquiry through conversation with any who would join him, and he honestly believed that his informal intercourse with the Athenian man-in-the-street was a divine commission of vital concern to Athens. The only life worth living, he insisted, was the life based on values formulated through rigorous, honest, personal self-examination. Through such individual self-examination alone might come about eventual moral regeneration in the state.

Once condemned, Socrates refused the option of voluntary exile and obstinately insisted that only death would make him cease from his customary activities in Athens, whereupon the jury felt compelled to sentence him to execution by poison. During the interval between his trial and death, he conversed freely with his disciples, who sought to persuade him to go into exile. Plato's *Crito* gives Socrates' reason for resisting these entreaties: the command of the state, which he had heeded throughout his life, must be heeded now even though the condemnation was unjust.

The death of Socrates is dramatically portrayed in the *Phaedo* of Plato. Ostensibly the dialogue is concerned with the immortality of the soul, but its essential purpose is to exalt the pattern of philosophic life consummated in Socrates' death to a transcendent ideal for all men.

Pertinent Literature

Taylor, A. E. *Socrates.* London: Davies, 1932. Reprinted in paperback by Doubleday Anchor Books.

While the facts concerning the trial and execution of Socrates are reasonably clear and beyond dispute, the character of Socrates and the actual nature of his thought are not.

Since Socrates himself left no written documents, a portrait of his career must be drawn from the conflicting accounts of Aristophanes, Xenophon, and Plato. The outstanding question is whether the celebrated "Doctrine of Ideas" formulated in the *Phaedo* was the distinct creation of Socrates himself or rather the distillation by Plato of metaphysical implications of the Socratic dialectic method of clarification and definition. One of the more significant answers to this question is that formulated by John Burnet and A. E. Taylor and expressed in the popular biography by Taylor, *Socrates*.

Taylor seeks to harmonize the evidence of the witnesses by postulating two distinct phases in the life of Socrates. Relying heavily on the autobiographical narrative in the central portion of the *Phaedo* and on the *Clouds* of Aristophanes, Taylor argues for a youthful association of Socrates with Anaxagoras and his disciple Archelaus, and suggests that Socrates must have been a scholarch, perhaps a successor to Archelaus, with a circle of disciples. During this period Socrates associated freely with Sophists visiting Athens and with the intellectual circles of Pericles and Aspasia, thus gaining a reputation as one of the wisest men in Greece.

Taylor suggests that this phase lasted until about the beginning of the Peloponnesian War in 431 B.C. and was brought to a close by the negative response of the oracle at Delphi to a question put by Chaerephon: "Is there any man wiser than Socrates?" Brooding upon the oracle, Socrates experienced a spiritual crisis and henceforth set out on the mission he describes in the *Apology*, urging every Athenian to attend to his own soul and its health. He developed the "Orphic" concept of the personal soul into a new notion of a moral center of personality. The essential function of the soul is to know the good; the health of the soul, or "virtue," is the knowledge and obligatory performance of the good as recognized by the soul. Hence arise the ethical postulates accepted by all scholars as genuinely Socratic: virtue is knowledge; vice is ignorance; wrongdoing is always involuntary. The problem of the human condition is that men are ignorant of the good which is transcendent and apprehended only in earnest dialogue with others or in searching one's own soul. Taylor argues that Socrates himself formulated the Doctrine of Ideas by fusing the Orphic notion of an eternal personal soul, the Pythagorean notion of eternal mathematical objects of knowledge, and the notion suggested, but not developed, by Anaxagoras of a teleological order of nature governed by a universal Mind. The soul, in a process of dialogue and self-examination, comes to distinguish in clear intellectual vision the eternal and absolute moral standards through knowledge of which it may rationally order personal life. Socrates himself seems to have concerned himself primarily with the knowledge of transcendent moral standards, but the Doctrine of Ideas as developed in the Platonic dialogues is of course much more inclusive in its applicability to all kinds of knowledge. Many scholars today, perhaps the majority, question the argument that the Doctrine of Ideas was thus fully formulated by Socrates himself at the time of his death. Taylor's thesis is plausible, but it depends on the absolute reliability of the *Phaedo* as a witness of Socrates' own ideas rather than to those of Plato.

Jaeger, Werner. "The Memory of Socrates," in *Paideia, the Ideals of Greek Culture*. Vol. II, Bk. 3, ch. 2. Oxford: Basil Blackwell, 1947.

Set within the context of his monumental study of the history of Greek ideals, Werner Jaeger's discussion of the character of Socrates begins with a brief review of the work of critical scholars. He insists that neither the Scottish school of Burnet and Taylor nor the Berlin philosopher Heinrich Maier has adequately explained the dual role of Socrates as moral paradigm and intellectual midwife. Jaeger himself sees Socrates primarily as a teacher interested in developing the moral potentialities of his fellow Athenians, and in his chapter on Socrates he concentrates more on the attitudes and methods of the teacher than upon his theological and metaphysical doctrines, which he feels are products of Plato's efforts to make explicit what is latent in these attitudes and methods.

Like any thoughtful Athenian of his day, Socrates knew the doctrines of the current natural philosophers, but his own approach to natural science was always anthropocentric and akin to that of the medical scientists whose influence on him was much more significant. The autobiographical passage in the *Phaedo* indicates that teleological explanations appealed to him even before he read Anaxagoras for the first time. Certainly his conception of wisdom was practical rather than theoretical; its model was the *techne* of the craftsmen and physicians: an organized body of principles underlying the achievement of distinct goals.

Jaeger denies any serious influence of Orphism, a religious movement much disputed as to date and character, upon the Socratic notion of the soul. Without speculating on its ontological status, Socrates urged each man he met to tend to the health of his own soul as the center of knowing and willing moral personality. It was self-consciousness, an intense awareness of personal goals in the light of rigorous rational criticism, that he sought to arouse in his young friends.

Like the Sophists, Socrates discussed political questions frequently and intensely, but the keynote of his treatment of these matters was internalization, a focus on ends as well as on means. Thus the virtues of a general or a ruler were reduced to fundamental virtues of leadership, of mastery over one's own person in the light of clearly defined goals.

Jaeger accepts the judgment of Aristotle that Socrates did not formulate the Doctrine of Ideas, but he notes that Xenophon as much as Plato depicts Socrates as trying to define morality in concepts harmonious with experience yet free from inner contradiction. Socrates challenged his partner to lay down a general hypothesis, and then proceeded to subject it to rigorous logical analysis. By this method, he sought to draw out of his partner a feeling for moral truth which he optimistically felt was innate in every human soul.

The Socratic postulates that virtue is knowledge, that all virtues are ultimately identical, and that no man willingly does evil were not enunciated as dogmas; they emerged during discussions as assumptions which alone seemed plausible and free from inner contradictions, thereby providing the basis for fruitful analysis of moral questions. It is from these postulates and from Socrates' dialectic method that the metaphysics and epistemology of Plato were developed later. The fundamental achievement of Socrates, in Jaeger's view, was the advance of moral education through introspection and the new focus on the goals of human life. *—Carl W. Conrad*

Additional Recommended Reading

Cornford, Francis Macdonald. *Before and After Socrates.* Cambridge: The University Press, 1932, reprinted 1962. Lectures on the impact on Greek cosmological tradition of the teleology implicit in Socrates' "morality of aspiration."

Levin, Richard, ed. *The Question of Socrates.* New York: Harcourt, Brace & World, Inc., 1961. A collection of ancient source material on Socrates.

Spiegelberg, Herbert, and B. Q. Morgan, eds. *The Socratic Enigma*. Indianapolis: Bobbs-Merrill Company, Inc., 1964. A collection of testimonies concerning the character and influence of Socrates from antiquity to the present day.

Stone, Isidor F. *The Trial of Socrates*. Boston: Little, Brown, 1988. Investigative journalist I. F. Stone draws on extant historical sources in his examination of Socrates' trial by the city of Athens in an attempt to explain the social and political climate that led to the trial and its infamous outcome.

Versenyi, Laszlo. *Socratic Humanism*. New Haven: Yale University Press, 1963. An emphasis on the humanism and irony of Socrates, relying heavily on the early Platonic dialogues and rejecting the mystical elements of the middle group of Platonic dialogues.

Winspear, Alban D., and Tom Silverberg. *Who Was Socrates?* 2nd ed. New York: Russell & Russell, 1960. A critical restudy of evidence of the opposition aroused by Socrates, with special consideration being given to its nature.

ORIGIN OF *MUNICIPIA*

Type of event: Political: development in diplomatic relations
Time: 340-338 B.C.
Locale: Rome, Latium, and Campania in Central Italy

Principal personage:
TITUS MANLIUS TORQUATUS, military tribune 362; dictator 353, 349; consul 347, 344, 340; and general in 340 against the Latin League

Summary of Event

Vital to the expansion of Roman dominance in Italy and for its later imperial development and organization was the discovery of a way to cement close relationships with other small neighboring states. Although the bonds gradually forged with Italian towns and tribal groups were diverse in character, a highly significant step in Roman diplomacy can be identified about 338 B.C. when Rome granted limited Roman citizenship to several cities of Latium and Campania.

In the middle of the fourth century B.C., Rome was becoming the strongest state in central Italy although encircled by unfriendly and ambitious rivals. Gallic tribes, which had captured Rome in 390 B.C., continued to invade the northern half of the peninsula. The most dangerous enemies of Rome, however, were the Samnite tribes in the southern Apennine mountains, which had more territory and a greater population than the Romans. The smaller states of central Italy, chiefly Etruscan and Latin, had been forced to seek Roman protection against both the plundering Gauls and the expanding Samnites, but these smaller neighbors resented and feared increasing Roman superiority.

Some thirty to forty smaller communities in the plain of Latium south of Rome had long been united in a league for mutual defense and common religious rites before Rome itself entered into agreement with them possibly as early as 493 B.C. by renouncing all claims to domination and by exchanging some citizenship privileges such as intermarriage and recognition of commercial contracts. Nevertheless about 358 B.C. several Latin League towns supported an attack by mountain tribes against Rome, and in 340 the entire league took up arms against Roman hegemony. Led by Titus Manlius Torquatus, hero of a famous duel in 361 against a giant Gaul, the Romans suppressed this revolt and in 338 proceeded to dissolve the league, making separate peace treaties with each of the former confederates. A few small towns near Rome were simply incorporated into the Roman state with full citizenship rights, while other Latin cities were given partial Roman citizenship but were required to supply troops for the Roman army.

Further south there were a number of populous communities that controlled the fertile lowland plain called Campania, situated between the Samnites to the East and South, and the Romans to the North. Capua, the largest city in Campania, appealed in 343 for Roman aid against Samnite aggression and received help. During the Latin Revolt of 340-338, citizens of Capua and other Campanian communities assisted the Latins against Rome, but the upper-class Campanian Cavalry remained loyal to Rome. Rome consequently rewarded the nobles of Capua and several smaller towns in Campania with what the historian Livy calls *civitas romana*, that

84

is, Roman citizenship. Also described as *civitas sine suffragio,* or "citizenship without suffrage," this qualified citizenship, similar to the kind granted earlier to Latin cities, specifically excluded the right to vote in Roman elections or to hold offices in Rome, but it did include the obligation to serve with the Roman legions when called upon to do so. Communities whose leading citizens were so bound came to be called *municipia* after 338. One or more Etruscan cities near Rome were given similar status.

This partial Roman citizenship subordinated the *municipia* to the military and diplomatic dominance of Rome, but it also allowed Italian cities to retain almost complete freedom in local self-government. Inscriptions show that Capua continued to be governed by its own traditional magistrates.

Since it was in the period after 338 B.C. that Roman power expanded most rapidly, it seems evident that the *municipium* relationship proved advantageous for Rome and also for the towns drawn into such close relationship. An increasing number of Italian towns became *municipia,* many of them forced to accept the status after being conquered by Roman armies. However, most of the towns showed remarkable loyalty during the Sam-

nite Wars between 327 and 303 and again between 298 and 290, as well as during Hannibal's invasion of Italy. Apparently Rome gave the *municipia* more security and less freedom than an alliance between equals, yet the *municipia* had the opportunity to share some of the fruits of Roman military victories and at the same time preserve their own self-government.

As Rome's domination extended in later centuries beyond Italy, terms such as *municipia* changed in meaning. By 80 B.C., all peoples living in Italy had been granted full Roman citizenship and all towns in Italy came to be called *municipia.* Moreover, by the Imperial period, independent Greek allies together with cities in Gaul and Spain came to be treated in much the same way as towns in Italy and were called *municipia.*

A major factor in the stability and longevity of the Roman Empire was the system which grew out of the *municipium* concept which originated about 338 B.C. Hundreds of cities were each given control of their own local affairs while the citizens were also Roman citizens with strong loyalties to the Empire. The concept was later to develop into the idea of a city being a corporation with a charter of its own.

Pertinent Literature

Sherwin-White, Adrian N. *The Roman Citizenship.* Oxford: The Clarendon Press, 1939.

This book was the first thorough study in English on how and why the Romans gradually extended their rights of citizenship throughout Italy and the provinces. The author carefully examines many German and Italian studies in Roman political forms, and skillfully sifts ancient literary and epigraphic sources. No later English scholar has attempted any sharply different interpretation of the confusing records of the early Republic.

Sherwin-White accepts as generally accu-

rate the tradition used by Livy which describes the reorganization of Rome's confederation after the Latin Revolt of 340-338 B.C. He concludes that Rome used ingenious and flexible diplomacy to secure the support of allies and conquered neighbors, arguing that the partial citizenship granted to several Latin city-states in 338 was the "first large breach in the older conception of a city-state." He rejects as a later confusion Livy's story that the non-Latin city of Caere, about fifteen miles north of Rome, had been given limited

Roman citizenship before 350.

In a chapter on "The Settlement of 338 B.C. and the Origin of the Municeps," Sherwin-White examines the status of the Campanian towns made *municipia* in 338. At first a generous extension of the older "Latin rights" to non-Latin allies, their partial citizenship was subtly downgraded with the advance of Roman prestige. He states that originally citizens of these *municipia* could claim full rights as Romans if they migrated to Rome, and that later, as a result of support given to Hannibal, the Campanian towns lost some of their status when Roman officials were sent to share with local authorities in the governing of their towns. Although it is debatable how regularly the Romans sent "prefects" to supervise the *municipia*, Sherwin-White argues that such actions were infrequent before the invasion by Hannibal. Nevertheless, local autonomy was never entirely abolished, and as the number of *municipia* increased in Italy, they gradually came to be treated much as were the more fully incorporated Latin towns.

The author traces in detail the extension of the *municipium* until it included by the final century of the Republic military and "Latin" colonies. The military colonists were Roman citizen-soldiers sent out by Rome, and eventually they were treated much like the *municipia*. Various "allies" throughout Italy also became self-governing *municipia*, incorporated into Roman citizenship as communities rather than as individuals. Extension of the franchise in 89 B.C. along with grants of citizenship by Sulla and Julius Caesar fully municipalized Italy by 80 B.C. When the model of *municipium* was extended to communities outside Italy, it had come to mean "a self-governing community, irrespective of its origin." Eventually "free cities" in Greece, Asia, and Africa were equated with the *municipia* in Italy. By the second century of the Empire, *municipia* grew even along the banks of the Danube River out of army camps, but after the decree early in the third century which granted citizenship to all residents of the Empire, only places of secondary importance remained *municipia*; cities obtained more renown by being called *coloniae*, a status which allowed them more freedom.

Finally, Sherwin-White discusses how far and why Rome managed to win genuine loyalty in its provinces. He points to some evidences of continuing tension in eastern areas between Hellenistic and Roman traditions, but he declares that the development of the "municipal system" was Rome's most valuable accomplishment politically.

Badian, E. *Foreign Clientelae (264-70 B.C.).* Oxford: The Clarendon Press, 1958.

This review of the patron-client relationship in Roman diplomacy includes a chapter which considers Rome's relationships with other cities in Italy before the Hannibalic War. Although Badian recognizes Sherwin-White's *Roman Citizenship* as "the standard work" on this subject in English, and states that the origins of the concept of *municipium* are "wrapped in obscurity," he disagrees sharply with Sherwin-White's judgment on the earliest known instance of a non-Latin city being granted partial Roman citizenship.

Badian believes it likely that Caere, an Etrurian neighbor of Rome north of the Tiber River, was the first city to receive the status *civitas sine suffragio*, or "citizenship without suffrage." Since the Caerites had aided Rome against the Gauls in 390 B.C., Rome treated Caere generously after defeating the city in war about the middle of the fourth century. Badian, accepting as authentic an old description of a Roman list of Caerite citizens drawn up by Roman censors, considers that the treatment of Caere by Rome was the original pattern which was later copied in regard to Campanian cities in 338 and thereafter.

Another point on which Badian disagrees with earlier studies involves the *foedus iniquum*, or "unequal alliance," a Roman device which Sherwin-White calls "the chief instrument in the formation of the federation of allies." Badian doubts whether this unequal alliance was ever actually articulated in any early Roman treaties, despite the fact that Rome from very early times considered many allies subject in some degree to Roman authority. However, Badian considers that it was no more than a "natural development" in any alliance between a powerful and a weaker state. The same thing happened in Greece during the fifth century when Athens predominated in the Delian League.

By correlating the patron-client concept with other diplomatic forms, Badian clarifies many changes which took place in Roman foreign policy, especially when Rome became dominant in the eastern Mediterranean. He argues that Greek cities such as Naples were first accepted as independent allies of Rome, but when Rome claimed the right to "protect" its allies, the *municipium* concept originating in Italy in the fourth century B.C. was subsequently blended with ideas of "free cities" and "client states" through which Rome was able to dominate Greek cities. Hence Badian's perspective on many incidents in Roman foreign policy differs from that of earlier historians who gave little attention to the patron-client relationship, ingrained in Roman private life, which Badian sees as being applied analogously to interstate liaisons, especially after Rome became the predominant military force in the Mediterranean world. Although Badian's focus is wider than most earlier studies, including Sherwin-White's, his book offers valuable insights even in the earliest of Rome's diplomatic negotiations in Italy.

—Roger B. McShane

Additional Recommended Reading

Abbott, Frank F., and Allan C. Johnson. *Municipal Administration in the Roman Empire.* Princeton: Princeton University Press, 1926. A compendium of more than two hundred documents illustrating Roman municipal development, without full English translation but with careful notes.

Adcock, F. E. "The Conquest of Central Italy," in *The Cambridge Ancient History.* Vol. VII, ch. XVIII. Cambridge: The University Press, 1928. A detailed account of Roman wars and diplomacy from 360 to 290 B.C.

Heitland, W. E. *The Roman Republic.* Vol. I, chs. XVII-XIX. Cambridge: The University Press, 1923. A study of Roman conquests from 366 to 265 B.C., with the correlative development of politico-diplomatic forms.

Pinsent, John. "The Original Meaning of Municeps," in *Classical Quarterly.* n.s. 4 (1954), 158-164. A linguistic study of Republican usage of vital terms relating to *municipia.*

Reid, James S. *The Municipalities of the Roman Empire.* Cambridge: The University Press, 1913. A valuable account of the development of cities in the Republic and Empire, although it lacks precise definition of terms and references to ancient sources.

Yeo, Cedric A. "The Founding and Function of Roman Colonies," in *The Classical World.* 52 (1959), 104-107, 129-130. A study of the earliest *municipia* and their relationship to the colonies established by the Republic.

BATTLE OF CHAERONEA

Type of event: Military: Macedonian victory which heralded the dawn of Hellenistic times
Time: August 2, 338 B.C.
Locale: Chaeronea, in Boeotia northwest of Thebes

Principal personages:
PHILIP II, King of Macedon 359-336
ALEXANDER, son of Philip, King of Macedon 336-323
DEMOSTHENES, Athenian statesman and orator
ISOCRATES, Athenian publicist and rhetorician

Summary of Event

The Peloponnesian War ended Athens' hegemony in Greece; Spartan dominance replaced it. The result was the outbreak of new destructive wars aimed at the overthrow of the latter. At the Battle of Leuctra in 371, the Thebans, allies of Athens, inflicted a decisive defeat on the Spartans, and Greece passed to the hegemony of Thebes. It proved to be exceedingly short-lived. Athens changed sides, and in concert with Sparta and other states overcame Thebes in the closely fought Battle of Mantinea in 362. Athens, meanwhile, had revived the Delian confederacy, but most of her allies successfully revolted against her in the Social War of 357-355, and Athenian power was badly shaken.

Men who participated in these unsuccessful, melancholy wars for the hegemony of Greece called out for relief from them. The Athenian Isocrates advocated, as the vital necessity for escaping continual competition and bloodshed, the unification of Greece under the leadership of some strong state and some strong men. Demosthenes of Athens dreamed of an Athens revitalized culturally and militarily and preeminent in Greece. The philosopher Plato hoped for government by philosophers.

A more likely savior than one of Plato's scholars appeared in Philip of Macedon, who began his reign in 359 B.C. He set about to Hellenize and modernize Macedonia with in-

genuity and energy. He brought the factious nobility of his country to heel and taught them to serve him with heavy cavalry. He also created an infantry phalanx better drilled and more effective than that of the Greeks. His army was of professional quality, far superior to the citizen militias or hired mercenaries which made up the bulk of the armies of the Hellenic cities. The Macedonian army was, moreover, supported by efficient financial institutions. Philip intended to establish his own hegemony over Greece, although he wished it to be merciful and enlightened. Already in the 340's he began to penetrate southward through Thessaly. The principal Greek states of Athens, Sparta, and Thebes, distracted by their own perpetual feuds and weakened by their precarious fiscal circumstances, resisted Philip, but only halfheartedly.

In 340 B.C., the decisive war broke out between Macedonia and the Greeks. In August, 338, the Macedonian army of two thousand cavalry and thirty thousand infantry came face to face with the united Greek armies of weak cavalry and thirty-five thousand infantry near the small town of Chaeronea in northwestern Boeotia. The Greeks deployed with their right flank covered by a small stream; it was held by twelve thousand Thebans and Boeotians. The center was composed of various allies from central Greece and the Peloponnesus, and the left was made up of ten thousand Athenians. The Greek phalanx was to make its usual straightforward attack, hoping to crush the enemy by the weight of its charge. Philip, on the other side, was a master of more subtle tactics, combining the use of cavalry and infantry. His own left, opposite the Thebans, was headed by his cavalry, which was to thrust itself into a gap to be made in the Greek line. The gap would be opened by luring the Athenians into charging his own right as it purposefully drew back in pretended retreat.

It was probably on August 2, 338, that the battle was fought, and everything went according to Philip's plan. The Athenians rushed forward shouting, "On to Pella!" (the capital of Macedonia), and when the Greek center and the left of the Thebans moved obliquely forward to keep in close ranks with them, a hole opened in the ranks of the Thebans. Into it, resolutely led by the eighteen-year-old crown prince Alexander, the Macedonian heavy cavalry crashed, charging in wedge formation. They were followed by crack formations of infantry, which attacked the flanks on either side of the gap. The The-

bans, after heroic resistance, were beaten; the Greek center and left, panic-stricken, broke and ran. The result was a decisive victory for Philip.

During the next few weeks, the Greek states surrendered one after another. In 337, Philip organized them into a Hellenic League with its seat at Corinth. He was himself president of the league, and members were forced to follow his foreign policy. Wars among them were forbidden, as was internal constitutional change except by constitutional methods. Philip's intentions were to secure a tranquil and contented Greece as the necessary first step in his new plan to liberate the Greeks of Asia Minor from the Persian Empire.

The Battle of Chaeronea was the great event that destroyed the sovereignty of the Greek states. There was, it is true, a revolt against Macedonia in 323-321 called the "Lamian War," and several more in the third century which brought temporary freedom, but the era of the old, unbridled parochialism and imperialism of Athens, Sparta, and Thebes was over.

Pertinent Literature

Hammond, B. G. L. *A History of Greece to 332 B.C.* Oxford: The Clarendon Press, 1959.

Hammond's book covers Greek history from 3,000 B.C., when the ancestors of the Greeks were still living in southern Russia, to the year when Antipater and Craterus were on the verge of overcoming the Greek revolt of 323 against the control which Macedonia exercised as victor in the Battle of Chaeronea. It is a general history, including chapters on international relations, constitutional history, and the evolution of Hellenic art and thought. The first section on the Mycenean period is weak, but as Hammond approaches the fourth century B.C., the age with which he is most familiar, his inter-

pretation of events becomes more and more interesting.

The wars fought between 431 and 338 B.C. gave rise to considerable anguish in Athens and elsewhere, as well they might. Conflict was attended by social upheaval and economic depression. Isocrates of Athens became a pan-Hellenist, believing that the unity of Greece must be achieved at any cost to win freedom from bloodshed. This unity could be brought about only by a strong leader. As the power of Macedonia increased, Isocrates hailed Philip as the natural *hegemon* of Greece, a king who could unite the warring states and cement their alliance by leading them in a national crusade against Persia. Isocrates, however, was a rhetorician and publicist who took little part in politics, so that his influence on events was small.

It was far different with Demosthenes, a leading politician at Athens, a figure of considerable oratorical skill and persuasive power, and an imperialist after the manner of Pericles. He was a proponent of Athens' resuming her role of leader of Greece, both in a military sense as *hegemon* of a revived naval confederacy, and in a cultural sense as the intellectual and moral school of Hellas. He saw that if Athens were to lead, she would inevitably come into conflict with Philip, and he never missed an occasion to denounce the King as an aggressor bent on the conquest of Athens to end her freedom. With Philip extending his power southward, collision was inevitable; the result was Chaeronea.

Hammond concludes his book with a short discussion of what the word "freedom" meant to the Greeks and to the Greek states. Freedom was a word always on the lips of Athenian statesmen, who, like Pericles, praised to the skies the men who had preserved the freedom of Athens at Marathon and Salamis, or who, like Demosthenes, exhorted their listeners to defend the freedom of Athens once more on the eve of Chaeronea. Hammond believes that there were two kinds of freedom, the old-fashioned freedom of Demosthenes, and the new kind of freedom preached by Isocrates and practiced by Philip through the Hellenic League. The old freedom meant the right of each of the major Greek states to exercise its full sovereignty. In actuality this meant the right of each to coerce or attack weaker states, making them parts of an empire, ending their freedom, and inflicting garrisons and tribute on them. As far as the Greeks of the lesser states were concerned, freedom for Athens or Thebes meant subjection for them. Unhappily, experience showed conclusively that none of the major city-states was strong enough to conquer the other permanently. The result was continual marching, fighting, bloodshed, and agony. The new freedom of Philip and the Hellenic League was freedom from interstate war, freedom from domestic revolution, and freedom to work for the prosperity of Hellas.

Tarn, Sir William, and G. T. Griffith. *Hellenistic Civilization.* 3rd ed. London: Edward Arnold, 1952.

The Battle of Chaeronea cast down the classical city-states from their central position in Hellenic affairs, and gave Macedonia the leadership during the following generation which ushered in a new age and a new style of Greek culture. *Hellenistic Civilization* has justly been called a classic book, and it is certainly among the best one-volume introductions to this period of history. Sir William Tarn was, in fact, a respected British scholar who enriched our knowledge and enhanced our understanding of the Hellenistic Age. This edition of the book is a revision made by G. T. Griffith.

The first chapter is a brief, hard-to-digest chronological outline of the major political and military events of the period. Once past this point, one encounters the marvelously diverse, rich account of Hellenistic history. The political, social, and economic institutions of the Greek cities are reviewed. Here there is a wealth of fascinating detail, including a sketch of the unsuccessful but interesting attempts to found utopian communities in which all citizens were political and economic equals.

Tarn next surveys the Asian empire of the Seleucids, a vast monarchy stretching at its widest extent from the banks of the Indus River to the shores of the Aegean Sea and including among its subjects the Greeks of its teeming cities, the robed Persian grandees of Iran, and the scarcely civilized hill men of eastern Anatolia and northern Iraq. Then the author presents a description of the highly centralized Egypt of the Ptolemies, with its complex system of economic exploitation which, by means of planned planting controlled from a central bureau, caused a stream of grain to pour down the Nile into the royal warehouses at Alexandria for export to overseas markets at the best prices. Typically, Tarn adds the intimate detail that one of the finance ministers of this remarkable state thriftily offered for sale roses from his private garden.

Chapters follow on a wide variety of topics. "Trade and Exploration" tells how Pytheas of Massilia sailed into the North Sea, discovered the fjords of Norway and reported on them, only to be called a preposterous liar. It also reports that by the end of the second century B.C., regular contact by sea was maintained between Egypt and India. "Literature and Learning" presents the Hellenistic period as a time of tireless literary industry. The scholar Didymus wrote, it is said, thirty-five hundred books on biography

and literary criticism and well earned his nickname, "Brazen-Guts." Sober and gifted historians such as Polybius had to compete with writers of cheap scandal such as Aristippus. "Science and Art" is a particularly successful essay setting forth the extraordinary achievements of Hellenistic science. We are told of the great physician Erasistratus, whose astonishing accomplishments gave credit to the story that he had raised a man from the dead. We also see dark glimpses of vivisections performed on criminals condemned to death.

Finally there is "Philosophy and Religion," those rich tapestries of Hellenistic thought and feeling exemplified by the ethical philosophies of Epicurus and Zeno, and the complete skepticism of Pyrrho. There is the rise of new and emotional religions from the Orient, tamed, or partly tamed, by Hellenism. Some men begin the grotesque practice of magic, and other men create the god Sarapis.

Sir William's book has done much to rescue Hellenistic culture from the limbo where devotees of classical Hellenism have too often wished to assign it.—*Samuel K. Eddy*

Additional Recommended Reading

Cary, Max. *History of the Greek World from 323 to 146 B.C.* 2nd ed. London: Methuen & Co., 1951. A comprehensive survey of Greek history after the Lamian War.

Gomme, A. W. "The End of the City-State," in *Essays in Greek History and Literature.* Oxford: Basil Blackwell, 1937. A thesis that the liberty of the Greek cities was not ended by the Battle of Chaeronea, nor did it curtail the vigor of their political life.

Jaeger, Werner. "Demosthenes: The Death Struggle and Transfiguration of the City-State," and "Isocrates Defends His Paideia," in *Paideia.* Volume 3: *The Conflict of Cultural Ideals in the Age of Plato.* 2nd ed. London: Oxford University Press, 1945. An important exposition of the life and doctrine of this Athenian statesman.

Jones, A. H. M. "The Athens of Demosthenes," in *Athenian Democracy.* Oxford: Basil Blackwell, 1953. An argument that financial stringency caused Athens to hesitate about opposing Macedon in the 340's more than the "moral decay" which Demosthenes and some modern scholars have postulated.

FOUNDING OF ALEXANDRIA

Type of event: Political: the building of a new city
Time: January 20 (?), 331 B.C.
Locale: The Nile delta

Principal personages:
ALEXANDER THE GREAT, King of Macedonia 336-323, who founded
the city of Alexandria
DINOCRATES OF MACEDONIA, architect who planned the city
PTOLEMY I, King of Egypt 306-283/2
PTOLEMY II, King of Egypt 283/2-246
SOSTRATUS OF CNIDUS, architect of the lighthouse at Alexandria

Summary of Event

When Alexander the Great took Egypt from the Persians in 332 B.C., he had no intention of restoring the country as an independent kingdom. He meant to make it a province of his own, and he believed that a new Hellenic city would make a more suitable capital than one of the old Egyptian towns. This capital was to be named Alexandria in honor of himself as its founder. The site chosen was on the coast, on the western edge of the Nile delta, where the city would have easy communications with the interior by river and with the outside world by sea. Labor was conscripted from adjacent villages of Egyptian peasants and fishermen, and in 331 B.C. work began with impressive religious ceremonies. Greek seers prophesied that the city would become "large and prosperous, a source of nourishment to many lands." Construction of the metropolis took years to complete and was still proceeding in the time of Alexander's successors, Ptolemy I and Ptolemy II.

The original plan of the city was prepared by the architect Dinocrates, who had it laid out on the grid-pattern developed in the fifth century. It was divided into four large quarters by two broad avenues. Canopus Street, a processional boulevard one hundred feet wide, ran east and west along the long axis; a lesser

street running north and south bisected it. At this intersection was the civic center containing the Court of Justice; the Gymnasium, a handsome, colonnaded building two hundred yards along its front; a series of sacred groves; and, most remarkable of all, an artificial hill dedicated to the god Pan. Its summit could easily be reached by a spiral path, and, from this point, visitors—and we know there were many—could survey the entire metropolis.

The most striking characteristic of Alexandria was its size. By the third century B.C. its population had already reached perhaps half a million. By the beginning of the Christian era it stood at nearly a million, rivaling even the capital of the Roman Empire. One quarter of the city was inhabited mostly by Egyptians and half-caste Greeks, who had no civic rights and performed the menial labor of the city. Another quarter was the residence of the Jews, who came to Egypt in considerable numbers during the reign of Ptolemy I. They enjoyed a certain autonomy under their own ethnarch and council and constituted one of the most important Jewish settlements in all the ancient world.

The Greco-Macedonian quarter seems to have been near the sea breezes of the waterfront. It is probable that these Europeans were organized into *demes* and tribes, with an autonomous council and assembly. From east to west along the waterfront stretched warehouses and harbors which received merchantmen from up-river, from Mediterranean ports, and even, via a canal connecting the Nile River with the Red Sea, from the Orient. By the second century B.C. there was contact with India, and the streets of the port felt the gentle tread of Buddhist missionaries. Here, too, were the efficient dockyards of the Ptolemaic Navy.

The Royal Quarter was the most imposing of all. It was ornamented with the palaces of the Ptolemies and the nearby monumental tomb of the great Alexander. Here also was the great Serapeum, a magnificent temple dedicated to the dynasty's new god. The palace complex contained the famous Library and Museum, where the first two Ptolemies gathered the most distinguished minds of the third century for the furtherance of science and scholarship.

Dominating the skyline and even overshadowing the palace itself, rose the great stone lighthouse designed by Sostratus of Cnidus. It stood on the island of Pharos, which was connected to the mainland by a man-made mole nearly three-quarters of a mile long, pierced by two bridged channels for ships. The tower was over four hundred feet high, and was provided with a windlass so that firewood could be drawn to the top. Here fires blazed by night in front of a reflec-

tor of polished bronze.

In the third century the culture of this brilliant city eclipsed even that of Athens. The scholarship of Aristophanes of Byzantium, the astronomy of Aristarchus, the poetry of Callimachus, and the medical studies of Erasistratus all were the gifts of Alexandria to the world. The city was also an important bridge between the cultures of Greeks and Jews. The Septuagint, the Greek translation of the Old Testament, was begun here in the third century, and here the famous Philo worked later.

Alexandria was a forceful expression of both the good and evil qualities of Hellenistic culture. While the city was the birthplace of much that was good, it was also infected with hideous urban ills. Mobs of the poor sometimes rioted against the government and perpetrated scenes of frightful massacre. The city's pleasure domes housed the most sophisticated debauchery; its slums, the most sordid depravity. There was conflict between ethnic groups for the usual reasons. Egyptians swelled the ranks of the proletariat. The Greeks were the perfumed rich. Egyptians were prevented by law from marrying Greeks. Many Egyptians, therefore, could not regard the metropolis as a beneficent "source of nourishment," but hoped instead, as one oracle put it, that it could be made a dank place where fishermen dried their nets, as it had been before the coming of Alexander.

Pertinent Literature

Jones, A. H. M. *The Greek City from Alexander to Justinian*. Oxford: The Clarendon Press, 1940.

Greek emigration overseas began about 750 B.C. and did not cease until around 200 B.C. One of the great folk-migrations of history, it carried the civilization of the Hellenes into almost every corner of the Mediterranean. The last wave followed the trium-

phant campaign of Alexander into Asia Minor, Syria, and Egypt, and built magnificent new cities such as Alexandria.

The city was the institution through which Hellenism expressed itself. Jones carries out his exposition on the nature and importance of the Greek city under five broad subject headings: (1) the diffusion of cities in the Orient, (2) their degree of dependence upon the suzerain when there was one, (3) their political organization, (4) the services they provided, and (5) their economic and cultural achievements. Each topic is discussed chronologically from the Hellenistic period through Roman Imperial times to the Byzantine age.

In the Hellenistic era a city was not only a physical collection of buildings; it was also a formal political institution with some degree of chartered autonomy. There was a council, or *Boule*, and usually an assembly, or *Ecclesia*, which had charge of local affairs. Civic institutions included gymnasia, which were formally organized clubs for practicing Greek athletics and also for propagating the more important forms of Greek culture such as musical competitions, public reading of great literary works of past and present, and philosophical discussions. These functions were so important that civic magistrates called *gymansiarchs* were responsible for controlling and encouraging their memberships. Cities were also equipped with theaters where plays and mimes educated or diverted the citizens. Repertory companies of actors organized as Worshippers of Dionysos traveled from city to city under international guarantee of safe passage to perform the admired dramas of the classical period. A few metropolitan centers, such as Alexandria, Pergamum, and Antioch, accumulated huge libraries to preserve and promote Greek knowledge and wisdom. Some cities paid for the education of their citizens, although public schools did not strike deep roots. Doctors, however, were maintained at public cost fairly widely. Sewers protected public health. Fire brigades were equipped with mobile water pumps. A few places boasted street lighting.

The achievement of these cities in bringing Hellenism to the East was significant. Not only was Hellenism extended, but another great cultural innovation came out of the Greek cities and the Hellenized Oriental towns of the East; Christianity was the city-bred child of Hellenism and Judaism. Jones reminds us, however, that the depth of the impact of Hellenism may be exaggerated. While the Greek language was supreme in both the institutions of high culture and in the chambers of government, it did not really penetrate to the peasantry except in western Asia Minor. The strength of Hellenism grew less inland from the coastal regions because the Greek immigrants were, after all, too few to impress their civilization deeply on the much more numerous and sometimes hostile Oriental populations.

Sandys, Sir John Edwin. *A History of Classical Scholarship.* Volume I: *From the Sixth Century B.C. to the End of the Middle Ages.* Cambridge: The University Press, 1903. Reprinted, New York: Hafner Publishing Co., 1964.

Scholarship is defined very specifically by Sir John Sandys as studying literature to establish the exact text of an author and also to elucidate his meaning. The Greeks of the Alexandrian Library were the first to develop rules of scholarship similar to those in use today. The reason they felt compelled to do so was to help Greek education, for literary instruction was as important a part of Hellenistic schooling as it is of our own. The most important books of Greek literature were the *Iliad* and *Odyssey*, attributed to Homer. These epics were deeply revered for their poetic portraits of the gods and their vivid pictures of the human condition, at once heroic and tragic; they are now believed to have taken formal shape about 700 B.C., although alterations of the original texts were constantly taking place. Some changes occurred in copying one manuscript from another, while others were consciously made by the *rhapsodes* reciting them in public, and by forgers. The texts of the plays of the Athenian dramatists, as useful for education as Shakespeare, were subject to interpolation or omission of lines by actors, who played an important part in transmitting versions from one generation to another.

Aristotle was perhaps the first Greek to concern himself seriously with these textual problems. He was the first Greek we know of who collected a large library of manuscripts from which to deduce facts on the dates plays were written, statements of authorship, and similar data to help with literary studies. The first important research library, however, was the one established at Alexandria by Ptolemy I with the assistance of the philosopher Demetrius of Phalerum in Attica, a student trained in Aristotle's school. The library was much enlarged by Ptolemy II. Eventually it held a large number of papyrus rolls, though sources for this information give numbers varying from 400,000 to 700,000. The first librarian was Zenodotus of Ephesus who was appointed in 284 and whose work must have consisted mainly of searching for old manuscripts. Callimachus of Cyrene, who died about 240 B.C., published a descriptive catalogue of the library which itself took up 120 rolls classified by subject: drama, epic and lyric poetry, law, philosophy, history, oratory, rhetoric, and miscellaneous. Zenodotus found time to publish a new text of the *Iliad* and the *Odyssey* in which he sought to remove spurious verses.

Aristophanes of Byzantium, who died about 180 B.C., followed him as librarian and produced a superior text of Homer. The resources of the library permitted him to understand Greek dialects, including the Ionic-Aeolic in which the two epics were originally written. He excised or corrected verses which appeared in other dialects, or rejected some after carefully comparing old manuscripts. He used accents and punctuation to aid interpretation, and he also published corrected editions of the dramas of Aristophanes and Euripides.

The greatest Alexandrian scholar was Aristarchus of Samothrace, who died about 145 B.C. He was a sober, judicious, and, above all, a cautious critic. By collating different versions of Homer from places as widely separated as Athens and Chios, he published recensions of the *Iliad* and the *Odyssey* along with learned commentaries explaining words and phrases when the meaning was not clear. He also issued new texts of the plays of Sophocles and Aristophanes.

What were the results of so much activity? Very little. The scholars of the Alexandrian Library had no great influence over the texts of Homer in daily use, and the versions which have come down to us are those of the *rhapsodes.—Samuel K. Eddy*

Additional Recommended Reading

Cadoux, C. J. *Ancient Smyrna. A History from the Earliest Times to 324 A.D.* Oxford: Basil Blackwell, 1938. A history of another major Greek city.

Davis, Simon. *Race Relations in Ancient Egypt.* London: Methuen & Co. Ltd., 1951. An interesting discussion of racial conflicts in Egypt and Alexandria and the various cultural backgrounds.

Downey, Glanville. *A History of Antioch in Syria.* Princeton: Princeton University Press, 1961. A detailed study of the capital city of the Seleucids.

Kenyon, Frederic G. *Books and Readers in Ancient Greece and Rome.* 2nd ed. Oxford: The Clarendon Press, 1951. A treatise on the making of ancient books or papyrus rolls, and the invention of the codex or modern leaved book, with some remarks on the book trade and literary tastes in ancient times.

Marrou, Henri I. *A History of Education in Antiquity.* Translated from the French by G. Lamb. New York: Sheed and Ward, 1956. An exhaustive and definitive account of the curricula and methods of ancient education.

Parsons, Edward A. *The Alexandrian Library.* New York: Elsevier Press, 1952. Many strange details of the library are included in this curious volume.

ALEXANDER'S VICTORY AT GAUGAMELA

Type of event: Military: execution of a decisive battle
Time: October 1, 331 B.C.
Locale: Mesopotamia

Principal personages:
ALEXANDER THE GREAT, King of Macedon 336-323
PARMENION, Macedonian general
DARIUS III, King of the Kings of the Persian Empire 336-330
BESSUS, Persian Satrap of Bactria, who after the death of Darius
ruled as Artaxerxes IV 330

Summary of Event

After King Philip II of Macedon had defeated the Greek states in the Battle of Chaeronea, he made plans to invade the Persian Empire. His assassination in 336 B.C., however, cut short the operation of this scheme until his son Alexander had made his succession to the throne secure. In 334, Alexander invaded Asia Minor and quickly defeated the Persians on the Granicus River. He advanced eastward and in 333 at Issus, in northern Syria, defeated King Darius III himself. In 332, he took the wealthy province of Egypt.

By 331, Alexander was ready for a second and deciding battle with Darius for the supremacy of Asia. The Persian King had been collecting a large army, and he came westward as far as the plains near the village of Gaugamela (Tel Gomel in modern Iraq), where he waited to be attacked. His army consisted mainly of cavalry posted in long lines on level ground. The left wing was made up of his good Iranian horsemen, the Persians, some heavily mailed Saca, and the Bactrians, all commanded by Bessus, the Satrap of Bactria. Syrian, Mesopotamian, and Median cavalry took stations on the right. Behind the cavalry was infantry, mostly troops of little fighting value who had been levied recently. Behind the center of the two fighting lines was Darius with his personal bodyguard and fifteen elephants. The Persian

forces numbered over fifty thousand men.

In the autumn Alexander arrived at Gaugamela, and on October 1, led his army out of camp. He had forty thousand infantry and seven thousand horsemen, both Greek and Macedonian. His army was also in long lines, with the infantry placed in the center and half the cavalry on either flank. Parmenion commanded on the left while Alexander himself took charge of the right with his best squadrons of Macedonian heavy cavalry. Alexander's chief virtues as a general were his understanding of how to use cavalry and infantry together, and his gift for inspiring his men, either in battle or in the relentless, disciplined pursuit of a disorganized and fleeing foe. He now slowly advanced to his right while studying the enemy's array until the Hypaspists, a brigade of crack Macedonian infantry, were facing some scythed chariots in front of the Persian center. He turned to face the enemy. Now Bessus sent the Saca charging at the extreme right of Alexander's cavalry. Alexander countered by bringing forward squadrons deployed behind them. There was a sharp fight with losses on both sides until Bessus' cavalry drew off to regroup. Meanwhile, the scythed chariots bounded forward against the Macedonian center, but here Alexander had posted troops armed with missiles, and these men shot

97

down most of the chariot horses with their arrows and javelins before they reached the phalanx. The chariots, which did little damage to the Macedonians, were routed.

The cavalry action on Alexander's front had opened a gap between Bessus and the center of the long line of Persian horsemen. As soon as Alexander had his own horsemen under control, he charged into this gap, the infantry phalanx following him on the run. This blow was irresistible, and the Persians' lines began to crumple and stream towards the rear. Darius for the second time turned to flee. His personal guard of two thousand Greek mercenaries stood their ground and lost five hundred men, killed to win time for Darius to escape. As Alexander was reforming to pursue the Persian monarch, he received distress messages from Parmenion that the Persian right was pressing him hard, and Alexander rushed across the field with his own cavalry to help. His timely arrival sent the Persian right reeling back, and the battle became a general rout. Alexander then drove his horsemen rapidly after the remnants of the Persian army, dispersing large numbers of fugitives, until he reached the

city of Arbela after nightfall. But he did not succeed in catching up with Darius.

The Battle of Arbela (Gaugamela) was decisive. The Persians' forces were so scattered that they could not be reorganized. The Persian nobles believed that Darius was responsible for the debacle, and they accordingly deposed and killed him. Bessus, whose troops were the only ones to withdraw in fairly good order, became king as Artaxerxes IV. He, however, could not collect enough men to oppose Alexander's swift and inexorable advance. The Persians quickly lost their wealthiest provinces. The rich plains of Babylonia surrendered without resistance. Persis, the heartland of the empire, fell, and Persepolis, its religious capital, was also taken, along with some fourteen years' worth of accumulated tribute. Alexander eventually caught Artaxerxes and had him executed, alleging the murder of Darius III as an excuse. He also burned the magnificent royal buildings at Persepolis. This act signaled the fall of the Persian Empire, the beginning of Alexander's own, and the subjugation of the East to Macedonian imperialism.

Pertinent Literature

Tarn, W. W. *Hellenistic Military and Naval Developments.* Cambridge: The University Press, 1930.

Alexander's conduct of his battles was a shining example to his junior officers, and they imitated so many features of his strategy that the Alexandrian military technique became the tactics of generals for the next century. The old-fashioned, straightforward melee of Classical Greece was finally obsolete. W. W. Tarn's small and readable book is an explanation of the new forms of warfare in Hellenistic times.

One important new feature, actually a development from the time of Alexander's father, was professionalism. Philip spent so

many years campaigning that his troops acquired the experience of a standing army. This quality was maintained through the military institutions of the Hellenistic monarchies, which granted land to military settlers, who seem to have been required to spend two years on active service before passing to a kind of reserve as civilians. Technical problems raised by the increasing use of machines, the building of giant warships, and the complex new tactics ended the day of the gentleman amateur in war, such as Themistocles or Pericles had been. Generals and admirals now had to be professional students of war and tactics. Instead of charging at the head of their men, generals kept out of at least the early stages of a battle to be better able to control all their forces. For example, on the plain of Gaugamela Alexander had fed in his cavalry against Bessus without involving himself personally until the decisive charge was made at the gap in the Persian line.

Battles on land became increasingly complex, since the combined use of different kinds of troops was vital. Cavalry, which had not been important in classical times, now became a decisive arm, capable of attacking and riding down infantry. It was still impossible for horsemen to charge formed infantry frontally, but masses of cavalry could now be hurled at the flanks of a phalanx or into a gap opened in its line, as was done at Gaugamela. Infantry became more and more diversified. The heavily armored hoplite remained the basic foot soldier, but he found a complement in the *peltast*, a man equipped with lighter arms and armor for greater speed and mobility. There were also javelin men, archers, and slingers. Arrow-fire was the best counterstroke to a charge of horse, as Alexander's strategy against Darius showed. In turn, slingers were used against archers; leaden sling-bullets had a greater effective range than ancient bows and arrows.

The third century B.C. was the age of the war elephant. Contrary to some commonly held opinions, elephants were seldom used as mobile battering-rams to charge fortified places; on the few occasions when such an attack was made, the animals were repulsed.

Against troops unfamiliar with elephants, especially against cavalry whose horses were unused to them, a charge of the great beasts could easily be decisive.

The technique of the siege became increasingly complicated. Covered battering-rams were used to attack walls; high, movable towers ("city-takers") were rolled forward against walls until bridges could be let down upon the top of the enemy's fortifications, whereupon assaulting infantry charged across the walls. Torsion engines of various sizes threw arrows, spears, or carefully rounded stones accurately up to an effective range of two hundred yards. A missile called a flame-carrier was invented; it was a cylinder filled with inflammable liquid for attack on wooden roofs or wooden siege engines. Iron armor was the main defense against it.

Navies were equipped with giant ships. The trireme was displaced by the quinquereme, a vessel with one bank of long, heavy oars, each pulled by five men. Flagships called "fifteens" were known, apparently gigantic triremes with three banks of rowers and five men on each oar. Such craft were large enough to carry torsion artillery for attack on seaports.

The Hellenistic period was thus a time of great inventiveness and growing sophistication in the art of war. The expense of organizing properly equipped armies and navies and the need to build massive defensive works of stone added to the financial burdens of the Hellenistic states, and made the development of new sources of revenue a necessity.

Tarn, W. W. *Alexander the Great.* Cambridge: The University Press, 1948. 2 vols.

The personality of Alexander, like that of many great men of antiquity, remains something of an enigma. We know much about what Alexander did, but less about why he did it. What led him to attack the Persian Empire? What were his intentions in 334? Sir William Tarn attempts to answer these questions and to give as detailed a biography of Alexander as the ancient sources allow. Volume I is a well-written narrative of Alexander's career. Volume II contains a series of complicated essays explaining in detail how the author reached the more important conclusions of Volume I.

Alexander attacked the Persian Empire in 334 because he inherited the war from his father Philip. No doubt Alexander was influenced by Panhellenic idealism, that is, a desire to liberate the Greek territory in Asia Minor which had been taken over by the Persians. Tarn holds that Alexander did not intend more than the conquest of Asia Minor. The rapid collapse of Persian resistance there possibly fired his adventurous imagination and led him on eastward, first into Syria and then on to Babylonia, Persis, and even India.

As a man, Alexander was an imperialist and conqueror. He had moments of cruel, dark passion when he was murderous towards even his friends. None of these facts can be denied. But he was at the same time much more. As an adolescent he had had no less a teacher than the great Aristotle, and if the philosopher taught him to despise non-Greeks as barbarians, a belief which Alexander outgrew as king, he also deeply influenced him to respect learning. Alexander's army escorted the first consciously organized scientific expedition of which we have record, made up of botanists, zoologists, geographers, historians, and philosophers whose task was to record important phenomena observed in the course of the King's march. The information collected was sent back to Aristotle, and it came to form a significant part of the corpus of data used by the remarkable Greek scholars of the third century B.C.

Towards the end of his life Alexander devised an idealistic policy of ethnic fusion as one important facet of his plan for ruling the enormous territory he had overrun. In such a policy he ran counter to the racial narrow-mindedness of Plato and Aristotle. He persuaded eighty reluctant Macedonian officers to marry Persian and Iranian aristocratic ladies, and it was unfortunate that after his death seventy-nine divorces ensued. It may have been the experience of crossing most of the then known world that broadened his outlook and led him to enunciate the idea that "all men are sons of one Father," that is, that they are all brothers. The exact meaning and originality of this notion are still argued, but some such idea was put forward by Alexander as the basis for the mixed Greco-Macedonian-Oriental government he began to shape for his polyglot empire.

Alexander passed his short life of thirty-three years in a world that he, more than any other man of antiquity, drastically changed. His stupendous march of conquest left an indelible impression on peoples everywhere. The world of the Greek was suddenly enlarged, and Greeks flocked after Alexander's standards into a new continent thrown open to them. The world of the Orient was plunged into subjection. Astonishingly enough, Alexander the imperialist became a folk hero in many Eastern lands. He became not only a Christian saint in the Abyssinian Church, but even a conquering hero of the Iranians whose empire he had pulled down.

—*Samuel K. Eddy*

Additional Recommended Reading

Brunt, P. A. "Persian Accounts of Alexander's Campaigns," in *Classical Quarterly.* Vol. XII (New Series, 1962), pp. 141-155. A study which shows that in our ancient Greek versions of Alexander's battles there is information derived from a source written from the Persian side.

Fuller, Major General J. F. C. *The Generalship of Alexander the Great.* New Brunswick:

Rutgers University Press, 1960. This study of Alexander's campaigns by one of Britain's greatest professional strategists is a useful supplement to the biographies of the professional historians.

Wilcken, Ulrich. *Alexander the Great.* Translated from the German by G. C. Richards. London: Chatto and Windus, 1932. A treatment of Alexander's life by an authoritative German scholar.

ISSUANCE OF THE *LEX HORTENSIA*

Type of event: Legal: enactment of constitutional legislation
Time: 287 B.C.
Locale: Rome

Principal personage:
QUINTUS HORTENSIUS, plebeian dictator in 287

Summary of Event

In the persistent class conflict which raged throughout the fifth and fourth centuries B.C. between the privileged patrician class and the plebeians over the distribution of political rights and powers, the plebeians managed to win increasing degrees of equality with the aristocrats. Through various laws they had gained recognition of intermarriage with patricians and the right of election to all major political offices. The patricians had also recognized the plebeians as a distinct political body within the state by granting to them the power of electing their own officials, the tribunes of the people. Most of these gains (essentially tactical concessions to the new economic and military power of the plebeians) were won only grudgingly from the patricians, who retained ultimate and decisive control over the state through control of the legislative process, among other things.

In the early Roman constitution a measure became law after it had been proposed to and ratified by a validly convened assembly, or *comitia*, of the community. Such assemblies had to be convoked by a consul or a praetor, could meet only on specified days after the performance of stipulated religious rituals, and could only vote "yes" or "no" to properly submitted proposals. Even after a proposal had been affirmed, it still required formal ratification by the patrician senators before it became valid. To ensure further patrician control over the legislative process, the main assembly in the early period was the *comitia centuriata*, in which the voting groups were unequal and a minority of wealthy patrician citizens could influence greatly the final ballot. Once a proposal had navigated this complex process, it became law and was binding on all members of the community regardless of class affiliation; but the restrictions on the autonomy of the legislative body allowed the predominantly patrician senate (which did not itself have the power to enact laws) to subordinate legislation to senatorial interests and programs.

From the earliest days of the Republic the plebeians had apparently formed their own assembly (the *Concilium Plebis*) which contained only plebeian members and attended to their interests alone. Although convened by its own legitimate authority, one of the tribunes, it was not considered to be a *comitia* since it was limited to the enactment of proposals which were validly binding only on the plebeians themselves. Such enactments were termed plebiscites and were rigidly distinguished from laws, which obligated everyone.

The first attempt to change this situation was contained in one of the provisions of the Valerio-Horatian laws of 449 B.C., which stipulated that validly enacted plebiscites were to enjoy the same standing as laws and bind the entire citizen populace. The ineffectiveness of this law required a similar enactment by Publilius Philo in 339 B.C., which again attempted to convert plebiscites into laws. Some historians have seen both these laws as fictitious anticipations of the later Hortensian

Law of 287 B.C., while others have argued that both laws were real enough but contained some qualifying condition, such as the necessity of senatorial ratification, before plebiscites became legally binding on everyone. It is likely, however, that both laws were passed without any qualification but were simply disregarded by the patricians as invalid since they had been passed without their approval.

This situation developed into a crisis in 287 B.C., when the plebeians, who had contributed greatly to the recent victory over the Samnites, imposed a general strike by withdrawing as a group from the city to force the patricians to meet their demands. In this emergency the extreme measure was taken of appointing as dictator the plebeian and oth-

erwise undistinguished Quintus Hortensius. Hortensius put through a law, called the *Lex Hortensia*, again making plebiscites equal to laws and enforceable on the entire community. The plebeians returned to the city after the acceptance of this constitutional reform by the patricians, and thereafter there was no further opposition to this particular issue by the patricians. Roman legal theorists treat subsequent plebiscites and laws as equivalent legislative enactments differing only in their point of origin. Armed with the power of making laws, the plebs became an influential part of Roman political life; the tribunate, as the initiator of plebiscites, grew into a more powerful office; and the democratic aspects of the Roman constitution became more evident and effective.

Pertinent Literature

Von Fritz, Kurt. "The Reorganization of the Roman Government in 366 B.C. and the So-called Licinio-Sextian Laws," in *Historia*. I (1951), 1-44.

Since the *Lex Hortensia* ended the struggle between the patricians and plebeians, it finds a central place in von Fritz's attempt to estimate the traditional constitutional reforms of 287 B.C. In dealing with this earlier period von Fritz demonstrates that the historical accounts of the struggle between the orders derive mainly from the time of the Gracchi, and that aspects and characteristics of the Gracchian turmoil have been projected back into the accounts of the earlier period. Since Livy used this tradition, his account is also flavored with energetic tribunes and tribunate intercessions, devices which probably became crucial only when used by the Gracchi. Von Fritz is also doubtful about many parts of the Licinio-Sextian rogations and says that one point needing elucidation is what form the rogations took. Were they laws? This raises the issue of the *plebiscitum*, since according to Livy these rogations were first approved by the plebeians.

It is quite clear that because of the Hortensian Law, a plebiscite and a law were almost exact equivalents after 287 B.C. The two earlier laws that had raised plebiscites to the level of law have either been rejected as outright historical fabrication or more commonly been accepted as genuine but containing some restrictive provision. This latter view was especially championed by the great German historian Mommsen, who relied heavily on a poorly documented part of Sulla's constitutional reforms during the last century of the Republic, which purportedly revived the earlier practice of a tribune's being unable to propose any measure for consideration by the plebeian assembly unless the senate had first given its permission. Mommsen argued that this earlier practice was the one constantly in effect until the Hortensian Law. Von Fritz thinks this obscure reference is heavily suspect, that Sulla's weakening of the tribunate was to forestall its future exploitation by reformers such as the Gracchi, and that even if Sulla did restrict the legislative capacity of the tribune, to describe such a restriction as the revival of an earlier practice may have been nothing more than propaganda to disguise the illegality of his proposal.

Von Fritz stresses instead the circumstances of the earlier plebiscites. The major ones are all associated with secessions of the plebeians in which they removed themselves bodily from Rome and imposed in effect a political strike on the state. Although there have been some recent efforts to deny any historical validity to these plebeian secessions, von Fritz points to the intriguing fact that no withdrawal is ever mentioned after 287 B.C., so that it was clearly not a later condition that historians could read back into the early period. Von Fritz goes on to accept the uniqueness of the Hortensian Law and sees two important conclusions arising from it. Plebiscites were extremely important even before 287 B.C., though before that date they did not have the force of laws; they were simply an expression of the will of the plebeians and were probably first used to announce the inviolability of the person of the plebeian tribune. Since this edict required only passive observance by the patricians, it did not raise any constitutional problems. The situation was different when the plebeians expressed their will on more concrete problems such as intermarriage or reduction of the interest on debts. Although the plebeian tribune had the power to assemble the plebeians and ascertain their will, there was no legal standing for this activity. The patricians were free to disregard it and obviously did so on numerous occasions. In this case, the only remaining response of the plebeians was to withdraw from communal life in order to force the patricians to accept the plebiscite as binding upon them. This procedure of plebiscite followed by secession resulted in a form of legalized revolution which only the Roman genius for compromise prevented from becoming bloody clashes. This potentially violent situation was completely eliminated by the Hortensian Law, which by raising plebiscites to full legal standing provided a constitutional outlet to forces which before the passage of the law were only partly regulated and often unruly. The beneficial effects of the law can be gauged from the total disappearance of plebeian secessions from Roman political life once the plebeians had gained a legal instrument for the execution of their aims.

Abbott, Frank Frost. *A History and Description of Roman Political Institutions.* Boston: Ginn & Co., 1910.

The age of this book has not diminished its usefulness as a descriptive guide through the maze of Roman constitutional developments and procedures. Because of its descriptive character, the book tends to accept as certainties many problematic aspects of Roman political history. The traditional accounts of the early period by the later Roman historians are generally accepted to permit concentration on the precise workings of the actual procedures in force. Thus, in the case of the lawmaking power of the plebeian assembly, Abbott, though skeptical that such power was given to it as early as 449 B.C. by the Valerio-Horatian laws, does accept the premise that the similar enactments of 339 and 287 B.C. reaffirmed a principle that had in some unspecified way already been established. This principle itself, however, requires the usual explanation for the historicity of the three laws; namely, that until 287 B.C. there were definite restrictions in the form of senatorial approval on the legislative capacity of the plebeian assembly. From 449

B.C. to 339 B.C., this approval was required after the plebeian assembly had acted favorably upon a legislative proposal. From 339 B.C. to 287 B.C., the approval of the patrician element of the senate was a prerequisite merely for the introduction of a measure before the plebeian assembly. The effect of the *Lex Hortensia* was to eliminate entirely all outside interference on the plebeian assembly.

From its start the plebeian assembly was open, of course, only to plebeians. As in the other assemblies, voting was conducted on a group basis by tribes. The original twenty-one tribes of the fifth century had expanded to thirty-five by 241 B.C., and remained at that number. Abbott believes that membership in the tribe was a privilege enjoyed only by the landed plebeians, and that poorer plebeians were only permitted entrance in the last decade of the fourth century. It now seems clear that all plebeians were enrolled in the various tribes from the beginning but that the plebeian inhabitants of Rome were confined to the four urban tribes. This still meant a disparity in the voting power since a vote in one of the urban tribes, with their much larger constituencies, would count for far less than a vote in the rustic tribes. An attempt was made in 307 B.C. to allow plebeians to register in any tribe they might choose, but this reform was rejected in 304 B.C. and the entire question of the precise distribution of new citizens into the tribes continued to be a matter of dispute until the end of the Republic.

Nor was this the only limitation on the legislative capacity of the plebeian assembly. Since only plebeian tribunes could propose a measure for consideration by the assembly, there was little likelihood of any radical enactments by the assembly as long as the senate was able to rely upon tribunes docile to its interests; we hear of none until the era of the Gracchi. A further imbalance resulted from the fact that the assembly had to meet within the confines of the city. This made meeting attendance more difficult for citizens who lived remote from Rome than for members of the urban populace. In addition, the size of the assembly, potentially between 250,000 and 300,000, made it unwieldy for taking a very decisive role in political matters, a condition that left the senate dominant. For these reasons, Abbott's conclusion is that the *Lex Hortensia* introduced only a modified form of democracy within Rome and left unimpaired the oligarchic character of the Roman constitution. Although this machinery was more than adequate in responding to the foreign dangers throughout the third century and the first half of the second, it was slow to adjust to the new conditions and problems of Rome itself. When decisive action was imperative, it originated in the office of the tribunes through their explosive courting of the plebeian assembly, and especially of its urban members. This development exposed Rome to an almost continuous period of violence and bloodshed.

—George M. Pepe

Additional Recommended Reading

Botsford, George W. *The Roman Assemblies.* New York: The Macmillan Company, 1909. An extremely detailed and scholarly account of the various Roman assemblies, with special attention to the ancient sources.

Jones, H. Stuart, and Hugh Last. "The Making of a United State," in *Cambridge Ancient History.* Vol. VII, Chapter XVI. Cambridge: The University Press, 1954. A reliable account of the *Lex Hortensia* emphasizing earlier developments.

Staverly, E. S. "Tribal Assemblies Before the Lex Hortensia," in *Athenaeum.* XXXIII (1955), 3 ff. An examination of the origin and early history of the tribal assemblies.

DECLARATION OF THE FIRST PUNIC WAR

Type of event: Political: use of military force
Time: 264 B.C.
Locale: Italy (especially Sicily) and Africa

Principal personages:
HIERO, King of Syracuse 265-215
APPIUS CLAUDIUS CAUDEX, consul in 264 and leader of the prowar faction in Rome, who led the first campaign into Sicily
MARCUS ATILIUS REGULUS, consul in 267 and 256, another leader of the war party who led the Roman invasion of Africa
HAMILCAR BARCA, Carthaginian general in Sicily at the end of the war, and father of Hannibal the Great

Summary of Event

The first Punic War was a milestone in Roman history. Entry into this conflict committed Rome to a policy of expansion on an altogether new scale; prosecution of the war marked the emergence of Rome as a world power; disposition of conquered territories reshaped its political condition domestically as well as in foreign affairs.

The Mediterranean world in the early third century B.C. consisted in the east of large territorial empires in areas conquered by Alexander the Great. In the west was Carthage, dominating the coasts of Africa and Spain, while Rome ruled a network of allied cities in central Italy. In the center was Sicily, the only portion of the Greek world where the imperial ideal had failed to replace the older system of numerous independent city-states. Sicily was an anachronism, certain to attract efforts on the part of the Hellenistic monarchies to attach it to one or another of the eastern Empires. Carthage and Rome were equally certain to resist the establishment of Hellenistic powers in the western Mediterranean. When Pyrrhus, King of Epirus, led his armies into Italy and Sicily, he first met the resistance of Rome, then of Carthage. The failure of his Sicilian campaign between 280 and 275 B.C. left a power vacuum little different from that which existed before, and it was only a matter of time before Rome and Carthage could be expected to come into conflict there.

The occasion of Roman involvement in Sicily, and the beginning of the First Punic War, may have seemed of relatively slight importance. The Mamertines, once mercenary soldiers of Syracuse who had seized the city of Messana and used it as a base of operations in northeast Sicily, found themselves threatened by the growing power of Hiero, King of Syracuse. They called on the Carthaginians for aid, but then, fearing domination by these traditional rivals, requested aid from Rome in order to expel the Carthaginian garrison. Rome was a land power with no navy. The Roman senate, fearing overseas campaigns against a naval power, refused to accept the Mamertines' overtures. But the Roman people, perhaps foreseeing the prosperity they might gain from involvement in the rich territories of Sicily, perhaps merely failing to foresee the extent of the military operations they were initiating, voted to aid the Mamertines. Appius Claudius Caudex, a leader in the prowar faction, was elected consul for the year 264 B.C. and led an expedition to Sicily.

In the first phase of the war, the Roman forces aided Messana, while Carthage supported Syracuse. But this phase, and with it the original pretext for the war, was soon over. Hiero of Syracuse had no interest in matching his power against Rome's, nor in being dominated by his erstwhile allies. In 263 B.C., Hiero made peace with Rome on terms that left him extensive territories as well as his independence. Messana was saved. But Carthage and Rome now were in a struggle that neither cared to give up.

Between 262 and 256, Rome pressed hard, driving the Carthaginians into a limited number of military strongholds, and mounting her first fleet, which met with surprising success against the experienced Carthaginian navy. In 256, under the consul Marcus Atilius Regulus, Rome transported an army into North Africa; it had initial successes, but the Carthaginians, directed by the Greek mercenary Xanthippus, succeeded the next year in destroying the forces of Rome.

Back in Sicily, the fortunes of war took many turns. On land, Rome controlled extensive territories but Carthage held her strongholds. At sea, the Roman navy was often victorious even though the loss of one fleet in battle and of others in storms weakened her position. By 247, both powers were fatigued.

Peace negotiations stalled, but military efforts were at a minimum for some years.

In 244, the Roman government, too exhausted to build a new fleet, allowed a number of private individuals to mount one with the understanding that they should be repaid if the war were brought to a successful conclusion. In 242 this fleet arrived in Sicily. When a convoy of transports bringing supplies to Carthage's troops was captured, Carthage came to terms. The Carthaginians agreed to evacuate Sicily and pay an enormous indemnity over a long period of time.

Sicily, or many of the territories in it, became Rome's first province. Her annexation of it as a subject, tribute-paying territory marked the start of developments that gained in importance through the remaining history of the Roman Republic. By annexing a Hellenic territory Rome became, in a sense, a Hellenistic state, a fact that had a profound effect upon Roman cultural life as well as upon foreign relations. Rome's development of naval capacity made possible commercial and military involvement with all the Mediterranean world. Its need to govern conquered territory caused it to modify city-state institutions and begin constitutional developments that would in the end undo the republican form of government in Rome.

Pertinent Literature

Frank, Tenney. "Rome and Carthage: The First Punic War," in *Cambridge Ancient History*. Vol. VII, ch. 21. New York: The Macmillan Company, 1928.

Frank's treatment of this subject includes, besides a chronological account of the military campaigns, a discussion of the causes and effects of the war with respect to political and military conditions at Rome. In describing the debate and hesitation that preceded Rome's decision to send an expedition to Sicily, the author points out that the question at hand was not one of war against Carthage, but one of alliance with Messana. Mes-

sana was at this time a leading power in Sicily, third, perhaps, after Syracuse and Carthage. Its domination of water routes, particularly of the straits between Italy and Sicily, made friendship worth cultivating. Messana was in danger of domination by Carthage whose help it had enlisted in order to resist the might of Syracuse; if Rome allowed Carthage to gain control of one Sicilian seaport after another, it could expect the Carthaginian policy of *mare clausum*, or "closed sea," to keep out non-Carthaginian ships and block Rome and hard-won Roman allies in south Italy from commerce with the rich nations of the Greek world.

The nobles who dominated the Roman senate, however, were, for the most part, landholders interested in a strong military security on land and not at all concerned about extension of trade and foreign commerce. These men hesitated to commit themselves to military operations against a naval power; they feared, too, loss of privilege to the new classes that might gain power if Rome became a seafaring nation. The conservative party prevailed in the senate, which refused to pass a resolution which would have meant sending an army to Sicily. But the Roman people, partly under the influence of the merchants and partly enticed by the prospect of booty from campaigns in the rich territories of Sicily, enacted the alliance with Messana.

The most important result of the First Punic War, in Frank's opinion, was the conversion of Rome to an imperial nation. As Rome conquered territories already accustomed to foreign rule, it gave up its eighty-year-old policy of basing its power upon alliances with federated states, and adopted the Hellenistic forms of territorial control already in effect in most of the Mediterranean world. The results of the adoption of this foreign idea of territorial sovereignty, involving the creation of provincial administration, the use of standing armies, and the collection of tithes, were to have far reaching effects upon political conditions in Rome itself.

Frank draws attention to two other ways in which the First Punic War affected conditions in Rome. A new nobility of men rose to prominence during the war. As families such as the Manilii, the Aurelii, and the Lutatii gained senatorial status during this period, a change was effected in the make-up of the Roman senate, and therefore in the directions of Roman policy. Furthermore, the cultural life of Rome was stimulated by the experiences of vast numbers of Romans serving extended tours of duty in the Greek territories of Sicily; Roman literature had its start in the years following the war, developing Hellenic forms, chiefly dramatic and epic, in the Latin tongue. The other arts were similarly affected.

Picard, Gilbert Charles, and Collete Picard. *The Life and Death of Carthage.* Translated by Dominique Collon. London: Sidgwick & Jackson, 1968.

The difficulty in writing a history of Carthage is that Carthaginian accounts are nonexistent. The Picards have taken the trouble to collect the epigraphical and archaeological materials from Carthage and her territories and to compare these carefully with Greek and Latin sources relating to Carthaginian affairs. The Picards' account of the Punic Wars, relating these events to conditions in Carthage itself, forms a useful supplement to the traditional histories that take the Roman viewpoint throughout.

The authors review the history of Carthaginian activities in Sicily under the early kings, and again under the oligarchic regime that governed Carthage after the early fourth century. Although Carthage was a major power in Sicily in the early third century, taking, for instance, a leading role in the repulsing of the invasion by Pyrrhus in 280 B.C., its position at the start of the First Punic War was not substantially different from what it had been for some time past. The Picards ascribe the opening of hostilities, and indeed the prosecution of the war throughout, to the initiative of the Romans.

A review of Roman politics before and during the First Punic War shows that the prowar faction was led by noble families of Campania admitted to the Roman senate during the Samnite wars, and by some few native Roman nobles who had connections or landed interests in the south of Italy. The antiwar faction was led by those whose interests lay to the north. The degree of vigor with which the war was prosecuted varied from time to time as political developments in Rome favored one family or another.

The Second Punic War, in contrast to the First, was chiefly prosecuted by the Carthaginians on their own initiative, and much of the interest of the Picards' book lies in their account of how the First Punic War affected conditions in Carthage in such a way as to lead to a resumption of hostilities with Rome after a period of some twenty years.

The young general Hamilcar Barca had been left to conclude the war in Sicily after the oligarchic government in Carthage had largely lost interest in it. During the Mercenary War of 241/40, when a revolt broke out among Carthaginian troops as they returned home to be paid off and disbanded, Hamilcar was called up by the popular party to replace the oligarchs' generals and pacify the troops. He was successful in this endeavor, winning many of the mercenary troops to a per-

sonal loyalty to himself. The popular party that had called on him was able to break the power of the oligarchs in Carthage so that the civil government there, henceforth headed by popularly elected magistrates, remained on friendly terms with Hamilcar and allowed him the generalship of large armies for extended periods of time.

Hamilcar used his troops to pacify large territories in Spain. His purpose in so doing was partly to gain control of Spanish mines as a means of enabling Carthage to pay the enormous war indemnities imposed upon her by the Romans. But he also wanted to create a strong military and naval base from which to resist further Roman advances, and his control of the Spanish territories was so personal as to make of them almost an independent kingdom. Killed in battle in 229 B.C., Hamilcar was succeeded as general of the Spanish armies by his son-in-law Hasdrubal, who devoted his administrative talents to consolidating Hamilcar's military gains. Hasdrubal, assassinated in 222, was succeeded by Hamilcar Barca's son, Hannibal the Great, to whom Spain was not so much a kingdom to rule as a base of military operations against the hereditary enemy, Rome.

—Zola M. Packman

Additional Recommended Reading

Grant, Michael. *The Ancient Mediterranean.* New York: Charles Scribner's Sons, 1969. A general history of the Mediterranean world from prehistoric times through the achievement of Roman domination.

Grimal, Pierre, Hermann Bengtson, *et al. Hellenism and the Rise of Rome.* Translated by A. M. Sheridan Smith and Carla Wartenburg. London: Weidenfeld and Nicolson, 1968. A survey of the Mediterranean world in the third century B.C.

Heitland, W. E. *The Roman Republic.* Cambridge: The University Press, 1923. A thorough, three-volume study of the political and military history of the Roman Republic.

Toynbee, Arnold J. *Hannibal's Legacy.* Oxford: The University Press, 1965. A two-volume account of the struggles between Rome and Carthage, and their effects on Italy and Rome.

Warmington, Brian Herbert. *Carthage.* New York: Praeger, 1960. A description and history of Carthage.

REVENUE LAWS OF PTOLEMY PHILADELPHUS

Type of event: Economic: publication of regulations for a state economy
Time: 259 B.C.
Locale: Alexandria

Principal personages:
PTOLEMY II (PHILADELPHUS), King of Egypt 283/2-246
APOLLONIUS, his Minister of Finance

Summary of Event

The Ptolemies, who controlled Egypt after the end of the fourth century B.C., inherited a well-articulated system for managing the economy of the country. The Pharoahs had treated the land as their personal property and had organized a bureaucracy to oversee it. It is uncertain to what extent the Ptolemies altered this system or what changes were made by which Ptolemy. Ptolemy I, however, seems to have been preoccupied with building up his army and navy, while his son Ptolemy II certainly refined the economic institutions which supported them. It is likely that the Macedonians' modifications were in the direction of a stricter and more sophisticated system. They created a corps of supervisors, clerks, and counter-checkers to keep highly detailed records of economic activity of all sorts. They put the country for the first time on a money economy, caused iron tools to be used far more extensively than before, and brought about technical improvements such as the introduction of better machines for irrigation.

The economic life of Egypt was directed from Alexandria to bring in as much money in taxes as possible. Part of a copy of the impressively complicated *Revenue Laws of Ptolemy Philadelphus* of May/June, 259 B.C., has been found. They were issued by the Ministry of Finance, headed by a certain Apollonius, whose responsibility it was to formulate and carry out the state's economic policies. The best preserved sections are regulations for the government's monopoly on oil-bearing plants. Sesame oil was an edible cooking oil, and castor oil was used for lighting. The laws laid down that the amount of land to be sown annually with oleaginous plants would be determined in advance at Alexandria by the *dioecetes*, or finance ministers. Out in the villages peasants formally contracted with the state to grow a stipulated crop. These cultivators could sell their harvest in the presence of a clerk only to men whom the state licensed to trade. The growers were paid a price fixed by the government, and the king took a quarter of the crop as tax. The licensed buyers processed the remainder at a registered, state-owned oil press, and then sold the finished oil at a price also determined by the Finance Ministry. The laws provided a comprehensive schedule of fines for persons who interfered in any way with the exercise of this royal monopoly, from the lowly Egyptian peasant up to the Greek district supervisor. We can put together enough scattered pieces of evidence to show that detailed regulations also applied to other sectors of the economy including manufacturing, fishing, and trade.

To organize the state economy, Egypt was divided into provinces called *nomes*, each governed by a *strategos*, or general, who maintained law and order, with economic affairs being administered by an *oeconomos*. Most *nomes* were divided into *topoi*, or "places," supervised by *toparchs*, and the *topoi* were

110

subdivided into the basic *comae*, or "villages," presided over by a *comarch*. Comarchs were usually bilingual Egyptian clerks, but the higher officials were almost always monolingual Greeks. The *comarchs* kept registers of the land around their villages and classified it according to quality, also maintaining lists of cattle and other animals of value. Copies of these registers were sent to the *toparchs* who in turn compiled registers of their districts and sent copies to the *oeconomoi*. Registers for each *nome* went to the *dioecetes* in Alexandria, where from the master register the annual planting plan was prepared for wheat, barley, sesame, castor, and other crops; orders for carrying out the master plan were then dispatched down the chain of command.

The greater part of the labor force was made up of Egyptian peasants called "royal farmers." Though not serfs, they were not free men either, as they were required to remain in their villages during the growing season. Some land was used by temples of the great Egyptian high gods with most of the income going to maintaining the cults and buildings, but the priests were also subject to the master planting plan, and had to turn over any surplus to the state. Cleruchic land was granted to Greeks and Macedonians who served in the armed forces or departments of state; it was farmed by Egyptians while the Europeans performed military or administrative functions.

In western Asia the Seleucid dynasty controlled a kingdom much larger and more heterogeneous than the Ptolemaic. While they had economic policies of their own, what little we know of them shows that the Seleucid Empire was less centralized and less strict than the Egyptian. In western Asia Minor, the kingdom of the Attalids of Pergamum seems to have been consciously modeled on Ptolemaic practice, and control of peasants and workmen was as strict as it was in Egypt.

Pertinent Literature

Rostovtzeff, M. I. *The Social and Economic History of the Hellenistic World.* Oxford: The Clarendon Press, 1941. 3 vols.

Professor Rostovtzeff was a man of many linguistic skills, enormous learning, and prodigious power of research. His books have contributed enormously to our understanding of the social and economic history of the Hellenistic period and the age of the Roman Empire immediately following.

Rostovtzeff believed that the principal reason the Ptolemies treated Egypt as a money-making machine was to secure the means of importing the timber and metals which Egypt lacked, and of hiring mercenaries in time of war without which Egypt could not have competed with other well-organized Hellenistic states. He held that the Macedonian modification of the Pharaonic system was begun by Ptolemy I, and was greatly elaborated and rationalized by Ptolemy II. He regarded the organization as "marvelous in its logic and clearness of conception," although he was well aware of the ethnic injustice it caused. He argued that the Ptolemies were obliged to develop a state dominated by Europeans. The army had to be Greco-Macedonian because only Greeks and Macedonians understood the military technique invented by Philip and Alexander, whose campaigns had proved that it was greatly superior to Egyptian or Persian methods. Furthermore, the loyalty of Egyptian soldiers could scarcely be trusted. The same was true in the economic sphere. In Greece during the fourth century there had been a steady evolution of methods of state financial management. Once the Macedonians had learned how the Pharaonic system operated, they combined selected Egyptian customs with such elements of Greek practice which seemed best suited to produce the most efficient exploitation of the agricultural, mineral, and human resources of the country. While some Egyptians became Hellenized and entered into the life of the state on nearly the same terms as Greeks, the overwhelming mass of the Egyptians did not, and society was divided into a fairly small number of Macedonians and Greeks with the best jobs, a class of Greeks and mixed Greco-Egyptians who had inferior or even bad jobs, and the Egyptian masses, who tended almost always to be diggers of ditches and keepers of pigs.

Rostovtzeff admired the rational organization of the state, and paid a warm tribute to the men who worked in the creative atmosphere of Alexandria. The clever schemes of drainage and land reclamation put into effect made an area of wasteland over into a whole new *nome*. Crop rotation was enforced. Seed grains of various kinds were imported, acclimatized, and planted to increase yields. Better strains of animals were introduced and crossbreeding was practiced.

Our knowledge of some districts in Egypt is so minutely detailed that we can hazard, by extension, rough estimates of the population and income of the country as a whole. Rostovtzeff suggested that the population of Egypt at the beginning of the Christian era was about seven and a half million, not counting Alexandria whose people numbered close to one million. All these agents, soldiers, and workers toiled to support themselves and enrich the state. Rostovtzeff accepted the statement of Jerome that the annual income of Ptolemy II from Egypt alone was 14,800 talents in money. This figure does not include income in kind or taxes from overseas possessions, which were large. This figure may be compared with that for Athens in 431 B.C., when she was at the height of her power: 350,000 Athenians enjoyed a state income of one thousand talents in money from both foreign and domestic sources. The difference between Athens and Egypt shows how drastically the power of the old city-states had shrunk by the third century B.C.

Bell, Sir H. Idris. *Egypt from Alexander the Great to the Arab Conquest.* Oxford: The Clarendon Press, 1948.

Bell's small book is a masterly presentation of the history of Egypt with emphasis on the early diffusion and subsequent decay of Hellenism throughout the country. The Ptolemies, he says, organized their system of planned economy to realize a maximum income for a minimum of expenditure. Under the first three Ptolemies, vigorous and energetic men, the system worked well; but under Ptolemy IV, a weaker leader, the system began to break down. Without a strong hand on the controls, the bureaucracy grew more and more incompetent and corrupt. The Egyptian peasants, treated as inferiors by Greek officials who all too often acted like *Herrenvolk*, began under the leadership of the native priesthood, to revolt against the foreign regime. Patriotic uprisings continued sporadically throughout the second and first centuries B.C. and sapped the strength of the state, which, in 30 B.C., was taken by Rome.

The Romans reorganized their new province only slightly. A prefect was appointed to take the place of Ptolemy. Tight supervision of the Egyptian temples was begun. The Romans moved to protect Hellenism in Egypt, and a Greco-Macedonian elite continued to monopolize most of the high offices. The bureaucracy was purged of incompetents and more honest men took their places, but the government and the economic system kept essentially the same form that the Ptolemies had given it. Bell thinks that the very efficiency infused into the system by the new men appointed by the Romans was one cause of fresh troubles with the Egyptian peasants. A second reason was that, although the Ptolemies had exploited the country, much of their profit was reinvested in it. The Romans now efficiently exploited Egypt's resources themselves but as absentee landlords, and they exported the country's wealth to feed their eastern armies and the Roman mob, or to embellish the palaces of the rich in Italy. By A.D. 20 many peasants fled to avoid work. Such a course was the only one left an Egyptian when the courts failed to protect him against oppression.

Enough persons fled their places in the first century A.D. for the Romans to resort to a regime of compulsory state service, including providing warships, collecting taxes, and cultivating land where lessees had decamped. From the reign of Vespasian through that of Antoninus Pius, A.D. 69-161, compulsion seems to have been applied locally and temporarily, but from the accession of Marcus Aurelius on it was more and more frequently resorted to on a broad scale. Under the military emperors of the third century it became common and provoked outbursts of anti-Hellenism and anti-Romanism. Egyptians prophesied the destruction of the hated capital Alexandria. A collection of martyrologies advertised the selfless patriotism of Greek citizens of Alexandria standing up to the cruel Latin emperors. Flight of Greek officials and Egyptian peasants alike became common, in turn bringing more compulsion, force, and repression. Rebellions broke out.

At the end of the third century A.D. the Roman Empire as a whole faced a series of political and economic crises, and the Emperors Diocletian, A.D. 284-305, and Constantine, A.D. 308-337, well aware of the bureaucratic system organized in Egypt, decided to enforce some of its institutions on the Empire as a whole. As had been the case in Ptolemaic Egypt, Diocletian decreed the separation of military and civil power in the provincial organization; the estimation of necessary state income in advance; a severe rationalization of the taxing system; the rating of land for taxation according to quality; and the fixing of prices, as the old Finance Ministry of Apollonius had done. Constantine attempted to enforce a system of serfdom throughout the Empire by compelling agricultural labor to remain on the land in perpetuity. The reforms of Diocletian and Constantine largely failed, and in the fourth century, native passions rose in Egypt, expressing themselves through the creation of Egyptian Coptic literature, and the strongly anti-Hellenic mobs of riotous Christian monks. — *Samuel K. Eddy*

Additional Recommended Reading

Grenfell, B. P., and J. P. Mahaffy. *The Revenue Laws of Ptolemy Philadelphus.* Oxford: The Clarendon Press, 1968. A study containing the Greek text, English translation, notes, and commentary.

Kraemer, C. J. "Bureaucracy and Petty Graft in Ancient Egypt," in *Classical Weekly.* Vol. 20 (1927), 163-168. A sketch of administrative malpractice in Greco-Roman Egypt.

Marcus, Ralph. "Antisemitism in the Hellenistic World," in *Essays on Antisemitism.* Edited by K. S. Pinson. 2nd ed. New York: Conference on Jewish Relations, 1946. A brief outline of anti-Semitism in the ethnic struggles in Alexandria.

Musurillo, Herbert A. *Acta Alexandrinorum. The Acts of the Pagan Martyrs.* Oxford: The Clarendon Press, 1954. An excellent book containing all that is known of the anti-Roman and anti-Semitic patriots of Greek Alexandria.

Rostovtzeff, M. I. *A Large Estate in Egypt in the Third Century B.C.* Madison: University of Wisconsin Press, 1922. A description of the management of Apollonius' holdings.

Westermann, W. L. "The Ptolemies and the Welfare of Their Subjects," in *American Historical Review.* Vol. 43 (1938), 270-287. Argues that the Ptolemies sincerely attempted to remove the oppression caused by their corrupt or brutal agents.

BATTLE OF ZAMA

Type of event: Military: engagement between Roman and Carthaginian armies
Time: 202 B.C.
Locale: About sixty miles southwest of Carthage in what is now Tunisia

Principal personages:
HANNIBAL, Carthaginian general
HASDRUBAL BARCA, younger brother of Hannibal
PUBLIUS CORNELIUS SCIPIO, Roman consul and general
MASSINISSA, King of eastern Numidia, and an ally of Rome
GAIUS LAELIUS, consul 190, and Roman commander under Scipio

Summary of Event

After Hannibal had finally been trapped in southern Italy by the "Fabian tactics" of Rome, the tide of the Second Punic War turned against him. Scipio's victories in Spain from 208 to 206, and the frustration of the efforts by Hasdrubal, Hannibal's younger brother, to reinforce Hannibal in 207, prepared the way for an invasion of Africa by Scipio in 204. It was then Rome's turn to ravish the enemy countryside as Hannibal had done for fifteen years in Italy. With a large and well-disciplined army, mostly volunteers, Scipio outwitted two defense forces collected by Carthage, captured the rural areas around the city, and damaged its economy. The Carthaginians offered a truce to gain time in order to effect Hannibal's return from Italy; he succeeded in getting away with a force of more than ten thousand veterans.

Hannibal spent the winter of 203-202 collecting and training an army for the decisive meeting with Scipio. Since both Roman and Carthaginian cavalry were limited, the rival generals each sent out appeals for aid to various African chieftains. Scipio turned to an old companion in arms, the wily desert sheik Massinissa, who had fought with the Romans in Spain. In 204-203 Scipio had helped Massinissa defeat a rival for control of a kingdom in Numidia, west of Carthage. But in 202 Massinissa was slower to respond to Scipio than were other African princes who brought cavalry and elephants to aid

Hannibal. So Scipio moved his army inland and westward to avoid a major battle until he had secured more cavalry.

Hannibal marched his army in pursuit of the Romans, hoping to force a confrontation before Scipio was ready. When the Carthaginian army came near the village of Zama, about five days' march southwest of Carthage, he sent scouts to search out Scipio's position. These spies were captured, but after being shown through the Roman camp they were released. Scipio by this device hoped that their reports would discourage an immediate Carthaginian attack. Polybius, the Greek historian who lived in the first half of the first century B.C., reports that before the battle the two generals actually had a dramatic face-to-face meeting, alone on a plain between two opposing hills where their armies were encamped. However, Hannibal's peace proposals were rejected by Scipio, who had recently been encouraged by the arrival of Massinissa with four thousand cavalrymen and other reinforcements.

On the following day the two armies were drawn up for battle. They were probably about equal in size, although some scholars estimate that Hannibal's force was as large as fifty thousand men while Scipio's was as small as twenty-three thousand. Certainly the Roman cavalry was stronger. Hannibal placed his eighty elephants in front of his first-line troops, who were experienced mercenaries from Europe and Africa. Scipio's front line was divided into separate fighting units with gaps between them to allow the elephants to pass through without disarranging the line. When the battle began, bugles stampeded the elephants, which turned sideways onto Hannibal's own cavalry stationed on the wings. The Roman cavalry under Laelius and Massinissa took advantage of the confusion to drive the Carthaginian cavalry off the battlefield.

During the infantry battle which ensued, the disciplined front rank of Roman legionnaires, closely supported by their second-rank comrades, managed to penetrate Hannibal's line in places. The second-line troops of Carthage, apparently not as well coordinated, allowed both Punic lines to be driven back with heavy casualties. Hannibal had kept in reserve a strong third line of veterans, intending to attack with this fresh force when the Romans were exhausted, but he allowed a fatal pause during which Scipio regrouped his detachments. The final stage of the battle raged indecisively until the cavalry of Laelius and Massinissa returned to the field to attack the Carthaginians in the rear and destroy most of those encircled by this maneuver. Polybius reports twenty thousand Carthaginian casualties compared to only fifteen hundred Romans killed.

Hannibal escaped, but Carthage was exhausted and surrendered without a siege, accepting peace terms which took away all Carthaginian possessions outside Africa, imposed a heavy indemnity, and guaranteed the autonomy of Massinissa's kingdom. Scipio returned in triumph to Rome where he was awarded the title "Africanus." Remarkably undaunted by defeat, Hannibal led Carthage within a few years to economic recovery; later he was forced by Rome into exile, and he fled eastward to aid adversaries of Rome in further wars.

By their victory at Zama, the Romans gained supremacy in the western Mediterranean and launched an imperialistic program which eventually made them dominant throughout most of Europe and the Near East, repressing eastern leadership until the rise of Moslem power.

Pertinent Literature

Scullard, H. H. *Scipio Africanus: Soldier and Politician.* Ithaca: Cornell University Press, 1970.

This work is a definitive biography of Scipio. While the author has great respect for Africanus, he finds it unprofitable to speculate on his rank among the world's great generals as did Liddell Hart in his commendable study, *A Greater than Napoleon: Scipio Africanus.* This later British soldier and military analyst devotes some sixty pages to Scipio's African campaign which ended at Zama, and gives only begrudging acknowledgment to Hannibal's skill.

Scullard agrees with Liddell Hart that Scipio was a great man. His basic claim to distinction, according to Scullard, was his realization that Rome could no longer depend upon her traditional citizen levies, commanded each year by a different general, to defeat Hannibal. A professional army was required. Scipio realized that establishment of such an army involved attacking "Republican formalities"; to pit the individual against the *mos maiorum* and the corporate body was an appalling effrontery to his fellow noble traditionalists. Consequently if Hannibal had to fight a short-sighted government, Scipio had to overcome the Roman establishment. Fortunately he made no constitutional threats against his foes in the senate, and instead of becoming a demagogue he retired voluntarily after his victory into exile. In his role as an exceptional commander, however, he foreshadowed the later military dictators of Rome.

Scipio moreover understood that the Roman army had to be mobile so that it could not be outflanked as it was at Cannae. He preferred to arrange his forces in independent units in a decentralized organization which put a premium on the self-reliance of individual lieutenants for quick action.

Scullard would like to see in Scipio a precocious, idealistic imperialist. As such Scipio supposedly saw that Fabius' guerrilla tactics could solve nothing. Hannibal and later Antiochus had to be defeated in the open field on their own ground to make the world safe for Rome; Carthage had to be eliminated in order to lay the foundation for the later Empire.

Scullard attributes to Scipio's farsighted imperial outlook his policy of withdrawing troops and treating conquered countries mildly to foster in them the devotion to Rome which would make them loyal provinces in the future. Unlike Hannibal, Scipio came not to destroy but to offer culture and civilization without threats or fear to those who would profit by such treatment. Scipio's settlement of veterans close to the pillars of Hercules instead of near Rome reveals his confidence in Rome's mission as a future imperial power. It is interesting to note that he called his settlement "Italica" rather than naming it after himself in the manner of Hellenistic rulers.

Scipio's greatness rests in his encouragement of a new culture blending together the best of Greece and Rome. His interest in literature was a new departure among his noble colleagues in politics; his daughter Cornelia was provided with an exceptionally good education. Scullard admits that Scipio's part in the Hellenization of Rome is difficult to assess and document. He asks whether Scipio was a Grecophile in philosophy, or sincere in claiming divine guidance. Was he a Greek skeptic or atheist exploiting the religious aura surrounding him by fostering a false belief in his divine mission? Or was he a bona fide mystic trusting in divine communication? Scullard is inclined to believe in Scipio's own inner integrity. Polybius apparently judged him to be an extreme rationalist, projecting his own personal judgments rather than those of contemporary Romans who were at that time basically religious.

Scipio was in time compared to Alexander. Dante saw the hand of God in his victory at Zama which made possible the future glory of Rome. The Renaissance saw him as a bridge between the classical world and the Christian, a man having a fine sense of morality serving in Roman times the ends of Divine Providence. Petrarch was much influenced by Cicero's *Scipio's Dream* and he glorified Scipio in his *Africa* as an inspiration in the dream of Humanism to rediscover the ancient world.

Dodge, T. A. *Hannibal.* Boston: Houghton Mifflin Co., 1891. 2 vols.

This fascinating old study of Hannibal is self-opinionated and undocumented, but it remains interesting as a eulogy of the great Carthaginian general who was defeated at the Battle of Zama. In nearly seven hundred pages Dodge admires Hannibal in great detail, and while it is unfair to isolate his strong generalizations from their context, some of his conclusions follow.

Dodge's position regarding Scipio is equivocal. He recognizes the merits of the man as a great general and politician, but he regards him as inferior to Hannibal in generalship. The author reminds his readers that history has eulogistic Roman historians such as Livy to thank for Scipio's unearned reputation.

Dodge moreover believes that Scipio was exceptionally fortunate in having about him able lieutenants such as Laelius and Silvanus in Spain for whose work he reaped the credit. Scipio enjoyed "marked good fortune" throughout his career which caused his ultimate success as much as his "fine abilities." Dodge regards Scipio as a brilliant but not a great general.

Scipio's reputation derives in part from his popularity despite his "many and serious errors." He entered history dramatically by saving his father's life at Trebia and by heroically presenting himself as the only volunteer to lead the dangerous assignment in Spain. He was admittedly handsome, manly, enthusiastic, courageous, intelligent, self-confident, honorable, considerate, generous, educated, and refined. But he was born under a lucky star. "When he failed from the result of his own errors, Fortune always came to his rescue." Fortune was indeed as good to him as to Alexander, although the latter did far more to deserve such favors. Because he was a great, almost obnoxious, believer in his own destiny, he was haughty and considered himself to be above criticism. It is fortunate that he was never called upon to account for his high-handedness. Livy records how he blatantly threatened to bypass the senate and appeal to the people in order to gain acceptance for his resolution to take the war to Africa. He openly defied the senate and Fabius Maximus when he was asked to submit, saying that he would prefer to consult the "interests of the state" himself. Dodge suggests that such action shows he was more of a politician than a good military man dedicated to the service of the civil state. He was forced to collect his own supplies at first, and only later was he able to persuade the senate to allow him to draft some troops from Sicily.

It was not the superiority of Scipio over Hannibal which brought him victory at Zama. History shows that the best general does not always win. Scipio should be thankful that before Zama he had not faced an equal opponent except perhaps Hasdrubal, or else Fortune could not have saved him for Zama when Hannibal's forces and chances were already wrecked. Had Scipio met the great Carthaginian general earlier, he would surely have been defeated. At Zama, Carthage was almost defenseless with scarcely enough men to man her walls compared to the thirty-seven thousand enthusiastic troops under Scipio. His feeble attempts against Carthage earlier and his waste of time collecting and shipping booty to Rome should go a long way toward placing Scipio "where he fairly belongs in the ranks of generals." At Zama the Roman army won because its cavalry was superior; the victory was not the result of Scipio's brilliant generalship. Hannibal was superior in logistics and strategy, but he was handicapped by inferior forces and the stubbornness, stupidity, and short-sightedness of the Carthaginian senate. Rome had to win, not because it outgeneraled Carthage but because of the "strength of its organization and the soundness of its body politic" against the military corruption of Carthage. Had Rome not been victorious at Zama, it would have succeeded somewhere else. In fact Zama should be downgraded in importance along with Scipio, for Carthage lost long before the battle took place. When Hannibal was ordered back from Italy, the die was already cast. It was only Hannibal's genius which prolonged the struggle and made Zama possible at all.

Additional Recommended Reading

Baker, G. P. *Hannibal.* New York: Dodd, Mead & Company, 1929. A clear account of Zama with three maps to show different stages of the battle.

Battle of Zama

Cottrell, Leonard. *Hannibal, Enemy of Rome.* New York: Holt, Rinehart, and Winston, 1960, 1961. An interesting biography which provides clear battle diagrams.

De Beer, Gavin. *Hannibal.* New York: Viking Press, 1969. This handsomely illustrated biography gives only a brief account of the Battle of Zama.

Hallward, B. L. "Scipio and Victory," in *The Cambridge Ancient History.* Vol. 8, ch. 4. Cambridge: The University Press, 1928. In discussing the Battle of Zama, this account eulogizes Hannibal as the "consummate strategist" and statesman.

Liddell Hart, B. H. *A Greater than Napoleon: Scipio Africanus.* Edinburgh: William Blackwood and Sons, 1926. A semipopular but solid account lauding Scipio as greater than Caesar, Alexander, and Frederick the Great.

Russell, Francis H. "The Battlefield of Zama," in *Archaeology.* Vol. 23, no. 2 (April, 1970), 120-129. A beautifully illustrated study of the Battle of Zama.

Warmington, B. H. *Carthage.* London: Robert Hale Ltd., 1960. A history including a brief description of the Battle of Zama and its consequences for history.

ESTABLISHMENT OF THE *CURSUS HONORUM*

Type of event: Constitutional: postulation of regulations governing officeholders
Time: 180 B.C.
Locale: Rome

Principal personages:
PUBLIUS CORNELIUS SCIPIO AFRICANUS, consul in 205 B.C.
MARCUS PROCIUS CATO, a *novus homo* who achieved the
    consulship in 195 B.C. and the censorship in 184 B.C.
LUCIUS VILLIUS, plebeian tribune in 180 B.C.

Summary of Event

The growth of Rome from an insignificant river city to the administrative center of a far-flung empire brought with it numerous changes in the machinery of its government. Many of these changes were made gradually but some were concessions forced by new political situations. A significant stage in this process was marked by the law passed in 180 B.C., the *Lex Villia Annalis.* Understanding of its full significance, however, requires a historical description of the Roman magisterial offices.

Before the establishment of the Republic, all final political power in Rome resided in the person of the king, while the executive officers of the state acted solely as his personal representatives. With the overthrow of the monarchy, these officials, called magistrates by the Romans, became effective representatives of the entire community; their powers, duties, and privileges were thought to be derived from the senate and people conjointly, even though in the early period the people were limited solely to ratifying the election of patrician candidates. At that time the most powerful officials were the two consuls, elected for terms of one year. Only patricians were eligible for this office until the Licinian laws of 367 B.C. threw it open to the plebeians. So strong was the aristocratic domination of Roman political life, however, that only in 172 B.C. were both consuls ple-

beians. The duties of the consuls were diverse; they were charged with conducting the affairs of the senate, maintaining public order throughout Italy, and leading the army in time of war.

The second most powerful office was the praetorship. It seems probable that the first praetor was elected in 360 B.C., although there are some indications that the office may have formed part of the original constitution of the Republic. Plebeians first became eligible for it in 337 B.C. The praetor was above all the supreme civil judge. In 242 B.C. the number of annually elected praetors was raised to two, so that one could be placed in charge of lawsuits between Roman citizens and aliens. As Rome's overseas dominions increased, the number of praetors was raised to four in 227 B.C. allowing two praetors to serve as governors of the newly-formed provinces of Sicily and Sardinia, and in 197 B.C. the number was raised to six, the additional two officers being assigned to administer the two provinces of Spain.

An office not constitutionally essential for election to higher offices, but extremely influential in itself, was the aedileship. At the beginning of the Republic two aediles were appointed to supervise the temples and religious practices of the plebeians. Ultimately they were given control over public buildings, street maintenance, the distribution of the corn supply, and, above all, production of the public games. This capacity enabled ambitious politicians to stage lavish and spectacular games in an attempt to gain popularity with the urban electorate.

The lowest political office was the quaestorship. The office was probably created at the beginning of the Republic, with the number of annually elected quaestors raised to four in 421 B.C. At the same time plebeians were also made eligible for the office. Ultimately the number of quaestors was fixed at twenty. Two of the quaestors had charge of the state treasury and official archives. The others were attached as aides either to generals on campaign or to provincial governors. Their duties were diverse: financial, judicial, and military.

These four offices formed the so-called *cursus honorum*, the order in which political offices had to be held, although strictly speaking the aedileship was not a prerequisite for election to any other office. The *cursus honorum* did not exist before 180 B.C., since until that time there were no age qualifications assigned to any of these offices, nor was the holding of any one office a necessary condition for election to another higher office. Thus Scipio Africanus, the conqueror of Hannibal, was elected consul for 205 B.C. at the age of thirty-one and Flaminius, the victor at Cynoscephalae in 197 B.C., was elected consul in 198 B.C. at a similarly early age. This situation was drastically altered by the law carried in 180 B.C. by the tribune Lucius Villius, which set fixed age qualifications for the various offices. The probable age limits established were forty for the praetor and forty-three for the consul. Although no minimum age was placed on the quaestors it was generally understood that candidates who stood for this office would have already completed their ten-year military obligation and thus be approximately twenty-eight. Through these strictures, a regular and restrained order was placed over the advancement of all political careers.

Pertinent Literature

Scullard, H. H. *Roman Politics 220-150 B.C.* Oxford: The Clarendon Press, 1951.

This work relies extensively on a method of investigating Roman history that was developed in Germany during the first quarter of the twentieth century. Called "prosopography," it involves an accurate and all-inclusive determination of the definite relationships existing among prominent Romans during periods where such information is retrievable. These relationships were brought about either by birth, marriage, or intimate friendship. Once the relationships have been worked out, there emerge distinct groupings of individuals into purportedly political alliances and associations with their own programs and strategies.

Scullard has applied this methodology of historical research to the period between the opening of the Second Punic War and the middle of the first century, when Roman domination had been extended to practically every shore of the Mediterranean. Scullard's book provides a detailed catalogue of political maneuvers and feuds against which the urgency and impact of the *Lex Annalis* clearly stand out.

Marriage patterns and verifiable friendship disclose three prime groups vying for political eminence in this period: (1) a traditional, conservative right, headed by Valerius Flaccus, best embodied and articulated by the energetic newcomer Marcus Porcius Cato; (2) a philhellenic, expansionist group led by the illustrious hero of the Punic War, Cornelius Scipio Africanus; and (3) a middle-of-the-road faction centered around the families of the Claudii and the Fulvii.

There is general agreement that it is anachronistic to describe these alliances as traditional political parties. Their membership was susceptible to desertion as a result of divorce or personal animosity; nor did the separate groups devise firm ideologies or advance concrete political and economic programs. What they held in common was a membership drawn almost exclusively from the *nobilitas*, the recently formed oligarchic circle that had exercised political dominance at Rome since the middle of the third century. No longer split into plebeian and patrician factions, the nobles identified themselves as the descendants of ancestors who had attained consular offices. Considering that this pedigree made them the only qualified and competent candidates for political authority, the nobles contested among themselves for political prominence, manipulating matrimonial and personal relationships to ensure their own advancement. They were united in their desire to exclude from successful political careers men whose family trees did not include previous holders of the consulship, the so-called "new men" or *novi homines*. Their solidarity against such upstarts sometimes weakened in the face of their even greater fear of the too-rapid success of any member of their own class. Thus

the Valerii backed the career of the new man Cato to offset the sudden ascendancy of Scipio Africanus.

This was the general background for the passage of the *Lex Annalis* in 180 B.C. Scullard considers that the law specified the minimum age requirements for each office, set up a mandatory sequence of offices, and ordered a minimal two-year interval between offices. Since this law prevented precipitous political advancement by ambitious young nobles, and in effect subordinated the individual noble to the code of his class, Scullard sees its main intent as tightening the oligarchs' control of the state by reducing friction among them. He points out, however, that both this law and other measures designed to check the increasing electoral corruption through bribery were passed during a period when plebeian "new men," such as Cato, were prominent in office. From this standpoint, the law, presumably facilitating the gradual rise of a *novus homo*, appears as a deliberate antidote to the nobles' monopoly of political office. This reform quite possibly contributed to the general internal stability of the following fifty years but the careers of the brothers Gracchi eventually exposed the weaknesses of Roman political life which were far too basic for solely electoral reforms to eradicate.

Greenidge, A.H.E. *Roman Political Life.* London: Macmillan & Company, 1901.

The overthrow of the Republic can be ascribed in large part to the failure of the Roman constitution to provide an adequate system of government for the expanded Empire. Although the constitution underwent numerous reforms and renovations as in the case of the *Lex Annalis*, some of its features, especially its structure of magisterial offices, were never modified sufficiently to ensure the political health of the Empire. The *Lex Annalis* corrected certain defects of the *cursus hon-*

orum by establishing an orderly sequence of office, but its limited aims prevented it from clearing up other more important and inherent shortcomings of the magisterial system. These shortcomings are readily apparent in the admirably detailed examination of the Roman magistracies available in Greenidge.

Roman politicians and theorists took pride in the mixed form of their constitution; supposedly, senate, people, and magistrates were all equipped with enough influence to prevent a usurpation of power by any one of the three. The pattern of checks and balances responsible for this internal equilibrium also characterized every Roman magistracy through the principle of collegiality of officers. Every Roman magistrate shared his executive authority with at least one other equally powerful partner. In the case of the quaestors with their circumscribed powers and extensive duties, the collegial system made possible an efficient division of labor. The provision for two consuls, however, with their untrammeled authority, was potentially anarchic and able to bring all governmental activity to a complete standstill. This difficulty could be avoided as long as the two consuls accepted the same political persuasions. Once rival political factions arose around the *optimates* and the *populares*, however, the consulship became one of the prime arenas of their violent opposition. Preferring time-honored, practical compromises rather than radical reforms, the Romans ludicrously decided that during military campaigns, the consuls should take daily turns as commanders of the expedition, to prevent their absolute veto power over one another from endangering the welfare of the army. This makeshift arrangement was alleviated somewhat by Sulla's reform which entrusted military power and responsibility to the proconsuls. In the end this reform only introduced a far more serious problem, as the career of Julius Caesar indicates.

Perhaps the most blatant weakness of the magisterial system was the office of plebeian tribune. Although the tribunate was not a requisite part of the *cursus honorum* since it was open only to plebeians, it nonetheless became a focal point of political strife because of its leverage over the other magistra-

cies. This leverage was also due to the frantic desire of the Romans to maintain equilibrium among all the sources of political power. In the case of the tribunate, however, through the personal inviolability of its holder and his extensive veto power over the activities of all the other magistrates, the Romans had in effect sanctioned legalized civil war within the state. Although the resources of the office were not fully exploited until the careers of the Gracchi, the nature of the resulting crisis can be gauged by the senatorial response which amounted to a practical declaration of war against the holders of the tribunate.

These repeated failures to adjust the constitution to changed conditions can only be grasped through an understanding of the Roman concept of *imperium*. Originally this term expressed the fullness of power that was possessed by the early kings. During the Republic, it was exercised by specially appointed dictators in grave emergencies. Under normal conditions, it was held by the consuls, but only after its scope had been significantly curtailed by the one-year term of office and the equal veto power. Behind these limitations was the fear of the return of the unlimited and arbitrary power of the kings. Although Roman statesmen made the return of monarchy unlikely, they restricted themselves in other respects, especially when the constitution was stretched to govern the expanded Empire. In this situation they failed to create a nonpartisan civil service; instead, they resorted to the *Lex Annalis* to ensure some diverse continuity to users of political power. This piecemeal and temporizing treatment of basic weaknesses in executive organization eventually led to the establishment of a dreaded unbounded *imperium* in the person of the emperor. —*George M. Pepe*

Additional Recommended Reading

Abbott, Frank Frost. *A History and Description of Roman Political Institutions.* Boston: Ginn & Co., 1901. A useful account of Roman executive offices, their powers and limitations.

Adcock, F. E. *Roman Political Ideas and Practice.* Ann Arbor: University of Michigan Press, 1959. A treatment of the theory and realities of Roman politics.

Astin, A. E. *The Lex Annalis Before Sulla.* Brussels: Collection Latomus XXXII. 1958. A survey of the *Lex Annalis* and its problems.

Frank, Tenney. "Rome," in *Cambridge Ancient History.* Vol. VIII, ch. XII, pp. 357-387. Cambridge: The University Press, 1930. A detailed account of the historical background of the *Lex Annalis.*

TRIBUNATE OF TIBERIUS SEMPRONIUS GRACCHUS

Type of event: Socio-political: attempt at government reform
Time: 133 B.C.
Locale: Rome

Principal personages:
TIBERIUS SEMPRONIUS GRACCHUS, Roman tribune
MARCUS OCTAVIUS, Roman tribune, 133, opponent of Tiberius
SCIPIO NASICA, Roman senator, chief opponent of Tiberius, consul
138

Summary of Event

By the 130's B.C., conditions in Roman Italy were changing for the worse. The acquisition of empire made necessary the posting of garrisons in distant provinces and a long-drawn-out war of pacification in Spain. Soldiers were conscripted for these duties from the citizens, and the long periods of time some of them had to spend overseas made it difficult or impossible for the less well-to-do to keep their farms going at home. The property of some of these soldiers was sold to creditors, and the land was then usually added to the wide plantations of the rich, who worked the land with non-Italian slaves taken in vast numbers during the provincial wars. For these reasons a few Roman military units had been on the verge of mutiny. Landless citizens swelled the growing numbers of the demoralized urban proletariat, who, without property, were no longer subject to military service with the Roman field armies. This tendency towards the pauperization of the small holders, who made up the bulk of the soldiers of the Roman army, was dangerous for the state. The few attempts which had been made to repair the situation had been stopped by the conservative Roman senate.

In December, 134 B.C., Tiberius Gracchus took office as one of the Tribunes of the People, and he proposed passage of the Sempronian Agrarian Law which had to do with public land, that is, land belonging to the state itself. The land was occupied, but not owned, by farmers and ranchers, many of whom were far from being poor. The bill stipulated that the amount of public land being used by any one man should not exceed three hundred acres. A man might work an additional one hundred and fifty acres for each of his first two sons. Areas above three hundred to six hundred acres the state would repossess, paying compensation for improvements made by the occupier, and this excess would be divided into allotments of about eighteen acres which the state would rent to landless citizens. Thus, the urban mob would be reduced and the numbers of men liable for overseas military service would be increased.

This statesmanlike plan was presented to the Assembly of the People, the *Consilium Plebis*, which voted it into law. At this point, however, another of the ten Tribunes, a certain Marcus Octavius, who was said to have enormous tracts of public land, vetoed the Assembly's act, as it was his legal right to do.

Tiberius, resolved to counterattack with a legal innovation, provoked a constitutional crisis of the first order. He argued that a Tribune of the People should not hold office if he acted against the interests of the people. Whether he did act against them should be decided by the people themselves, namely, the *Consilium Plebis*. Conservatives strongly opposed Tiberius' proposal, pointing out that tribunes were inviolable, and, by extension, not subject to recall; additionally, there was no precedent for the deposition of a tribune. Nonetheless, Tiberius presented his proposal to the *Consilium Plebis*, which voted overwhelmingly to recall Octavius. With that obstacle out of its way, the Assembly then voted the Agrarian Bill into law, and a commission, including Tiberius, his brother Gaius, and another relative, was set up to survey the public land and proceed with its reallotment.

To function, the commission required money, and the senate now proved to be a second stumbling block for Tiberius. By custom and precedent it controlled the state's finances, and it refused to grant sufficient funds for the commission to act. At this point the astonishing news arrived that Pergamum, one of the Hellenistic monarchies, had been willed to Rome by its recently deceased king, Attalus III. Tiberius, apparently with the approval of the *Consilium Plebis*, laid hands on part of the financial reserve of Pergamum and used it to finance the commission's work. This action, while necessary to give effect to the land law, was, to conservative Romans, an outrageous breach of constitutional practice and a serious challenge to the traditional authority of the senate, whose political experience and prestige had guided Rome for more than a century. The senate

determined to resist.

By now the time for the election of magistrates for the year 132 was approaching. Tiberius feared that his opponents would make a great effort to elect men friendly to their own views, and that they would try to repeal the Agrarian Law. To prevent this he presented himself for reelection. This action was also without precedent. Conservatives emotionally charged that Tiberius was collecting more and more power into his own hands to wield year after year and finally make himself king.

On polling day a crowd of senators and their clients gathered. When it became apparent that Tiberius was going to be returned to office, these men, led by Scipio Nasica, armed with staves and knives, stormed into the crowded voting areas, seized Tiberius, and clubbed him to death. Three hundred of his supporters shared his fate, and their bodies were flung like carrion into the Tiber.

Tiberius, in attempting to reform Roman society, had had to resort to extraconstitutional measures, which turned the senate sharply against him. It, however, instead of attempting some form of legal redress, resorted to the drastic expedient of murder. Thus was inaugurated an era of violence, gradually swelling until it turned into full-scale civil war.

Pertinent Literature

Last, Hugh. "Tiberius Gracchus," in *The Cambridge Ancient History*. Vol. 9. Cambridge: The University Press, 1932.

Last begins this chapter with a survey of the military and social problems which confronted Rome in 134 B.C., and then proceeds with an exposition of the measures which Tiberius undertook to meet them. His main object was to reduce the number of poor who were filling the slums of the capital and other cities of Italy. The population of Rome at this

time is unknown, but it is certain that it was growing rapidly and that the city was showing then most of the signs of urban sprawl and blight with which we are familiar today. Reconstructions of the appearance of the city in history books show the Rome of another age, the Rome of the Caesars, when the city had been rebuilt and ornamented with marble. The Agrarian Law was designed to reduce the size of the mob, increase the numbers from which the army was drawn, and correct grave social injustices. It would also, perhaps, reduce the number of foreign slaves on the large estates of Italy. Tiberius' motives, which were both practical and moral, were good.

Resistance to Tiberius came largely from wealthy senators who were in possession of considerable areas of public land. Octavius himself was accused of vetoing the bill because his own extensive holdings of public land were threatened by it. His opposition and that of the senate forced Tiberius to face the alternatives of abandoning his program, which he felt the good of Rome demanded, or of raising the issue of constitutional reform. He chose the latter. Last says that the method Tiberius used shows him to have been a young man carried away by enthusiasm. His proposals amounted to the launching of a doctrine of popular sovereignty, under which the *Consilium Plebis* was to become the supreme authority in the state. This was contrary to Roman legal tradition, which had laid down a regulation that legislation was to be agreed upon by an assembly summoned by a magistrate with the consent of the senate. Tiberius' acts not only made tribunes subject to recall by this assembly, but also overrode the authority of the senate. This solution had a streak of Hellenism in it; in democratic Greek cities, affairs were managed by a sovereign assembly of citizens which might elect or depose its leaders at will. A leader might hold office for many consecutive terms if the electors assented. Roman practice, on the other hand, insisted upon an interval of years, usually two, between the time a man might hold different offices in the *cursus honorum*, or regulation for office holding, and one of ten years between his holding of the same office twice. Roman practice also insisted upon the principle of collegiality, holding that the power of a magistracy was to be shared between the equal holders of that office, which was a principle Tiberius attacked by carrying out the deposition of Octavius. Tiberius was certainly influenced by two Greek friends, the famous rhetorician Diophanes of Mytilene (later condemned to death for complicity in the Gracchan program), and the Cynic philosopher Blossius of Cumae (who was condemned to exile for the same reason).

Last believes that Tiberius' doctrine of popular sovereignty was dangerous for a state which was not really a democracy but more like an aristocratic republic. It was bound to cause opposition. But Tiberius, he maintains, employed argument and reason to gain the assent of one of the great assemblies of the Roman people for his actions. The senatorial opposition abandoned argument and persuasion for lynch law, thereby setting the stage for the most brutal period in the history of the Republic.

Smith, R. E. *The Failure of the Roman Republic.* Cambridge: The University Press, 1955.

This short and interesting book is not for everyone. It contains a minimum of detailed, factual presentation of Roman history, and a maximum of interpretive argument which assumes prior knowledge of Roman political and economic history on the part of the reader. Smith discusses the causes of the collapse of the republican form of government at Rome and its replacement by the monarchy of Caesar and Augustus, and he regards the actions of Tiberius Gracchus as one of the significant causes.

The Roman state in the early 130's was dominated by the senate, which, in turn, was controlled by a small number of rich and noble families. Between 234 and 134, half the consuls came from only ten families. On the whole, the senate's governing of Italy was responsible and able. The senators' point of view was broadly shared by a society that was very conservative in religion, temperament, and outlook. Religion, especially, was an important force holding Roman society together, an important part of that conglomerate of precedent, law, and tradition which the Romans called the *mos maiorum*, "the custom of the ancestors." The most important political issue the Romans had to solve in the 130's was the problem of governing their growing empire. That sense of Roman superiority which had grown so strong by the middle of the century often expressed itself in a coarse contempt for foreigners; and the administration of provincial affairs was often corrupt, cynical, and cruel. This feeling of superiority created dangerous resentment and hatred for Rome; serious slave uprisings and provincial rebellions were imminent.

At this point Tiberius came on the scene. Smith holds that he wished to increase the number of small farmers liable to military service in order to solve problems connected with conscription. His answer, the Agrarian Law, Smith says, was the concept of a philosopher rather than the solution of a statesman. When the senators frustrated the application of the law, Tiberius impatiently challenged their authority by taking control of the Pergamene treasure, thereby infringing upon senatorial management of financial and foreign affairs. The senate had no obvious means of protecting its preeminent position, for there were no written laws defining its rights, only custom and precedent. Tiberius thus raised the question of who was to govern Rome, which was irrelevant to the main problem of finding more humane and sensible methods

of governing the Empire. Therefore, while a secondary issue was being fought out in Italy during succeeding decades, the Romans failed to realize that Rome had become a world power with the moral obligation for providing good administration for the provinces.

Tiberius Gracchus was an innovator in Roman politics. He was an individualist, impatient of tradition, and strongly influenced by Hellenism. The *mos maiorum* stressed *disciplina*, "obedience," and loyalty to the Roman way of life. The arrival of Greek ideas in Rome set up a rival schedule of intellectual and moral values. The Greek philosophers, in their quest for the Good, questioned Roman standards of right and wrong, and challenged the usefulness not only of unthinking *disciplina*, but also belief in traditional Roman religion. The result was a spiritual crisis. Tiberius Gracchus had to choose between either Roman precedent and the withdrawal of his vetoed bill, or the introduction of Greek values and the government of an urban mob. He chose the latter. To put it another way, the senate, upholder of the traditions of Rome, was challenged by new ideas flooding from the Greek world into Rome, a city inhabited by a demoralized proletariat uninhibited by moral or religious restraints. The schemes Tiberius favored undermined the traditional authority of the chief organ of the state itself, and nothing could take its place, ultimately, but armed force. Tiberius thus began the process which led in time to the outright collapse of Roman religion, morals, and decency which was the first cause of that long and sordid record of civil war and rebellion in Roman Italy.—*Samuel K. Eddy*

Additional Recommended Reading

Astin, A. E. *Scipio Aemilianus.* Oxford: The Clarendon Press, 1967. A biography of the life of this great contemporary of Tiberius Gracchus and of his role in the critical 130's B.C.

Boren, Henry C. "Numismatic Light on the Gracchan Crisis," in *American Journal of Philology.* Vol. 79 (1958), 140-55. This article argues from an analysis of surviving coins that the brothers Gracchus were concerned with the plight of the urban poor.

Greenidge, A. H. J. *A History of Rome During the Later Republic and Early Principate.* Vol. 1. London: Methuen & Co. Ltd., 1904. This book, now outmoded on details, nonetheless contains penetrating insights into the course of Roman history from 134 to 104 B.C.

Marsh, Frank B. *A History of the Roman World from 146 to 30 B.C.* London: Methuen & Co. Ltd., 1935. A competent survey of Roman history, including a sketch of conditions in the 130's and the results of Tiberius' abortive reforms.

Oman, Sir Charles. *Seven Roman Statesmen of the Later Republic.* London: Edward Arnold, 1914. Biographies of important Romans, including Tiberius Gracchus and his younger brother Gaius.

MARIUS' CREATION OF THE PRIVATE ARMY

Type of event: Military: innovation in recruitment and organization of the Roman army
Time: 107-101 B.C.
Locale: Rome, North Africa, and North Italy

Principal personages:
GAIUS MARIUS, commoner who gained high civilian status through
    military achievements
JUGURTHA, one of three princes who inherited the kingdom of
    Numidia in 118

Summary of Event

Marius' reforms of the Roman army were the culmination of developments arising out of Rome's emergence as an imperial power. They were the beginning of developments that were to lead to the civil wars of the late first century and the end of the Roman Republic.

From the earliest known period, the Roman army was recruited on an *ad hoc* basis for specific campaigns. Levies were held in each year in which military operations were proposed; recruits were conscripted from freeborn citizens whose properties enabled them to provide their own arms. Although the property qualifications for military service were often extended downward, and although the extended campaigns required from the time of the First Punic War brought about the institution of military pay for soldiers, the armies of Rome were still thought of, and in large part were still treated as, a citizen militia rather than a professional force. Possession of property, regarded as a pledge of good faith and commitment to the nation, remained a requirement for eligibility to serve.

During the third and second centuries B.C., the traditional system of recruitment was subjected to increasing strain. The requirements of empire created a need for larger numbers of troops recruited for longer periods of time. Small landholders, who made up the bulk

of the army, found it increasingly difficult to maintain their farms while fulfilling their military responsibilities. The importation of cheap grain from conquered territories created additional difficulties for small farmers, and small holdings fell more and more into the hands of large landowners, who operated their tracts with the help of slaves and tenants who were disqualified, by lack of property, from army service. In short, the need for troops was increasing while the class of citizens who supplied that need was diminishing.

The reforms of Tiberius and Gaius Gracchus, designed to reestablish the small farmer class, failed in their effect while creating a climate of mutual suspicion and hostility between the ruling senatorial order and the rest of the Roman population. When Gaius Marius, an experienced soldier unconnected with the senatorial order, offered to remove the conduct of the Jugurthine War from the hands of the senate-appointed generals, he was elected to office by a large popular majority. Moreover, over the objections of the senate, he was entrusted with the African campaign. Marius, seeing the difficulties of raising an army in the traditional way, and less bound by tradition than generals of higher birth, refused to order a conscription; instead, he called for volunteers, accepting all who appeared to be physically fit, with no

130

consideration of property qualifications.

Marius' action, superb in its simplicity, solved once and for all the problems of recruiting military forces. While the Roman countryside had been depleted of small farmers, the urban proletariat, the propertyless masses of the city, had grown large. From these, and from the rural proletariat who were chiefly tenant farmers, came an army of volunteers who regarded military service not as a civic obligation but as a means of earning a living.

The change from a citizen militia to a professional army, however, created difficulties of a new kind. Thereafter, the Roman army was not a force raised by the state, but one that had attached itself to a particular commander. Soldiers fought not to protect their possessions, but to earn a living. Their advantage lay not in a quick resolution of a specific campaign, but in the continuation of military action. The commander of such forces had to guarantee their pay and their booty; he also had to ensure them some form of pension, usually a small landholding, at the end of their service. To offer such guarantees, he had to maintain a high degree of control over Roman policies, both foreign and domestic. So Rome came under the twin threats of civil war and military dictatorship, a situation which was not resolved until the collapse of the Roman Republic, when military and civil government were combined under the emperors.

With the creation of a truly professional army came extensive reorganizations in tactics and equipment. The Roman legion, regarded as a standing force, was given an identity symbolized by a permanent name and a legionary standard. Armor and pack were improved and standardized; training and discipline received greater attention. The maniple, a tactical unit of some one hundred and twenty men of proven maneuverability against the larger and tighter Greek phalanx, was replaced by the cohort. This tactical unit of six hundred men proved itself more effective against the non-Greek forces that had become more common as opponents. Whatever its unfortunate effects upon the republican form of government, the professional army created by Marius served the Empire well for centuries of conquest, occupation, and defense.

Pertinent Literature

Perowne, Stewart. *Death of the Roman Republic.* Garden City, New York: Doubleday & Company, Inc., 1968.

The subtitle of Perowne's book is "From 146 B.C. to the Birth of the Roman Empire," but he begins with the beginnings of Rome. In five chapters he describes the rise of Rome, up to the end of the Third Punic War and the sack of Corinth. A sixth chapter, "The Fatal Flaw," assesses the weaknesses that were to lead to the decline of the Roman Republic. The rest of the book tells the story of that decline, beginning with the period of the Gracchi. It is an eminently readable account, made dramatic by the author's humane sympathy with the fortunes of institutions, societies, and, above all, individuals.

The social and military circumstances leading to Marius' rise play a large role in Perowne's story. The ruling nobles of the senate and the wealthy class of *equites*, the so-called "knights," had been estranged during the political strife of the period of the Gracchi, and this split had widened with the opening of the Jugurthine War. Originally a war of succession among three princes of an independent kingdom of North Africa, the conflict was supported by the *equites*, whose commercial interests were threatened by the conquests of Jugurtha. The senate, forced to manage a war in which its members had little interest, made slow work of it.

Gaius Marius, then a man in his middle years, was a commoner by origin. He had attracted the attention of Roman nobles by his long and capable service in the army, and he had gained admittance to the senate by being elected to the lower magistracies. Marius joined the Roman armies in Africa as second-in-command to the general Quintus Caecilius Metellus. Recognizing the alienation between nobles and commoners in the matter of the war, Marius returned to Rome against his commander's wishes, and entered into competition for the consulship, promising a vigorous prosecution of the war.

Marius was elected, and the popular assembly, overriding the decision of the senate to the contrary, authorized him to replace Metellus in command of the African campaign. It was under these circumstances that Marius enrolled his volunteer army, creating a force attached not to the senatorial government but to himself.

Marius' subsequent commands, and much of the tactical reorganization of the army, were held in the face of a different military threat. Hordes of barbarians from the north were pressing into Italy. Marius was re-elected to the consulate in the years following the conclusion of the Jugurthine War. His newly professionalized troops succeeded in outmaneuvering and outfighting the German hordes in two dazzling victories, and he himself was regarded as savior of the state.

Perowne correctly places Marius' position in the course of Roman history between the Gracchi and Sulla. As the Gracchi had prepared the way for Marius by attempting and failing to revitalize the class of independent peasants that had previously furnished the armies of Rome, so Marius prepared the way for the military dictatorship of Sulla by his creation of a professional army permanently attached to an individual commander. The title of the chapter Perowne devotes to Marius is "Inter Arma Silent Leges," that is, "When the fighting starts, the laws are silent," a remark attributed to Marius himself. It is ironic that Marius so failed to see the implications of his own military reforms that he never attempted to use his troops to gain control of Rome. Instead, he resigned his armies at the end of his campaigns, and entered politics in a more traditional manner, failing to make any lasting achievement in that sphere, and contributing to the disorder that precipitated the military dictatorship of Sulla.

Smith, R. E. *The Failure of the Roman Republic.* Cambridge: The University Press, 1955.

Smith's book is more of an interpretive essay than a straightforward history; his thesis is that the decline of the Roman Republic was due to a spiritual crisis precipitated by the Gracchi and elaborated in a vicious circle during the civil disturbances of the years between 133 and 31 B.C.

Smith begins with an account of the political, social, and cultural unity that prevailed in Rome during the first half of the second century B.C. The senate governed unchallenged with the consent of the people, whose right it was to confirm or reject proposals submitted to them in the voting assembly. Though the senate was dominated by, and the magistracies reserved to, the members of a limited number of great families, the common people were not disaffected. The client-patron relationship, whereby commoners were attached to great families in a condition of greater or less dependency, created such bonds between these classes that they found large areas of common interest. A rising class of wealthy merchants and entrepreneurs, largely independent of nobles and commoners alike, represented interests sometimes opposed to the senate's, but the three classes of society were able each to identify its interests with that of the state, and Smith finds second century Rome an uncommonly close-knit social and political body.

The destruction of Carthage in 146 B.C., removing the last supposed threat to her security, left Rome temporarily without a sense of national purpose. Domestic problems, by no means so severe that they could not have been dealt with by traditional means, came to occupy men's thoughts. The Gracchi, in attempting to deal with these domestic problems, resorted to methods that undermined the authority of the senate, disrupted the continuity of governmental policy, drove the nobles into a defensive and reactionary position, and created in the wealthy equestrians a political force specifically designed to oppose the senate. From this time forward, each social class in Rome regarded the aspirations of all other classes as hostile to its own. The harmony of the Roman state was shattered, and men identified themselves not as members of the Roman state but as members of this or that narrower group.

The Jugurthine War and the rise to power of Marius were natural results of this social disintegration. Entry into the war was forced by the wealthy *equites*, who saw in its prosecution prospects for wider and more profitable commercial activities. Senatorial opposition was overridden, and extraordinary methods were used in order to place Marius, the general commissioned by the *equites*, in charge of the African campaign. Marius' army reforms were undertaken, despite their far-reaching implications for Roman government and for Roman society, on his own authority without consultation with the senate.

The creation of a professional army is usually viewed as the cause of the civil disorders and military dictatorships that succeeded each other for the remaining years of the Roman Republic. Smith points out, however, that such an army, whose loyalties lay with its commander rather than with its government, could not have been created except in a state whose social structure had already disintegrated. "No man marches against his ideals; if a Roman army was prepared to march on Rome, it was because Rome stood for nothing that won their loyalty." The Roman soldier, as any other Roman, gave his loyalty to his group, not to his nation. His case was no different from that of the self-seeking noble, equestrian, or commoner. Marius' reforms did not cause the disintegration of Roman society. They merely reflected it, creating yet another group, the army, to compete with the others already exploiting Roman society for their own special interests.

—*Zola M. Packman*

Additional Recommended Reading

Adcock, F. E. *The Roman Art of War Under the Republic.* Cambridge: Harvard University Press, 1940. A description of the Roman military forces on land and at sea.

Andreski, Stanislav. *Military Organization and Society.* London: Routledge & Kegan Paul, Ltd., 1954. A sociological treatise describing the relationship between the social structure of society and military organization, with examples from many ages including ancient Rome.

Cook, S. A., F. E. Adcock, and M. P. Charlesworth, eds. *The Cambridge Ancient History.* Volume IX: *The Roman Republic, 133-44 B.C.* Cambridge: The University Press. The third chapter, by Hugh Last, provides an authoritative account of "The Wars of Marius."

Parker, H. M. D. *The Roman Legions.* Oxford: The Clarendon Press, 1928. A straightforward account of the development of the Roman army from Marius through the second century A.D.

ENACTMENT OF THE JULIAN LAW

Type of event: Legal: social reform
Time: 90 B.C.
Locale: Rome

Principal personages:
MARCUS LIVIUS DRUSUS, tribune in 91 B.C.
LUCIUS JULIUS CAESAR, consul 90 B.C.
SILO POMPAEDIUS, leader of the Italic allies
GNAEUS POMPEIUS STRABO, Roman military commander, consul
89 B.C.

Summary of Event

In political practice, the enjoyment of Roman citizenship conferred three distinct effects: the possession of duties, privileges, and rights. The foremost duties were the payment of various taxes and compulsory service in the military; the chief privilege was eligibility for elective public office. The rights of citizenship covered a wider area: *conubium*, the right to contract a valid marriage, *commercium*, the right to own private property and to enter into contracts that were enforceable in court, the right of appeal in the face of cruel and arbitrary punishment by a public official, and the right to vote on proposed legislation and on candidates for elective office. The internal history of the early Republic is dominated by the struggle between two opposite factions for an equitable distribution of the fruits of citizenship. In the later Republic an analogous struggle prevailed between Rome and certain cities of Italy.

By the end of the First Punic War, Rome had gained complete mastery over the peoples and cities of Italy, which had thereby lost their status as independent city-states. This development compelled Rome to devise a new political arrangement that recognized its altered relationship with the cities of Italy. As most peoples of antiquity, the Romans considered citizenship solely as a fact of birth. A child was restricted to the citizenship of his parents. To be a Roman citizen required descent from Roman parents on both sides. This traditional viewpoint prevented Rome from incorporating the conquered communities completely within the Roman state as full members endowed with all the effects of citizenship. Also prohibiting this simple solution was Rome's desire to maintain its own exclusive city-state status. Instead, a complex scheme was worked out so that the separate cities of Italy were treated in different ways.

In some cases, Rome broke with its own traditions and bestowed full citizenship outright on a few individual cities. This was a selective and limited process. Other cities were granted partial citizenship, enjoying *commercium* and *conubium* but not voting rights. Although such cities gradually came to receive voting rights as well, by the end of the second century their number remained small. Another common arrangement was the bestowal of the so-called "right of the Latin Name," which conferred on certain cities, generally racially and geographically close to Rome, *commercium* and *conubium* together with limited voting rights in Rome. An added feature was the granting of full citizenship to those who held local political office. This ingenius and not altogether disinterested provision ensured each city a small ruling class,

134

primarily loyal to Rome. The remaining cities of Italy were treated as allies, *socii*, who were bound to Rome by formal treaties that specified their obligations and rights. Such cities retained their local autonomy except in matters of foreign policy, where they had to follow the will of Rome. Although they were exempt from the payment of tribute and taxes, they had to provide troops at Rome's request even for wars which did not affect their own security directly. Furthermore they were under the vague and general obligation to respect Rome's dignity and to preserve its power.

This complex system with its fine gradations functioned smoothly in the beginning. Hannibal's efforts at fomenting insurrection among Rome's allies in the Second Punic War had insignificant results. In the course of the second century, however, the situation gradually worsened. The attitude of several Roman officials toward the allies was especially severe, and there are cases during this period of cruel and arbitrary treatment of allied citizens. Their repeated demands for the protection of full citizenship were rejected by the conservative senate and the jealous urban proletariat. In 125 B.C., when the tiny town of Fregellae revolted, Rome's response was the total destruction of the city and the resettlement of its inhabitants. Similar reprisals increased the grievances of the allies and rendered war more probable.

In 91 B.C., the tribune Marcus Livius Drusus undertook among his other reforms the enactment of legislation to extend citizenship to the allies. He was opposed on all sides, his program was rebuffed, and he himself was murdered. This failure made war inevitable. Under the leadership of a Marsian, Silo Pompaedius, the allies revolted and established their own confederation of *Italia* with its capital seat at Corfinium. They began issuing their own coinage and put a hundred-thousand-man army in the field. After initial military successes, the massive might of Rome began to wear them down. With the capture of the city of Asculum, a center of the revolt, by Pompeius Strabo (the father of Pompey the Great), and the defeat and death of Silo Pompaedius in 88 B.C., the war ceased gradually, hastened by political concessions on the part of the Romans. In 90 B.C., the consul Lucius Julius Caesar, the uncle of the more famous Gaius Julius Caesar, carried the *Lex Julia: De Civitate Latinis et Sociis Danda*, which granted full Roman citizenship to any community that had not joined in the revolt or which ceased its insurrection. Another law passed the following year, the *Lex Palutia-Papiria*, carried the same process even farther. The net effect was to make all inhabitants of Italy south of the river Po potential citizens of Rome. The internecine war was brought to a close, and the concept of citizenship was extended considerably beyond the geographic confines of the city of Rome, the first real step of an upward climb that ended in A.D. 212 with the bestowal of citizenship generally throughout the Empire.

Pertinent Literature

Sherwin-White, A. N. *The Roman Citizenship.* Oxford: The University Press, 1939.

This erudite study of all aspects of Roman citizenship devotes two chapters to the problem of Rome's relationship with other parts of Italy. The author emphasizes that it was above all a relationship between separate political states; the Romans did not consider or deal with the Italians as a single bloc of equal individuals, but only as members of distinct cities and municipalities. This outlook had the effect of casting the Italians in a dual role, on the one hand as citizens of their own municipalities with their own traditions and political structure, and on the other as partial Romans, depending on the degree of enfranchisement granted them. This degree of enfranchisement was heavily influenced by geographic, racial, and cultural considerations on the part of the Romans. While the various grades of citizenship extended to the Latins and other favored neighbors tended to overlap in certain key aspects, the treatment of allies remained a source of discontent and eventual insurrection.

The allies were those Italians that for all practical purposes the Romans regarded as foreigners. Rome established the same relationship with them as she employed towards the barbarian tribes which had been subdued. This sentiment was expressed in a treaty that contained the mutual obligations of the contracting parties without allowing room for an exchange of rights and genuine loyalties. In the case of the allies, such treaties were specific with regard to the inferior and disadvantaged position of the allies *vis-a-vis* Rome. In return for Rome's military protection, the allies renounced any independent foreign policy, agreed to assist in Rome's wars, and swore to preserve the power and dignity of Rome. These conditions were not onerous when both Rome and the allies faced the common danger of Hannibal and foreign domination. The second century, however, saw the virtual disappearance of such threats. Henceforth, the allies were called upon to support Rome's external and offensive campaigns in the East and in Spain.

This support, instrumental in the success of Roman imperialism, did not bring with it for the allies a share in the fruits of that success. It is in this context that the author sees the basis and aim of the allies' demands on Rome. They did not seek Roman citizenship outright, but social and political equality of treatment and opportunity in the new world they had materially helped Rome to win. Above all they sought relief from the oppressive superiority of the Romans, which was so conspicuous in the annihilation of Fregellae. A more ordinary manifestation of this oppression was continually at hand in the arbitrary and cruel punishment inflicted on the allies by Roman magistrates. The tragedy of the Social War is that this grievance could have been eliminated merely by extending to the allies the right of appeal which would have protected them from physical abuse. Rome refused even this minor concession because it endangered her status as an independent city-state, distinct from and dominant over the remainder of Italy. The war, however, forced Rome to adjust its concept of citizenship to the ideas that the allies had formed about it as a result of the unsuccessful reforms of Drusus.

Rome's response turned out to be a renewal of the earlier practice which she had employed towards her immediate neighbors and had allowed to slip into disuse. The effect was to introduce real unity throughout Italy, so that Rome ceased to be a traditional city-state, distinct from the other municipalities of Italy. This loss was offset by the emergence of the idea of Rome. Although the Italians took over the governing of Italy, Rome became and remained the symbol of their unity and the formal, if not physical, birthplace of all Italians.

Hammond, Mason. *City-State and World State.* Cambridge: Harvard University Press, 1951.

This book provides a good balance to the work of Sherwin-White, whose chief concern is with the theoretical and technical effects of the *Lex Julia* on the status and concept of Roman citizenship. Hammond examines the larger topic of the Social War within the context of the decline of the Roman Republic. His concern is to isolate the general tendencies of Roman political life that led to the outbreak of the war. This makes easier an analysis of the different effects of the war, both those whose impact was immediately felt and those which ultimately changed the tenor of life in Italy.

The generic causes of the war are to be found in the destructive tendencies that permeated Roman political behavior as a result of her recent conquests. The dominant aristocracy that had directed this successful expansion degenerated into an exclusive oligarchy, jealous of its new-found wealth and power, and suspicious of anyone who might upset its supremacy. Ambitious individuals who were cut off from political advancement by the oligarchic monopoly sought new avenues of power; they curried favor with the lower classes and secured independent military commands so that the victorious army owed allegiance not to the state but to its successful commander. The short-sighted exclusivity of the oligarchs and the unrestrained ambition of the generals encouraged a disregard for the interests of the average citizen and especially of the Italian allies, who found their vague treaty rights increasingly violated. When proposals for reform encountered continual senatorial opposition, the frustrated allies abandoned the expectation of the orderly redress of their grievances, and turned to rebellion and war.

The *Lex Julia* and the war itself brought significant changes for the future of Italy. Rome was compelled to renounce its preferred position and to admit all loyal Italian communities to equality of citizenship, which meant almost the total elimination of the manifold cultures which had persisted among the Italian towns that had shared only tenuous ties with Rome. While some local traditions and dialects maintained their independence, a gradual homogenization of culture spread throughout the peninsula. The "Romanization" of Italy bore fruit in a common language, law, and citizenship.

These effects, however, required time to become beneficial. A more immediate result was intensification of the already critical condition of Roman society. Although the extension of citizenship throughout Italy theoretically implied the end of Rome's status as a city-state, it produced little change in the actual mechanics of government, since the election of the chief magistrates and the ratification of legislation were still conducted exclusively in Rome. To exercise his rights and obligations, a Roman citizen had to come to Rome. Since the citizenship had been extended well beyond the limits of easy and convenient access to the capital, the conduct of affairs remained as before in the votes of the urban populace, which could still be either cajoled or intimidated by ambitious politicians. In this respect, the war only magnified the incapability of the city to provide the Empire with efficient and peaceful government.

Furthermore, the opposing political factions found in the unsettled conditions of the war new opportunities to achieve dominance. The military necessities of the war required the conscription of whole new armies, and trained commanders to lead them. The veteran general Marius was again called into service, but his troops fought not only the allies but also the senatorial forces under the command of Sulla. This internecine strife came to an end with Sulla's victory at the Colline Gates in 82 B.C., a battle which also signaled the end of the last resistance among the few remaining allies still opposed to Rome. Less than forty years later, this truce dissolved into an even more catastrophic civil war. The allies had won the equality of citizenship, but they had to wait until the principate of Augustus for real peace and the enjoyment of their gains. —*George M. Pepe*

Additional Recommended Reading

Badian, E. *Foreign Clientelae.* Oxford: The Clarendon Press, 1958. A valuable analysis of the interaction between the demand of the Italians for citizenship and the struggles of the political factions of Rome.

Gruen, Erich. "Political Prosecutions in the 90's B.C.," in *Historia.* XV (1966), 32-65. A study tracing the internal political problems of Rome which brought into the open issues that exploded into the Social War.

Last, Hugh, and R. Gardiner. "The Enfranchisement of Italy," in *Cambridge Ancient History,* Vol. IX, ch. V. Cambridge: The University Press, 1932. The most authoritative account of the events of the Social War.

Smith, R. E. *The Failure of the Roman Republic.* Cambridge: The University Press, 1955. An attempt to diagnose the Social War as symptomatic of the diseased condition of the Roman Republic caused by the proposed reforms and careers of the Gracchi.

CAESAR'S CONQUEST OF GAUL

Type of event: Military: annexation of territory to Rome
Time: 58-51 B.C.
Locale: Modern central and northern France, Belgium, Britain, and the German Rhineland

Principal personages:

GAIUS JULIUS CAESAR, Roman politician and general

GNAEUS POMPEIUS MAGNUS (POMPEY), Roman politician and general, originally an ally but subsequently a rival of Caesar for power

MARCUS LICINIUS CRASSUS, "DIVES," wealthy Roman consul, triumvir with Caesar and Pompey, who was killed in an invasion of Parthia

VERCINGETORIX, Gallic king chosen in 52 to lead the Gauls against Caesar

AMBIORIX, Gallic chieftain whose troops slaughtered a Roman legion and who was never captured by the Romans

Summary of Event

Supported by Pompey and Crassus in the political coalition called the "First Triumvirate," Julius Caesar as consul in 59 B.C. secured the right to recruit an army of three legions along with proconsular authority for five years to govern northern Italy and "the Province," a strip of territory containing Massilia or modern Marseilles along what is now the French Riviera, which Rome had controlled for sixty years. North of "the Province" lay most of Gaul, a diverse but fertile area between the River Rhine and the Pyrenees and inhabited mostly by Celts. Divided into more than one hundred tribes, the Gauls were unstable politically, with a feuding nobility and rival factions even within tribes.

In the spring of 58 B.C. the Helvetii, a group of tribes in western Switzerland, were migrating in search of richer lands. They requested the right to pass through the Roman "Province" in southern Gaul. Perceiving an opportunity to use his newly formed legions and gain military renown, Caesar rushed from Rome to Geneva to block the Helvetii at the Rhone River. Those he did not annihilate he

forced to return to their Alpine homes. Later that year, under the pretext of defending Gallic allies, Caesar boldly marched northward to drive back across the Rhine a Germanic chieftain whose aggressions were threatening central Gaul.

Recruiting additional legions in the winter and gaining more Gallic allies, Caesar in 57 B.C. ravaged Belgic territory in northern Gaul, overwhelming one tribe after another. When one town resisted a siege, he sold over fifty thousand of the Belgae into slavery. The following year, building a fleet, Caesar crushed the Venetii who lived along the Atlantic coast. Thus by the end of 56 B.C. he had ruthlessly asserted Roman dominance in most of Gaul.

Back at Rome, Caesar's political enemies charged that he had far exceeded his authority. However, in 56 B.C. the triumvirs renewed their coalition and the extension of Caesar's proconsulship for another five years encouraged him to press on toward permanent occupation of northern Gaul.

In 55 B.C. two German tribes had crossed

the Rhine seeking land. When their leaders came to Caesar to negotiate, he detained them and by a surprise attack massacred the Germans, his cavalry hunting down even their women and children. Caesar's enemy Cato demanded in the Senate at Rome that Caesar be handed over to the Germans to atone for his butchery. Bridging the Rhine, Caesar's forces briefly invaded Germany, to forestall further Germanic inroads. That same summer he led two legions in a reconnaissance of Britain, and the following year, 54 B.C., he led a large-scale invasion army across the English Channel, receiving the nominal submission of a British king north of the Thames. Although he gained no lasting control in Britain or Germany, these expeditions were impressive features in Caesar's reports to Rome.

Many Gallic tribes refused to accept Roman rule, and in the years 54-52 B.C. Caesar faced a series of dangerous rebellions. One crafty chieftain, Ambiorix, wiped out a Roman legion; Roman merchants as well as Roman supply trains were butchered by Gauls. Enlarging his army to ten legions or about sixty thousand men, Caesar vowed vengeance. But a new Gallic leader, Vercingetorix, unified a rebel coalition. His "scorched-earth" policy forced the Romans to besiege Gallic hill forts. Frustrated, Caesar's men massacred the inhabitants of several towns. His

siege of a stronghold at Gergovia, however, failed miserably, encouraging further desertions by Gauls who had been supporting Rome. Only by employing German mercenary cavalry and by dogged discipline and shrewd strategy did Caesar finally outmaneuver and corner Vercingetorix. After a bitter and bloody siege the Gallic hero surrendered.

By clemency to some larger enemy tribes, Caesar won their allegiance and pacified an exhausted Gaul. The country was devastated, with over half of its men of military age slaughtered or enslaved. Its agriculture and towns were badly damaged.

For Caesar this eight-year campaign brought wealth and glory. His reports to Rome cleverly justified his actions, and his veteran army, intensely loyal to him, enabled him to return to Italy to seize sole power after a civil war. Even more significant to Rome in the long run was the conquest of a populous new territory. Economically and culturally Gaul became the heart of the western Roman Empire, its virile people fully adopting Roman culture and playing a vital role in transmitting that culture to the modern world. In a sense, too, the conquest pointed Rome, hitherto a strictly Mediterranean society, geographically toward a European locus.

Pertinent Literature

Holmes, Thomas Rice. *Caesar's Conquest of Gaul.* London: Oxford University Press, 1911.

This masterly work of British scholarship is the fullest study in English of Caesar's campaigns in Gaul. It is reprinted almost verbatim in the second volume of Holmes's *The Roman Republic* and supplemented by the same author's *Ancient Britain and the Invasions of Julius Caesar.* An eminent classicist, Holmes skillfully interweaves the ancient historical evidence with well-reasoned commentary. His elaborate critical notes on

debated questions are a rich mine for continuing study, as he analyzes the opinions of literally hundreds of previous writers on a wide variety of topics such as topography and battle strategies.

Accepting Caesar's own reports as a highly trustworthy record, in spite of minor errors of fact, Holmes seems less able to evaluate Caesar himself objectively than have more recent scholars. He considers him to be "the greatest man in the world" and "the greatest man of action who ever lived." Not seriously disturbed over Caesar's bloody extermination of Gauls by the hundreds of thousands, Holmes at several points defends the military necessity for Caesar's trickery and ruthlessness in much the same way that Victorian Englishmen were accustomed to view the military necessities of the British Empire. Caesar conquered Gaul with the aid of Gauls, he noted, just as the British conquered India with the help of Indians.

His admiration of Caesar's military skills is also considered by some recent historians to be excessive. He describes Caesar's secret service as "perfectly organized" even though he admits that Caesar was frequently surprised and often badly informed. Where raw Roman recruits were lured into ambush, Holmes following Caesar's *Commentaries* blames the error on subordinate officers. Caesar's moderation and generosity always loom large, in Holmes' account.

For full factual detail, with maps, illustration, and scrupulous documentation, none of the numerous English studies of Caesar's campaigns compare with the technical precision of this remarkable and definitive study by Holmes, one whose outlook is doubtless reflecting the fascination of conquest inspired by the imperialism of the late nineteenth century continuing into the early twentieth.

Fuller, John F. C. *Julius Caesar, Man, Soldier, and Tyrant.* New Brunswick: Rutgers University Press, 1965.

This general review of the life of Julius Caesar includes two lengthy chapters on his expedition into Gaul. Without undertaking to discuss many of the questions already debated by Holmes and other writers, Fuller attempts a different portrait of Caesar as an "amoral" politician and a far less brilliant strategist than most historians have pictured. Fuller argues that the apotheosis of Caesar as a superman is not based on ancient sources; it arrived at full form only in the Renaissance and subsequently became a myth distorting Shakespeare's drama and many modern historical accounts.

There is much truth in Fuller's statement that Caesar's stature developed in later history. In the period of nation building during the nineteenth century, German scholars tended to take a sharp view of both Cicero and Caesar. After the disillusionment of 1848, Cicero, the hero of the Renaissance, was judged in the light of the hopeless speeches, debates, and assemblies which failed to bring unity to Germany. He became a voluble, empty talker, out of touch with reality and unable to bring order to government in his own day. Caesar, by contrast, became the symbol of the man-of-the-hour, the real politician, the Bismarck who could proceed by blood and iron. Much of this reputation as a great civil leader seems to have been transferred to his military career.

In his narrative of the Gallic campaigns Fuller stresses the brutality and treachery of Caesar, as well as his frequent mistakes in strategy and the defeats suffered by the Romans. After citing Plutarch's charge that Caesar killed one million men in Gaul and took captive another million, Fuller judges that "the atrocities he perpetrated on unfortunate Gauls have seldom been exceeded by civilized soldiers."

After concluding his account of the career and death of Caesar, Fuller adds a chapter evaluating the famous Roman, chiefly reviewing his Gallic campaigns. Admitting that Caesar had notable abilities "as a demagogue" and "genius as a soldier," Fuller tries to point out serious deficiencies in Caesar's judgment, partly as a result of "an Olympian sense of superiority." He sees Caesar as "a supreme Machiavellian," whose invasions of

Britain were "amateurish" through lack of careful organization. His Gallic conquests were based on a strategy of annihilation, Fuller believes, and only through experiences in Gaul did Caesar learn the value of moderation.

Those interested in military history will find Fuller's analysis of Caesar's generalship more critical than that of most other writers; he concludes that Caesar was a "strategical Jekyll and Hyde." This lively and opinionated study of Caesar led Fuller to a somewhat startling theory: "that, at times, Caesar was not responsible for his actions and toward the end of his life not altogether sane."

—Roger B. McShane

Additional Recommended Reading

Balsdon, J. P. V. D. *Julius Caesar.* New York: Athenaeum, 1967. A short biography with a clear summary of the Gallic conquest defending Caesar against criticism.

Dodge, Thomas A. *Caesar: A History of the Art of War Among the Romans.* Vol. 1. Boston: Houghton Mifflin Co., 1892. A work giving details, with one hundred and fifty maps, charts, and illustrations, of the Gallic conquest.

Fowler, W. W. *Julius Caesar.* New York and London: G. P. Putnam's Sons, 1891, 1908. More than one hundred pages and fifteen illustrations and maps are devoted to the Gallic Wars.

Gelzer, Matthias. *Caesar: Politician and Statesman.* Translated by P. Needham. Cambridge: Harvard University Press, 1968. A careful popular account, viewing Caesar in heroic proportions.

Grant, Michael. *Julius Caesar.* New York: McGraw-Hill Book Company, 1969. This well-illustrated study is critical of Caesar's "atrocities."

Walter, Gerard. *Caesar: A Biography.* Translated by Emma Crawford. New York: Charles Scribner's Sons, 1952. A large section, with good documentation, deals with the conquest of Gaul.

PROSCRIPTIONS OF THE SECOND TRIUMVIRATE

Type of event: Political: purge of enemies and wealthy citizens
Time: 43 B.C.
Locale: Rome

Principal personages:
GAIUS JULIUS CAESAR OCTAVIANUS (AUGUSTUS), heir of Julius
Caesar, first Roman Emperor 63 B.C.-A.D. 14
MARCUS ANTONIUS (MARK ANTONY), colleague and later rival of
Octavian
MARCUS AEMILIUS LEPIDUS, member of the Second Triumvirate
who was ultimately deposed
MARCUS TULLIUS CICERO, statesman, orator, and philosopher who
was a victim of the proscriptions

Summary of Event

The Roman Republic came more and more to experience a time of troubles after 135 B.C. The inadequacy of its city-state constitution for a growing empire, the stranglehold of great families on its offices, the rise of the equites and the consequent class struggle, and the twisting of its constitution initiated already by the Gracchi between 130 and 120 and by Marius and Sulla between 100 and 80, all contributed to the Republic's travail. Especially significant were the great rivals born in the decade between 110 and 100, men such as Pompey, Crassus, Caesar, Cicero, Catiline, and Sertorius, who were ready to fulfill their ambitions between 70 and 60. Most of them proved to be too big for the constitution to contain. The rise of private armies, extraordinary commands, absentee governorships, extended tenures of office, bribery, demagoguery, political manipulation, and outright violence became more and more commonplace. Marius and Sulla even dared to liquidate each other's adherents by outright proscriptions, or purges, a precedent set for the leaders who were to emerge as the Second Triumvirate. Their proscriptions, in turn, by decimating the old patrician stock and silencing Republican sentiments, brought an end to the civil wars by enabling Octavian in the long run to become the first Emperor of Rome.

The formation of the Second Triumvirate by Octavian, Antony, and Lepidus in 43 B.C. was a pragmatic arrangement of three leaders who were united only because of their common enemies: a faction under the leadership of Brutus and Cassius and another under the leadership of Sextus Pompey, the son of Pompey the Great. Unlike the First Triumvirate, this three-man dictatorship was given legal sanction. The three leaders met on a small island in a river near Bologna, and formulated a joint policy. Although in effect they established a three-man dictatorship, of necessity they avoided the term, since Antony, when consul, had abolished the office of dictator for all time. They formed themselves into an executive committee which was to hold absolute power for five years in order to rebuild the Roman state. The triumvirs planned to unite their armies for a war against the Republican forces in the East. The West, already under their control, was divided among themselves, Lepidus keeping his provinces in Spain and Transalpine Gaul, Antony taking the newly conquered parts of Gaul together with the Cisalpine province, and the junior member, Octavian, being assigned North Africa, Sardinia, Corsica, and Sicily, territories largely held by Pompeian adherents. Italy itself was to be under their combined rule.

At the same meeting the triumvirs determined to insure the success of their rule by declaring a proscription against their Republican enemies. In this purge, hundreds of senators and about two thousand wealthy equites were marked for destruction. Livy gives one hundred and twenty as the number of senators proscribed; Appian gives three hundred; and Plutarch gives two hundred to three hundred. The names of almost one hundred of the proscribed have been recorded. Not all were killed; a few obtained pardon and many successfully escaped from Italy. In most cases the victims suffered only the confiscation of their properties.

In the official proclamation of the proscription, the triumvirs emphasized the injustices suffered at the hands of the enemies of the state and pointed out the necessity of removing a threat to peace at home while they were away fighting against the Republican armies. To justify their position and gain for it some semblance of respectability,

they pointed out that when Julius Caesar had adopted a policy of clemency towards his enemies, he had paid for that policy by forfeiting his life.

While personal vengeance and political pragmatism played a part in the proscriptions, there is no doubt that the unadmitted reasons were largely economic. Octavian, Antony, and Lepidus had bought the support of their troops with lavish promises, and it was imperative that they pay them with more than words. Altogether, the triumvirs commanded forty-three legions, and they needed their support in the impending campaign against Brutus and Cassius.

In drawing up the lists, each of the three triumvirs had to give up some of his friends to satisfy the vengeance of one or the other of his colleagues. So it was that the most famous of the victims, Cicero, was found on the list of the condemned. Octavian would have spared the famous orator, but Antony insisted on his death. While many of the proscribed acted quickly and escaped, Cicero dallied, uncertain of the best course to take, and died as a result. The historian Livy has given a full account of his death.

Pertinent Literature

Syme, R. *The Roman Revolution.* Oxford: The University Press, 1939.

Syme's book treats the critical period of the fall of the Roman Republic and the first years of the Principate which succeeded it. Spanning the seventy-five years between 60 B.C. and A.D. 14, it centers on the career of Augustus and the establishment of his rule. The book has a clear thesis, namely, that there never could have been a restoration of the Republic, that Augustus, expert in *Realpolitik*, was ruthless as the leader of a faction in winning his power at the expense of the aristocracy and basing it ultimately on a wide basis of support: the people and the

army. In accord with this thesis, the proscriptions appear to be perfectly logical.

Logical or not, they were undoubtedly a traumatic experience of horror, as Appian and Suetonius attest through Syme's pages. The effect on Rome was terrifying. The early proscriptions of Sulla could still be remembered by many who could only fear that the new ones would be more ruthless than ever. If the total number of victims has been exaggerated, Roman feelings were shocked when the triumvirs sacrificed, as a pledge of solidarity to terrorize their enemies, their own friends such as Cicero, and their own relatives such as Lepidus' brother and Antony's uncle. Following Appian, Syme notes, too, the terror tactic of the triumvirs in beginning the proscriptions by the sacrilegious arrest and execution of a tribune of the Roman people. There were, fortunately, compensating instances of bravery and devotion. In Cales the citizens manned the walls and refused to surrender a certain Sittius who had patronized the town, and slaves were known even to substitute willingly for their condemned masters.

The proscriptions were pitiless and calculated. The abolition of the private rights of citizenship by the triumvirs seemed to them "no disproportionate revenge" for having been declared public enemies. Of the three members of the Second Triumvirate, Octavian was, if not the most ruthless, certainly not the puppet of Antony. In Syme's view he was "a chill and mature terrorist" who had good reason to try later to exonerate himself. His success was the work of fraud, bloodshed, rapacity, and ambition, a monument to his cleverness and skill in using opportunities and methods introduced by others, and eventually in employing effective subalterns to compensate for his inadequacies.

In keeping with the prevailing view of historians that the motive for the proscriptions was the need for money, that they were essentially a levy on capital rather than desire for revenge, Syme tells of a number of the proscribed whose only crime was their affluence. "The triumvirs declared a regular vendetta against the rich, whether dim, inactive Senators or pacific knights, anxiously abstaining from Roman politics." Retirement proved no defense, as for instance in the case of the old, innocuous Pompeian Varro. Moreover, lesser rivals took occasion, by feigning cooperation with the triumvirs, to settle private scores and to liquidate wealthy enemies, all serving to greatly expand the extent of the proscription.

Because the confiscated lands did not bring in the anticipated returns on the open market, the purge was followed by a number of novel taxes, a portent at the beginning of the Principate of a situation which was to be a major factor in Rome's eventual decline. Another effect of the proscription was the depletion of the senate and its replenishment with minions of the triumvirs, men with little or no ability for government. Syme concludes his chapter on the proscriptions with the statement that the Republic had been permanently abolished. "Despotism ruled, supported by violence and confiscation. The best men were dead or proscribed." To him the proscriptions are a watershed in the history of Roman civilization.

Buchan, J. *Augustus.* Boston: Houghton Mifflin Co., 1937.

This widely acclaimed biography of Octavian Augustus is less interested in the political and economic causes of the proscriptions than in the personal role Octavian played in them. In trying to assess his motives from evidence of his character and personality, the book is remarkable for the level of its analysis, especially since it was written before the trend toward psychohistorical studies had developed very far. Besides the penetrating study of Octavian's role in the proscriptions there is also a finely nuanced estimate of Cicero, the triumvirs' most famous victim. For his views Buchan draws data not only from secondary studies but from the Latin sources he knows so well and uses with discrimination: Seneca, Suetonius, and Macrobius.

Some writers have suggested that Octavian had a split personality; Seneca claimed that Octavian's later moderation could be attributed to sheer satiety with evil. Buchan develops a more complex explanation. Octavian, he claims, was a man who matured unevenly. His emotional development was exceptionally slow, and his capacity for affection was highly restricted. In his early years he regarded most men with suspicion, and under the circumstances, this attitude is not surprising. However, it was neither callousness nor careless politics which made Octavian so ready a party to the purge of 43 B.C. Rather, the proscriptions were a logical outcome of Octavian's feeling that it was his destiny to reconstruct the state. He was motivated by three principles: the need to avenge the death of Julius Caesar, a determination to bring order out of political chaos, and finally, the conviction that no sacrifice was too great to carry out his mission. Octavian was ready to give up happiness, friendship, ease, and common morality; Buchan says that he acted on the premise that only violence could curb violence. "To this task he brought both the stony-heartedness of self-absorbed youth, and the moral opportunism of the fanatic. His view was that of Horace Walpole: 'No great country was ever saved by good men, because good men will not go to the lengths that may be necessary.'"

Buchan goes on to explain the reasonableness—if moral scruples are disregarded—of Octavian's action by noting that Octavian's archenemies would have done the same

to him had they been granted the opportunity, and furthermore, that a policy of mercy would have been equivalent to the surrender of all the hopes which Octavian had cultivated since boyhood.

Moreover, contemporary historical circumstances must be considered: Brutus and Cassius were still in the East, senatorial and Republican enemies were everywhere, and assassins lurked in all corners. Considering, too, the bloody backlog of civil wars, shocking assassinations, and a series of political murders from the Gracchi to Julius as well as earlier proscriptions, Octavian can scarcely be judged by modern standards. Even in his relationship with Cicero, it must be remembered that they were never really friends, that Cicero was the brains of those who would restore the Republic, that he was ungrateful to Julius and so exulted over the Ides of March that he made gods of the assassins, and finally, that he, too, wanted to use Octavian as a tool.

Buchan does not explain away the proscriptions, which remain "the darkest stain upon Octavian's record." Instead, he attempts to interpret them in terms of Roman culture, not according to modern standards. He succeeds in his task, and for this reason he contributes to a better understanding of a particularly black page in the annals of Roman history. — *Mary Evelyn Jegen*

Additional Recommended Reading

Cary, M. *A History of Rome.* 2nd ed. London: Macmillan & Company, 1954. A lively narrative of events leading to the proscriptions, with special attention being given to Cicero.

Cowell, F. R. *The Revolutions of Ancient Rome.* London: Thames & Hudson Ltd., 1962. A tendentious account of the Second Triumvirate as the outcome of a bargain between "thieves and murderers."

Rostovtzeff, M. *Rome.* Translated from the Russian by I. D. Duff. New York: Oxford University Press, 1928, reissued 1960. A classic study of Rome which has little to say specifically about the proscriptions but which supplies details about conditions which existed at the time.

Scullard, H. H. *From the Gracchi to Nero: A History of Rome from 133 B.C. to A.D. 68.* 2nd ed.

London: Methuen and Co., 1964. A standard work placing the proscriptions in a fully developed context.

Weigall, A. *The Life and Times of Marc Antony.* London: Thornton Butterworth Limited, 1931. A work interpreting the proscriptions as a means of placating the antiaristocratic sentiments of the Roman mob.

BATTLE OF ACTIUM

Type of event: Military: naval engagement
Time: September 2, 31 B.C.
Locale: The Ambracian Gulf, on the west coast of northern Greece

Principal personages:

MARCUS ANTONIUS (MARK ANTONY), Roman general, member of
the Second Triumvirate

GAIUS JULIUS CAESAR OCTAVIANUS (OCTAVIAN), grandnephew of
Julius Caesar, later called Augustus

CLEOPATRA VII, Queen of Egypt, consort of Mark Antony

MARCUS VIPSANIUS AGRIPPA, general and admiral serving Octavian

Summary of Event

In the decade following the assassination of Julius Caesar in 44 B.C., a political struggle developed between Mark Antony and Octavian. Alternately rivals for power and reluctant allies, they became bitter enemies after Antony in 34 B.C. openly attached himself to Cleopatra, thus repudiating his legal wife who was Octavian's sister. In Italy Octavian's supporters excoriated Antony's liaison with the Oriental enchantress and published a purported will of Antony deposited with the Vestal Virgins by which Antony donated eastern territories to Cleopatra and her children. In 32 B.C. the two consuls and three hundred senators went east to join Antony, thus terminating negotiations between him and Octavian.

Antony had recruited a heterogeneous army, variously estimated from forty thousand to a hundred thousand men, while Octavian raised an Italian force almost as large. Battle strategy eventually depended on navies, with Octavian's admiral Agrippa the most experienced commander at sea. Antony's fleet, perhaps at first slightly greater in size, was composed of larger, slower ships, some of his "sea castles" having eight or ten banks of oars.

In 31 B.C. Octavian with his army and navy crossed to Epirus, just north of Greece.

Meanwhile Antony had stationed his forces so as to block the eastward passage of his adversary, most of his navy occupying the Gulf of Arta and his army fortifying the nearby sandy promontory of Actium, one of two peninsulas which pointed toward each other across the mouth of the gulf. After several months of skirmishing and entrenching, Octavian's army held the northernmost peninsula and his navy seized crucial bases to the south, thus cutting off Antony's supply routes. The morale of Antony's troops was lowered by hunger and malaria, and he suffered significant desertions.

In a council held in Antony's camp on September 1, 31 B.C., his officers were divided over strategy. A Roman faction advocated retreat by land; Cleopatra with some supporters favored a naval attack or an escape to Egypt. While Antony's enigmatic aims and actions are variously reported by later historians, it seems less likely that Antony wanted a showdown by naval action than that he hoped to break out of the blockade in order to fight later in a more favorable situation. Any ships he may have burned were probably unusable. All records agree that he left some of his troops ashore to retreat by an inland route, and that he kept aboard his ships the masts and sails, which

148

were ordinarily jettisoned before action, in order to allow his fleet either to escape if the battle went against it or else pursue its defeated enemy.

The following day's battle was a chaotic imbroglio, shrouded from our view in conflicting accounts. Antony's ships advanced through the narrow exit from the gulf, aligned so as to take advantage of an expected shift in the wind at midday. The Caesarian fleet blocked their passage. One squadron of sixty ships under Cleopatra was placed in the rear, carrying the treasure chest which undoubtedly belonged to her more than to Antony. After several hours of tense inactivity one wing of Antony's fleet was drawn into conflict, forcing Antony to commit the remainder of his forces. His soldiers aboard the large ships hurled missiles and shot arrows into Octavian's smaller vessels, which attempted to ram or surround and capture their clumsy opponents. Except for the use of oars, the battle vaguely resembled the one fought later between the sixteenth century Spanish Armada and the small English ships of Francis Drake.

Suddenly, at the height of the conflict,

when a breeze rose from the northwest, Cleopatra's reserve squadron hoisted purple sails and moved through the battle line, in evident flight southward. Although Antony's flagship was entrapped, he transferred to a smaller ship and with a small portion of his fleet followed Cleopatra. Plutarch vividly portrays the gloom of defeat on the escaping ships.

Abandoned by their leader, the remnants of Antony's fleet backed into the gulf. Over five thousand men had been killed or drowned. Octavian and Agrippa made little attempt to pursue Antony; instead, they kept their ships at sea to bottle up the enemy and thus prevented further escape. Within about a week the ships and soldiers left behind by Antony surrendered. Octavian claimed to have captured three hundred vessels.

Antony and Cleopatra returned to Egypt, where some final desperate expedients were contemplated but not effectively carried out. The next year Octavian came to Egypt where he met little resistance and precipitated the romanticized suicides of both Antony and Cleopatra. The civil wars and the Republic were at an end, for Octavian was now the undisputed ruler of the Mediterranean world.

Pertinent Literature

Tarn, W. W. "The Battle of Actium," in *The Journal of Roman Studies*. 21 (1931), 173-199.

This highly respected British scholar proposes an explanation of the tantalizing Battle of Actium which differs sharply from theories previously accepted. In particular he considers that treachery in Antony's fleet was the primary reason for the victory of Octavian. Reviewing carefully the numerous ancient authors who describe the battle, among them Velleius Paterculus, Plutarch, and Dio Cassius, and also examining the works of modern authors on the subject, Tarn concludes that Antony intended to wage a hard and decisive battle and that escape was contemplated only as a last resort and not as a

primary objective.

Ingeniously reconstructing the fragments of evidence, Tarn argues that the fleets were roughly equal in size and that Antony employed all usable ships, without burning any significant part of his fleet before the battle, as Plutarch reported. Tarn rejects Plutarch's account as a confusion arising from the later burning of ships by Octavian. Antony's strategy, in Tarn's view, was to wait for the wind to veer from west to northwest about noon, then to turn Octavian's fleet left, thus gaining the momentum of the wind in order to drive Octavian's fleet south away from his army and camp. This plan required sails, and so Antony took sails aboard. After a period of inaction, Tarn believes that the battle became a race between Octavian's left wing under Agrippa and Antony's right wing, to see which could gain position windward of the other. Therefore, Antony himself commanded the three squadrons of the right wing in this endeavor, which proved indecisive when Agrippa's left wing countered the attempt and grappled with Antony's ships.

Concerning this critical stage in the battle, at the point when other historians believe that Cleopatra's retreat decided the issue, Tarn theorizes that the three central squadrons composing Antony's center and left wings, not yet actively engaged, now backed into the gulf, unwilling to fight. Tarn bases this reconstruction of the turning point of the battle on two lines of Horace's poem about Actium which referred to retreat by some of Antony's ships. He argues that it was only because of this mass desertion by most of their fleet that Antony and Cleopatra carried out their alternate plan, to escape to Egypt.

Thus Cleopatra really deserved little blame for the defeat; indeed, she had been left in reserve because Antony trusted her loyalty; her squadron was to move into the breach in the line left by Antony's windward movement. When such a gap did open, Cleopatra moved forward, not intending flight but rather action. However, seeing the desertion of a major section of their fleet, Cleopatra continued southward with the wind, followed by Antony.

Tarn argues that Antony's decision to keep sails aboard his ships may have unsettled his officers, who doubted his determination to fight a decisive battle and were suspicious that they were fighting for Cleopatra and Egypt rather than for Antony and Rome. Since such a conflict involved personal ambition rather than patriotic principle, and since Roman soldiers were usually reluctant to slaughter other Romans, Tarn does offer an appealing solution to the puzzle of Actium.

According to Tarn, Octavian and later historians concealed the mutiny of Antony's fleet in order to make the Caesarian victory more glorious, and because it served Octavian's purposes to portray Cleopatra in a bad light as a traitress and coward.

Unfortunately Tarn's scholarly article is difficult for most readers to follow. He includes no charts of his reconstruction of the battle, and his argument turns on such obscure fragments of evidence that what he presents, although influencing subsequent popular narratives of this pivotal and dramatic event, leaves most historians dissatisfied with his conclusions.

Richardson, G. W. "Actium," in *The Journal of Roman Studies.* Vol. 27 (1937), 153-164.

Almost directly contradicting Tarn's theory of the Battle of Actium, which was given wide circulation in the 1934 edition of Volume X of *The Cambridge Ancient History*, Professor Richardson prefers to accept the more traditional reconstruction of the evidence by giving weight to "secondary" ancient accounts by Plutarch, Dio Cassius, Florus, and Orosius, writers largely rejected by Tarn. Richardson believes that Antony never intended to make a hard-fought battle at Actium; that Antony's fleet had not been fully concentrated at Actium but was partly dispersed elsewhere; and that, since his fleet was already inferior in size to Octavian's, Antony did indeed burn many of his slower ships the night before the battle, accepting the advice of Cleopatra to attempt to escape with a major part of his fleet but without the stigma of defeat.

Rejecting entirely Tarn's theory about treachery or desertion by a major part of Antony's fleet in the midst of the battle, Richardson argues that Antony, expecting a more aggressive attack by Octavian's fleet, was surprised when Octavian's ships refused to engage and blocked his exit from the gulf, thereby forcing him to advance into the open sea where Octavian's larger fleet and more mobile ships had the advantage. Richardson agrees with Tarn's view that Cleopatra was neither cowardly nor overly hasty in retreat; he believes that once Octavian had drawn Antony's fleet into action, the skill and speed of Agrippa's ships allowed them almost to surround Antony's smaller fleet.

Thus, Richardson claims, the battle did not develop along lines of a strategic plan by Antony, as Tarn had theorized, but rather as a frustrated struggle by Antony to elude the Caesarian fleet and get his own fleet away in order to fight another day. If sections of Antony's fleet did retreat in the midst of the battle, Richardson considers that it was not desertion but an effort to regroup or to seek safety in the gulf. He supposes that Octavian and Agrippa, in blocking Antony's escape, turned their formation so as to leave a gap in their line. At this point, Richardson believes,

Antony in desperation signaled Cleopatra and she responded by hoisting sail and moving forward through the gap to escape southward, followed by a few ships accompanying Antony.

Later reports that Actium was a hard-fought battle could not have been mere inventions or exaggerations by Octavian and his propagandists, in Richardson's reasoning. When hundreds of senators and thousands of soldiers knew the truth, why would Caesarian eulogists not have accepted and indeed publicized the unwillingness of Antony's forces to support him, if this were the truth? If such betrayals on a large scale had really taken place, Richardson argues, it would not have been necessary to create an imaginary battle but only to report what actually happened.

Richardson's article supports several non-English scholars who have replied to Tarn, and his viewpoint is the most widely accepted interpretation of the Battle of Actium. Yet since it involves a complex synthesis of scraps of evidence and leaves numerous questions unanswered, it has not definitely settled the issues. — *Roger B. McShane*

Additional Recommended Reading

Holmes, T. Rice. *The Architect of the Roman Empire.* Pp. 136-168 and 246-260. Oxford: The Clarendon Press, 1928. This careful scholar narrates in detail the struggle between Antony and Octavian.

Tarn, W. W., and M. P. Charlesworth. "The War of the East Against the West," in *The Cambridge Ancient History.* Vol. X, ch. 3, pp. 66-111. Cambridge: The University Press, 1934. An account of the period from 37 B.C. to the death of Antony and Cleopatra which incorporates Tarn's theories about Cleopatra's aims and the battle strategy at Actium.

Weigall, Arthur, E. P. B. *The Life and Times of Cleopatra, Queen of Egypt.* New York and London: G. P. Putnam's Sons, 1924. The traditional interpretation with some imaginative details.

DEFEAT IN TEUTOBURGER FOREST

Type of event: Military: ambush of three Roman legions
Time: A.D. 9
Locale: Northwest Germany

Principal personages:
PUBLIUS QUINTILIUS VARUS, consul in 13 B.C., Roman general
assigned to the Roman province between the Rhine and Elbe
rivers in A.D. 7, died A.D. 9
ARMINIUS, chieftain of the Cherusci, a small Germanic tribe
OCTAVIAN AUGUSTUS, Roman Emperor 27 B.C.-A.D. 14
ASPRENAS, consul A.D. 6, Varus' nephew and legate who led two
legions to Mainz to check the German advance
TIBERIUS, future Emperor and successor to Augustus who led his
troops to the Rhineland to help recover Varus' losses

Summary of Event

After the Battle of Actium in 31 B.C. and
the subsequent Roman conquest of Egypt,
the Emperor Augustus cut the Roman army
to almost half its former strength, leaving
only twenty-eight legions in service. This was
the period of the famous *Pax Romana*, which
some historians see as a period of national
fatigue and inertia rather than as a time of
good will.

Because it was difficult to maintain equilibrium on the northern frontier, Augustus'
policy called for an expansion into Germanic
territory. By A.D. 6 the region north of the
Main River between the Rhine and the Elbe
was a Roman province administered by Publius Quintilius Varus, a general chosen by Augustus, and married to the Emperor's grand-
niece. In A.D. 9 three legions under Varus
were defeated in the Teutoburger Forest by
Arminius, a chieftain of the Cherusci, a small
Germanic tribe, in a battle which marks a
watershed in the history of the Roman Empire. From this time on, the open secret of
Roman policy in the territory beyond the
Rhine was to divide, not conquer. Rome had
changed from an offensive to a defensive
position vis à vis the Germanic peoples.

The frontier problem was related to one
of the major defects in the Roman Imperial
system, namely, the nature of the Imperial
succession. Since the principle of succession
by heredity was not firmly established in the
early years of the Empire, the ambiguity of
the succession process played into the hands
of strong leaders in the army, men who had
little reason to be loyal to a Roman tradition
which, in many cases, they did not even know.
While it was many years before a barbarian
general ascended the Imperial throne, the
victory of Arminius signaled the growing
political function of the Roman barbarized
army.

Arminius himself was Roman-trained and
at the time of his victory over Varus the
leader of only a faction of his tribe, the Cherusci. Varus' appointment as governor was
an unfortunate choice. He tactlessly treated
the high-spirited Germans as inferior and tried
to Romanize them against their will. This
policy roused resentment in the Cherusci and
led to Varus' disastrous defeat. Enticed by
the report of an uprising, Varus led the seventeenth, eighteenth, and nineteenth legions
out of summer quarters into the Teutoburger

152

Forest, probably somewhere between Osnabrück and Detmold. There the army was ambushed and massacred, and Varus himself committed suicide. The episode can hardly be classified as a battle, for the Germans had the odds in their favor as they fell on the Roman columns encumbered by their baggage train in wooded country. The Roman cavalry attempted to escape but did not succeed.

After the rout of Varus, the Germans swept on to capture Roman forts east of the Rhine. Asprenas, Varus' legate, led two legions to Mainz, but here the enemy did not attempt to cross. Tiberius, the future Emperor, who had just succeeded after three years of difficult fighting in quelling a major revolt in Pannonia, was forced to postpone a triumph in Rome and hurry instead to the Rhine, where the garrison was raised to eight legions. To bring the forces to this level, two legions were withdrawn from Raetia and four from Spain and Illyricum.

While the Rhine defenses were thus strengthened, the three lost legions were not replaced in the army, so that its total strength was reduced to twenty-five legions, and any thought of further expansion beyond the Elbe was abandoned. Even before the disaster of the Teutoburger Forest, slaves were being pressed into military service, a practice which revealed a serious shortage of manpower.

Augustus himself mourned the loss of his three irreplaceable legions. Seventy-two years old at the time of the disaster, he never recovered from the shock. He even developed an aversion to his loyal German bodyguards and dismissed them from his service. Suetonius tells us that he kept the anniversary as a day of mourning, and that at night he could be heard murmuring, "Quintilius Varus, give me back my legions." Whether the story is true or not, it is certain that from this period Rome, for the most part, stopped expanding territorially, except in cases of frontier rectifications. It turned its energies inward, while the Germanic barbarians continued to develop their strength and to infiltrate the Empire. Germans regard the battle as a major event assuring the future development of a pure *Deutsche Kultur* uncontaminated by Romanization.

Pertinent Literature

Fuller, J. F. C. *A Military History of the Western World.* 3 vols. Vol. I: *From the Earliest Times to the Battle of Lepanto.* New York: Funk and Wagnalls, 1954.

Fuller's plan is to focus on the battles he considers decisive, and to weave around such battles the wars of which they were a part. He also draws some conclusions about the influence of these battles on subsequent events. Each account of a battle is preceded by a résumé of events leading up to it and an attempt to assess its political origins.

The Battle of Teutoburger Forest is the only engagement treated between the Battle of Actium, 31 B.C., and the Battle of Adrianople, A.D. 378. A transitional chapter after the account of Actium discusses the establishment of the Imperial frontiers. Fuller uses Caesar's Commentaries on the Gallic Wars to draw a graphic picture of the Germans as a restless, seminomadic people, and he recounts Tacitus' description of their weapons and methods of fighting. According to Tacitus, the Germans relied not on swords or lances, but on short spears which could be hurled or used at close quarters. According to Strabo, mistrust was the best defense against such people, for "those who were trusted effected the most mischief." The Battle of Teutoburger Forest corroborated these views of Caesar, Tacitus, and Strabo.

Fuller does not concur with the view which pictures Varus as an oppressive governor. He sees him rather as a weak one, basing his opinion on Velleius Paterculus, who portrayed Varus as a mild, quiet man, slow in mind and body, and "more accustomed to the leisure of the camp than to actual service in war." Fuller claims that the mistakes attributed to Varus (for example, his harshness and clumsiness in dealing with the Germans) were accusations made against him after his defeat, when wounded Roman pride was looking for a scapegoat. While he must agree that Varus' military disaster was preceded and perhaps caused by his administrative blunders, he insists that "stupidity rather than oppression would seem to have been his main defect" and that, more bureaucrat than soldier, he headed an administration that was weak rather than deliberately oppressive.

Among the motives that led Arminius to attack the Romans, Fuller lists revenge, not against Varus, but against a fellow German, Segestes, Arminius' own uncle. Segestes had refused to give Arminius his daughter Thusnelda in marriage. Segestes, also a loyal supporter of Varus, informed the Roman general of Arminius' plot. It was a warning Varus chose to ignore.

Velleius Paterculus and Dio Cassius are the two early authorities on whom Fuller relies most heavily for his account of the battle itself, noting that the information provided by these two writers does not warrant the full description of the battle given by some later authors. Fuller places the battle sometime in September or October. He estimates that some twenty thousand Roman soldiers were involved, besides the baggage train and the soldiers' families. Julius Caesar and Drusus, he notes, had both been in worse situations when attacked, "but then, they were leaders of men and Varus was but a camp attorney." The battle itself lasted over two days, according to Fuller's calculations, during which there were such heavy rains that by the second day the soldiers could neither advance nor even stand securely, nor could they use their water-soaked bows or shields. Dio Cassius says that Varus was not alone in his suicide, but that his more prominent officers also killed themselves.

Fuller's interpretation of the significance of the battle is in agreement with the view of many historians who see the event as a turning point in Roman history, because Roman prestige had received a blow from which it never recovered. Both the Romans and the Germans now knew Roman arms were not invincible. Yet the fact that the three lost legions were not replaced is more significant than their defeat, because the failure to replace them was proof that Rome was losing her vigor.

Where other historians see complex economic and social causes for this Roman loss of vitality, Fuller sees the deepest cause in the character of Augustus himself, who was "a splendid rather than an heroic figure . . . a tolerant opportunist" who became a bourgeois managing director rather than the monarch of his Empire. In this final verdict, Fuller offers a minority view which he fails to substantiate with sufficient evidence.

Finally, the author speculates on the long-range significance of the German victory over the Roman legions, suggesting that had the Elbe boundary been maintained and had the Germans not infiltrated farther west, "one culture and not two in unending conflict would have dominated the western world. There would have been no Franco-German problem, or at least a totally different one. There would have been no Charlemagne, no Louis XIV, no Napoleon, no Kaiser William II, and no Hitler." While the value of this kind of reasoning from the "ifs" of history can be questioned, in this instance the exercise helps the author make the point that the Battle of Teutoburger Forest had consequences stretching far into the future.

Defeat in Teutoburger Forest

Mitchell, Lt. Col. Joseph B., and Sir Edward S. Creasy. *Twenty Decisive Battles of the World.* New York: The Macmillan Company, 1964.

This book is a major revision of Creasy's *Fifteen Decisive Battles of The World,* published in 1851. Mitchell accepts Creasy's choice of battles, though he corrects details in the accounts in the light of research since the work was first published, adding five battles since Waterloo, and supplying excellent maps. As in other works of this kind, the battles are linked by synopses of events taking place between military engagements treated as decisive. Thus, the Battle of Teutoburger Forest is preceded by a synopsis of events after the Battle of Metaurus, in 207 B.C., and followed by one leading up to the Battle of Châlons in A.D. 451. Creasy and his modernizer are interested in the battles not as isolated events, but for their lasting effects, since, in Creasy's words, "the effect of those collisions is not limited to a single age, but may give an impulse which will sway the fortunes of successive generations of mankind."

The authors see the Battle of Teutoburger Forest as indicative of a decline in the Roman army since the Second Punic War, in 218-201 B.C. In the two-hundred-year period, Roman pride in a citizen army deteriorated until army service was seen as a duty rather than a privilege. In Augustus' time certain reforms were introduced or extended, including definite rates of pay and a discharge bonus. The army was becoming increasingly professional and decreasingly Roman, as the noncitizen population, particularly on the frontiers of the Empire, was brought into service to provide needed auxiliaries. Another of Augustus' aims was to acquire natural frontiers north of the Alps. To this end he wanted to secure the Elbe-Danube line, rather than the Rhine-Danube line, on the theory that the former would be easier to defend. The victory of Arminius over Varus was a fatal blow to this design.

The Mitchell-Creasy account emphasizes the fact that Arminius was no rude savage. He knew Roman tactics because he had served in Roman armies; he had been granted Roman citizenship and was a member of the equestrian order. At the time of the attack on Varus and his three legions, Arminius and his men were actually escorting the Roman troops, and when the battle became critical, Varus' light-armed auxiliaries, who were Germans, deserted. Thus, as the account makes clear, the Battle of Teutoburger Forest was not a simple case of rude barbarians pitted against a Roman army.

The graphic description of the actual encounter between the forces of Varus and Arminius is more colorful than convincing because the authors do not cite the early sources on which they base their account. Reference to Dio Cassius, however, is made in describing the effect of the battle on Augustus. Terrified that the Germans and Gauls might push into Italy, Augustus tried to increase the army, "and when none of the citizens of military age were willing to enlist, he made them cast lots, and punished by confiscation of goods and disfranchisement every fifth man among those under thirty-five, and every tenth man of those above that age." When this plan failed, he made conscripts of discharged veterans and emancipated slaves.

In explaining the decisiveness and far-reaching influence of the Battle of Teutoburger Forest, the authors claim that Arminius' victory "secured at once and forever the independence of the Teutonic race." This is an exceedingly sweeping claim. More in line with the facts is the observation that if the Elbe-Danube line had been achieved, the Germans between the Rhine and the Elbe would have been Latinized as were the Gauls and the Spaniards. Instead, the Rhine became the acknowledged boundary of the Roman Em-

155

pire in the West until the fifth century, a sufficiently important reason for regarding the Battle of Teutoburger Forest as a decisive

event in the history of Western civilization.

—Mary Evelyn Jegen

Additional Recommended Reading

Cook, S. A., F. E. Adcock, and M. P. Charlesworth. *The Cambridge Ancient History.* Volume X: *The Augustan Empire 44 B.C.-A.D. 70.* New York: The Macmillan Company, 1934. A study containing a discussion of the Battle of Teutoburger Forest with an evaluation of the early sources.

Jones, A. H. M. *The Decline of the Ancient World.* New York: Holt, Rinehart and Winston, 1966. An excellent abridgement of the author's four-volume work.

Lissner, Ivar. *The Caesars—Might and Madness.* Translated by J. Maxwell Brownjohn. New York: Capricorn Books, 1958. A chapter on Augustus describes the effect on the Emperor of the Battle of Teutoburger Forest.

ROMAN CONQUEST OF BRITAIN

Type of event: Military: subjugation of Celtic tribes
Time: A.D. 46
Locale: Britain south of Hadrian's wall from the River Tyne to the Solway Firth

Principal personages:
JULIUS CAESAR, first Roman invader of Britain, 55-54 B.C.
CLAUDIUS, Roman Emperor A.D. 41-54
AGRICOLA, Governor of Britain A.D. 76-84
HADRIAN, Roman Emperor A.D. 117-138
ANTONINUS PIUS, Roman Emperor A.D. 138-161

Summary of Event

Britannia, the Roman name for England, Wales, and southern Scotland, at the beginning of the Christian era had an Iron Age culture in the south and east below a line from the River Tyne to the River Exe. Before the sixth century B.C. waves of Celts had crossed the English Channel from the Continent, and by the time of Julius Caesar nearly all the inhabitants of Britain were Celtic in speech and customs. They dwelt in hill forts or villages of round huts, created art similar to that of the La Tène culture, and had considerable commercial relations with the tribes of northwest Europe. During his conquest of Gaul, Caesar's defeat of the northern tribe of the Nervii led him in 55 B.C. to make an expedition across the Channel against their British allies. With a small force he landed on the Kentish coast, but storm damage to his fleet and British resistance forced his withdrawal that fall. In the next year he returned, however, to defeat the native chieftain Cassivellaunus and his army, take hostages, and require the payment of a tribute. When Caesar returned to Gaul subsequent events there and in Rome prevented him and his successors from further large-scale operations in Britain for almost a century.

Augustus Caesar planned the incorporation of Britannia into the Empire, but both he and his successor Tiberius remained oc-cupied with the problems and defenses of more important areas. It was not until A.D. 43 that an invasion in force was mounted under the leadership of the Emperor Claudius and his general Aulus Plautius. A well-equipped army of four legions, some forty thousand troops in all, landed in Kent, crossed the Thames, and captured Camulodunum, now Colchester in Essex. With this capital city and Londinium (London) as bases, three army corps fanned out to overrun the British lowlands. On the left Legio II Augusta pacified the southern region under the command of Vespasian, who later ruled as emperor from A.D. 70 to 79. The legions XIV Gemina and XX Valeria thrust into the Midlands, and IX Hispana marched on the right up the east coast. By the year 47, the new province embraced lands south of the River Humber and east of the River Severn, but progress then became much more difficult because of high-land terrain and stiffening opposition. The Silures in east Wales and the Brigantes in Yorkshire proved to be intractable, and then in 61, the tribal queen Boudicca led a revolt in which Camulodunum, Londinium, and Verulamium (St. Albans) were sacked before the rebels were suppressed. With the eleva-tion of Vespasian to imperial power there came a succession of able governors to Brit-ain, one of whom, Agricola, is well known

157

because of the biography written by his son-in-law, the historian Tacitus. By 81, Agricola had advanced to the Forth-Clyde line in Scotland.

The history of the next thirty-five years is dim, but about 117 a revolt in the north resulted in the annihilation of Legio IX Hispana, stationed at Eboracum (York). In the wake of this disaster the Emperor Hadrian in 121 brought Legio VI Victrix as a replacement and initiated the building of the famous Wall of Hadrian, a frontier barrier running some eighty Roman miles from coast to coast from the mouth of the River Tyne to Solway Firth. The construction of this rampart with forts at regular intervals signaled the end of Roman expansion in the north, at a time when similar decisions were made concerning other boundaries of the Empire. It is noteworthy that in Britain Roman power last advanced, and there it first began to recede.

In the reign of Hadrian's successor, Antoninus Pius, Scotland was invaded and on the narrower Forth-Clyde line the legions built another barrier known as the Antonine Wall, but this was broken during a revolt in 180-184 and then abandoned. The remaining centuries of Roman rule saw defense entrusted partly to semiautonomous tribes on the borders, a system that worked well against attacks from Ireland and Scotland but was of little use against Saxon raiders on the south and east coasts. After the Teutonic conquest of Gaul at the beginning of the fifth century, Britannia was isolated; finally in 410, the Emperor Honorius informed the municipalities of the province that in the future they would have to arrange for their own security.

A last appeal to Rome for help failed in 446, and thereafter tribal princes gradually asserted their own power and control. Anglo-Saxons and Jutes began to settle in the lowlands, while in the highlands of the north and west the old Celtic culture revived.

Britannia was a typical province of the Empire, for behind the various border defenses a civilized culture developed in the southern and eastern lowlands. Its two chief features were the towns and the country villas. Eventually there were four *coloniae* or municipalities of time-expired soldiers at Camulodunum (Colchester), Eboracum (York), Lindum (Lincoln), and Glevum (Gloucester). Native towns such as Verulamium (St. Albans) received the status of *municipium*, which granted legal rights of self-rule little different from that of the *colonia*, and new towns such as Calleva Atrebatum (Silchester) arose in the Roman style. Silchester, laid out on the grid system, had a forum, temples, baths, and an amphitheater. Besides the regional towns Londinium (London) was a prosperous trading center and port by virtue of its location on the Thames estuary, and Aquae Sulis (Bath) was a spa and pleasure resort with splendid buildings. At the height of development from the late second to the middle fourth century the people of the towns and the educated rural population all spoke Latin and saw themselves not as subjects of a foreign power but as Romans living in a Roman province, far superior to the barbarians to the north and across the seas to the west and northeast. Britannia was an excellent example of the effectiveness of Roman civilization and its imperial system.

Pertinent Literature

Frere, Sheppard. *Britannia: A History of Roman Britain.* Cambridge: Harvard University Press, 1967.

This comprehensive work, based on literary and epigraphic sources and on archae-ological discoveries, covers Roman Britain from the Iron Age to the last days of Roman rule. It should be noted, however, that the plan of the work does not include the archaeology of the period as such, and there are no general descriptions of the surviving sites or remains. The first three chapters embrace the Iron Age to Caesar's expeditions, and the next six cover the story of the period after Caesar: the conquest of Claudius and the rebellion of Boudicca, the Flavian period, the Hadrianic and Antonine walls, and Severus and the third century. At this point the historic approach gives way to analysis and Chapters 10 through 15 examine the administration of the province, the army, towns and countryside, trade and industry, and the process of Romanization. Chapters 16 and 17 conclude with the story of Carausius and the fourth century, and the end of Roman rule. There are also thirty-six plates at the end of the book, thirteen figures in the text, an excellent bibliography, and an index.

Amid innumerable topics of interest Hadrian's Wall claims special attention because of the motivating idea behind it and other examples of the type which history has to offer: the Great Wall of China, the Maginot Line, and the more recent Berlin Wall. Such artificial barriers appear to indicate a loss of nerve on the part of the builders and no such wall appears to have achieved its objective. As archaeologists have found and interpreted the remains, the Hadrianic frontier now consists of six elements: (1) the continuous wall, with a walkway atop it and a large V-shaped ditch twenty feet wide in front of it; (2) milecastles or fortlets for patrols, evenly spaced along the wall every 4860 feet or one Roman mile; (3) turrets, evenly spaced, with two between each milecastle; (4) sixteen garrison forts, located at various strategic points along the wall; (5) an earthwork, called the Vallum, a wide ditch with mounds on each side, located on the south or inner side of the barrier; and (6) the military way, a lateral connecting road south of the wall. Constructed between 122 and 130, the wall extended for eighty Roman miles from Wallsend-on-Tyne in the east to Bowness-on-Solway in the west. Its eastern forty-five miles were of stone, some fifteen feet high and ten feet thick, but the western section traversed an area devoid of limestone and so the wall here at first consisted of turf, about twenty feet wide at the base and twelve feet high. As the work progressed, minor changes were made in the dimensions, and by the end of the century the turf section had been completely replaced by stone.

The garrison in the forts, composed of auxiliary regiments, included fifty-five hundred infantry and two thousand cavalry. Though the question is disputed, it seems likely that the milecastles were held and the wall itself patrolled by some two thousand additional auxiliaries. Ninety miles to the south in the fortress at Eboracum stood the regulars of Legio VI Victrix, on call for any emergency. But Frere makes the point that the primary purpose of the wall was political, not military. In the light of the large and hostile populations on both sides, barbarians to the north and the recently conquered to the south, it was designed to observe and control group movements and to expedite communications. From the military viewpoint, the spacing of the forts, the heavy percentage of cavalry in the garrison, and the screening function of the wall itself all provided for quick strikes in force against enemy buildups and against marauders.

Collingwood, R. G., and J. N. L. Myres. *Roman Britain and the English Settlements.* 2nd ed. Oxford: The Clarendon Press, 1937.

This book is notable for Collingwood's lucid description of the Roman period in Britain and Myres' continuation of the story in the early settlements of the Anglo-Saxons.

This treatment of the two periods, so closely related yet seldom surveyed together, is useful and occurs partly because the book is Volume I of the *Oxford History of England*, edited by Sir George Clark. Collingwood divides his section of the work into four parts: "Britain before the Roman Conquest," which considers the geology and early cultures of the island, Caesar's invasions, and the period thereafter; "The Age of Conquest," which carries the story from the Claudian victory to the Antonine period; "Britain Under Roman Rule," which considers government, towns, rural areas, industry, commerce, art, and religion; and "The End of Roman Britain," covering events from the early third to the midfifth centuries. Myres concludes the book in a fifth section in which he treats the sources for his period, the Anglo-Saxon conquests in Kent and the southeast, settlements in the fenlands, East Anglia, Wessex, and the Humber estuary, and the nature of the conquest and the difficult problem concerning continuity between Roman Britannia and Saxon England.

Collingwood offers a brilliant analysis of a major aspect of the Romanization of Britain. He points out that the Mediterranean world is one of town-dwellers, and that every Greek and Roman would assent to the Aristotelian dictum that only by life in a city can man fulfill his higher, spiritual needs. Periclean Athens and Ciceronian Rome, both part reality and part ideal, embodied this civilizing role of *agora* and *forum*, *stoa* and *basilica*, and all the other aspects of a great city where man can truly test and develop his humanity. But for the peoples of northern Europe this was an alien doctrine, since they believed that man's higher faculties flourished only in his own household and in the freedom of the countryside. For them the

town, if it existed at all, was simply a collection of huts where men might barter, buy, or practice a trade—an economic locus but never a place to be preferred to meadows, fields, and homesteads. It is remarkable that this deeply inbred prejudice against the city and the idealizing of all things rural characterized American political life for generations following colonial times, and that the ensuing crisis of the American cities stems in some degree from this long-cherished myth of northern Europe. Julius Caesar was struck by the absence of towns when he invaded Britain in 55-54 B.C., and he notes that the only equivalents of urban centers were tracts of land fenced in against assault. In the literal sense of the word, therefore, the Romans civilized Britain by building towns in their newest province.

By the time of the Antonines in the latter half of the second century town life had reached its apogee. There were a dozen tribal capitals such as Canterbury, Winchester, Dorchester, and Exeter south of the Thames, and Leicester and Caerwent north of it. London was the largest of all, with its walls enclosing some three hundred acres and holding a population of about fifteen thousand, and by this time it was almost certainly the seat of government. Because of its role as a port it was probably more cosmopolitan than British in the quality of its life, even though natives comprised the greater part of its populace. To the west stood the luxurious and fashionable resort of Bath, and there were also the military colonies originally settled by Roman veterans, but becoming increasingly British as the numbers of natives increased in the army. Some fifty other towns are known, running from regional and industrial centers to mere way-stations along the main highways built by the Romans.—*Kevin Herbert*

Additional Recommended Reading

Cottrell, Leonard. *A Guide to Roman Britain.* Philadelphia: Chilton Books, 1966. A useful guide for the armchair or actual tourist.

H. M. Ordnance Survey. *Map of Roman Britain.* Chessington: H. M. Ordnance Survey, 1956. A large map, superbly rendered, on a scale of sixteen miles to the inch, with an introduction, tables, and notes.

Holmes, T. Rice. *Ancient Britain and the Invasions of Julius Caesar.* Oxford: The Clarendon Press, 1907. The fullest treatment of the subject.

CREATION OF THE IMPERIAL BUREAUCRACY

Type of event: Political: establishment of civil service reform
Time: c. A.D. 50
Locale: Rome and the Roman Empire

Principal personages:
AUGUSTUS, first Roman Emperor 27 B.C.–A.D. 14
CLAUDIUS, fourth Roman Emperor A.D. 41-54
PALLAS,
NARCISSUS, and
CALLISTUS, freedmen heads of bureaus under Claudius, and
    regarded by Roman tradition as archetypes of the all-powerful
    bureaucrat
HADRIAN, thirteenth Roman Emperor A.D. 117-138

Summary of Event

The Imperial bureaucracy was the creation of the early Roman emperors, especially of the first, Augustus, and the fourth, Claudius. Augustus' reorganization of Roman government provided the framework for the development of such a bureaucracy; Claudius' deliberate elaboration of the bureaucracy that had developed during preceding reigns brought this branch of government service to the peak of its power.

The Imperial bureaucracy was comparable to, and at first existed alongside, an older and less elaborate bureaucracy of the Republican period. The Republican magistrates had drawn their supporting staffs from two sources. One was the pool of permanent employees attached to the central government treasury. The other was each magistrate's personal staff. The Roman magistrate was invariably a man of property, and it was customary for such a person to apply to public as well as to private business the aid of his personal staff, composed in large part of his own slaves and freedmen.

Under the political settlement effected by Augustus, the government of Italy and of about half the provinces continued to be conducted according to Republican custom, by annually-elected magistrates whose supporting staffs were drawn from personal employees and from employees of the treasury, which remained under the control of the senate. In the remaining provinces, government was the personal responsibility of the Emperor, who governed through representatives appointed by himself. The Emperor's representatives, once again men of property and political standing, may have been assisted by their personal staffs but they were not provided with personnel from the central treasury. Instead, the supporting staff for administration of the Emperor's provinces was drawn from the Emperor's own household, and was composed, for the most part, of the Emperor's slaves and freedmen.

Our information about the development of the Imperial bureaucracy under Augustus and under his successors Tiberius and Caligula, or Gaius Caesar, is limited. We may assume that as an emperor gathered ever greater powers into his own hands, the bureaus that assisted him grew in number, complexity, and power. With Tiberius' retirement from Rome in his later years and with Caligula's erratic preoccupations, much of the business of the Empire must have been left to the

162

chiefs of bureaus. It is a tribute to the capabilities of the bureaucracy and of the bureaucrats that civilian government did not collapse, even under the burden of unrest and resentment that led to Caligula's assassination.

The importance of a capable Imperial bureaucracy did not escape the notice of the pedantic Claudius, and it is during his rule that we have much evidence of the consolidation and expansion of this organization. Claudius' personal agents collected certain taxes even in provinces governed, in theory, by elected magistrates. These financial agents were granted political powers, particularly the right to preside over certain kinds of litigation, that had formerly been reserved for elected officials. The Emperor's staff in Rome was organized into distinct bureaus whose chiefs, the Emperor's freedmen, were granted extraordinary dignity and authority. Five chief bureaus are known: *a rationibus* dealing with finance, *ab epistulis* dealing with state correspondence, *a libellis* with petitions, *a cognitionibus* with justice, and *a studiis* with culture.

In his elaboration of the Imperial bureaucracy, Claudius was no doubt motivated by the desire to achieve efficient central administration, and there is evidence that the Empire in general, and particularly the outlying regions, benefited from his reforms. But the population of Rome, jealous of its ancient privileges, resented the assumption of power by foreign-born former slaves. Claudius may in fact have granted his ministers enough power to govern even him. Narcissus, chief of the bureau *ab epistulis*, is said to have disposed of Claudius' wife Messalina more or less without his consent. Pallas, chief of *a rationibus*, was believed to have cooperated with Claudius' next wife, Agrippina, in bringing about the Emperor's death by poisoning, and in establishing as next emperor, not Claudius' son and heir-elect, Britannicus, but Agrippina's son, the infamous Nero who reigned from 41 to 68.

As Nero devoted himself increasingly to his own amusement, the Imperial bureaucracy continued to wield nearly unsupervised power, and there is little doubt that the abuses of the Emperor's freedmen contributed to the alienation that led to open revolt and warfare in A.D. 68-69. Succeeding emperors attempted to restrain their agents without enacting any major reform of the bureaucracy, which continued to function in the form given it by Claudius until the reign of Hadrian. By that time, the principle of one-man rule was well accepted, and the service of the emperor was recognized as the service of the state. Hadrian reorganized the Imperial bureaucracy accordingly, relying less on the services of his personal dependents and opening the more important positions to free-born Roman citizens. The rift between bureaucracy and citizenry was repaired without diminishing the usefulness of the bureaucracy itself.

Pertinent Literature

Mattingly, Harold B. *The Imperial Civil Service of Rome.* Cambridge: The University Press, 1910.

It is Mattingly's purpose in this slender volume to describe the administrative apparatus of the Roman Empire during the first two centuries of the Christian era, and particularly the positions and organizations which were not carried over from the Republican period but which were instituted and developed by the emperors themselves. The author's approach is developmental, beginning with a description of the administrative problems that faced the Empire at its inception, and ending with a brief evaluation of the institutions that had been developed in order to meet those problems. In the three chapters that form the chief substance of his work, he describes the major areas of the Roman emperor's administrative activity, the organization of his delegates and employees in these areas, and the classes of persons from which those delegates and employees were recruited, along with the major innovations and reforms of the various emperors.

In Mattingly's view, the chief failure of the Roman Republic, and hence the most urgent administrative problem of the early emperors, lay in the sphere of government finance. In the many territories made subject to Rome, the city-state institutions of the Roman Republic had proved inadequate to exercise a proper control both of provincials and of the Roman officials who were sent to govern them. It was these territories, the Roman provinces, that supplied, through payment of taxes, the support of the civil and military operations of the Empire. The need to assure and regularize the financial basis of his government caused Augustus to depart from Republican practice by placing in the hands of his personal employees the collection of taxes, formerly hired out to contractors, and the administration of funds, formerly undertaken by elected officials, in those provinces entrusted to his command. The need to maintain a central account of the emperor's various financial agents led to the development of the Bureau of Finance. The

employees of this central bureau, together with those engaged in financial administration of the provinces, formed the largest and perhaps the most influential of the departments of the Imperial civil service.

Finance was not, however, the only branch of civil administration in which the emperor was occupied. His juridical responsibilities as governor in chief of so many provinces, his diplomatic and political activity as the foremost member of the Roman government, his public works in Rome and Italy, all required the employment of a large personal staff. The various areas of the emperor's activity were reflected in the great bureaus patterned in part after the first and foremost of them, the Bureau of Finance.

Mattingly finds the effectiveness of the bureaus in Rome reduced by the degree in which they sometimes usurped the authority of the emperors they were meant to serve. Under the rule of Claudius, in particular, he finds that the growing importance and responsibility of the central bureaus were more the result of self-seeking by freedmen employees than of any intention of the Emperor. But a strong central control greatly increased the efficiency of administration in outlying areas. The provinces grew prosperous and supplied a good income to the Imperial coffers. The relative stability that resulted more than outweighed the complaints of the Republican nobility against the upstart bureaucrats.

Duff, A. M. *Freedmen in the Early Roman Empire.* Oxford: The University Press, 1928.

In this book the development of the Imperial bureaucracy is viewed in a social, rather than in an institutional, context. Duff's subject is the class of freedmen, former slaves who, assuming with their liberation the citizenship of their former masters, swelled the population of Rome and of Italy during the later years of the Roman Republic and the earlier years of the Empire. He begins by

describing the origins of Roman slaves in terms of the operation of the slave market; he next studies the ways in which large number of Roman and Italian slaves attained their liberty. Finally he deals with the legal, social, and political status which the freedmen attained. Against this broad background, Duff describes the activities of freedmen in business and industry, in public office whether religious or political or military, and in the service of the emperor.

It becomes apparent, in reading Duff's survey of the social and legal condition of the freedman, that a number of factors contributed to his usefulness in the Imperial bureaucracy, as well as in Roman society at large. First, his non-Roman origin gave him a culture and a personality different from, and often complementary to, that of the native Roman or Italian. Romans thought of themselves as a nation of farmers and soldiers. Although with increasing urbanization of Italy, many Romans engaged in some form of commerce or trade, Duff believes that the feeling was never quite lost that many occupations, including handiwork, however skilled or artistic, personal service, and public performance, were somehow unbecoming to the freeborn citizen. Freedmen, whose servile origin prevented such self-consciousness, and whose native cultures often placed higher value on skilled crafts and professions, were able to fulfill a great many functions both necessary and valuable to Roman society. The more able of them achieved great wealth or status, or both, as contractors of public works, as merchants and tradesmen, and as professional artists, physicians, teachers, or performers.

Freedmen practiced such professions and others, as often as not, under the patronage or in the employ of their former owners, to whom they were bound by almost filial obligation as well as by practical consideration. The strong bond of mutual obligation and dependence between freedmen and former masters, reinforced by legislation under Augustus and again under Claudius, created a climate in which the freedman was virtu-

ally certain to be his former master's most loyal and trustworthy employee. Great families might have dozens of such freedmen in their private employ; the greatest household of all, the emperor's, soon had hundreds.

The emperor's freedman, serving him in his official as well as in his private pursuits, formed an organization whose actual political power contrasted sharply with its private status and with the servile origin of its members, a situation which provoked extensive resentment on the part of freeborn Romans. In time as Republican traditions were forgotten and Rome learned to identify the emperor with the state, the official character of the Imperial bureaucracy was accepted more readily. At the same time, as the freeborn sons and grandsons of Imperial freedmen continued to serve the government while attaining ever higher social rank, employment in the emperor's service was no longer limited to men of servile and foreign origin; the division between native population and government employee was gradually eliminated.

Duff's book ends with an assessment of government policy towards freedmen and their impact on Roman society. He finds the policy of the early emperors partly conservative in attempting to limit the numbers and the influence of freedmen, and partly utilitarian in enlisting their services in public and private life alike. The effect of the introduction of large numbers of freedmen into Roman society and government was mixed: They added much to Rome's greatness in their pursuit of the arts and professions but contributed to her moral decline by undermining the character of the population and by a self-serving devotion to luxury.

—Zola M. Packman

Additional Recommended Reading

Cook, S. A., F. E. Adcock, and M. P. Charlesworth, eds. *The Cambridge Ancient History*, Volume X: *The Augustan Empire, 44 B.C.-A.D. 70.* Cambridge: The University Press, 1934. Chapter VII, "The Imperial Administration," by G. H. Stevenson, and Chapter XX, "Gaius and Claudius," by M. P. Charlesworth, are relevant to the subject of this paper.

Holmes, T. Rice. *The Architect of the Roman Empire.* Oxford: The University Press, 1928-1931. A two-volume history of Augustus' reign.

Mattingly, Harold B. *Roman Imperial Civilization.* New York: St. Martin's Press, 1957. A survey of public and private institutions in the Imperial period.

Momigliano, Arnaldo. *Claudius the Emperor and His Achievement.* Translated by W. D. Hogarth. Oxford: The University Press, 1934. A study of Claudius' religious and governmental policies.

Perowne, Stewart. *Hadrian.* London: Hodder and Stoughton, 1960. A thorough study of Hadrian's Imperial strategy.

NERO'S PERSECUTION OF THE CHRISTIANS

Type of event: Politico-religious: harassment of a religious group
Time: A.D. 64-67
Locale: Rome

Principal personages:
NERO, Roman Emperor 54-68
PETER, Apostle of Jesus
PAUL OF TARSUS, Apostle of Jesus

Summary of Event

Rome was a totalitarian state in the sense that no concept of sovereignty existed outside it. Consequently, religion in Rome was not a matter of individual devotion, or the making of an independent church, but rather the execution of a craft carried on in the name of the entire corporate body by the state through its official priestly colleges. As a result, foreign cults, and even philosophies, found themselves from time to time in awkward or even perilous positions. The state's response to this challenge of new religious "isms" seems to fall into three patterns: (1) to accept all polytheistic cults, as long as they were not gross enough to threaten public order, either by adding their gods to the state pantheon or by identifying them with individual official deities; (2) to tolerate bona-fide national religions of conquered people even when a particular religion is monotheistic as in the case of the Jews; (3) to regard a nonnational monotheism, such as the Christian religion, a foreign threat capable of establishing a sovereign body within the state and therefore incompatible with the established totalitarian order.

On the whole, Rome was tolerant though always watchful. It saw fit to purge the public rituals of Cybele, to repress and persecute the Bacchanals under senatorial decrees, and to harass the cult of Isis off and on over a hundred-year period. The Druids were dealt with harshly as cannibalistic. The Jews on the whole were treated well officially and even given enviable special consideration by such men as Pompey, Caesar, and Augustus, thanks to such wily collaborators as Herod the Great and Herod Agrippa. Local anti-Semitism, however, always smoldered against the Jews of the Dispersion especially in cities such as Alexandria, evoked, it was believed, by the Jews' supposed "hostility to the rest of mankind."

It is not easy to explain how the Christians got into trouble. The Apostle Paul surely enjoyed Roman protection, and many other instances of cooperation between Rome and Christendom are not difficult to list. One noble Christian lady, Pomponia Graecina, seems to have been persecuted as early as 57 for "foreign superstition." But it was not until 64 that difficulties definitely arose, when the great five-day holocaust starting in the shops near the Circus Maximus burned most of Rome.

Many questions arise over the incident. How was the attack on Christians carried out legally? What were the charges? How extensive was the affair? How many suffered? The evidence is slim. Tacitus in his cryptic way merely states that Christians were charged with incendiarism as scapegoats, and that large numbers confessed and were condemned for their antisocial tendencies. They were torn by dogs, crucified, and burned as torches while Nero paraded around at his garden party dressed as a charioteer. The public reaction, Tacitus adds, tended to pity the Christians as victims more of Nero's brutality than as perpetrators of crimes. Suetonius, the other classical authority, merely mentions that Christians were early driven out of Rome, and in no way does he associate Christians with the later fire.

The names of the martyrs under Nero are unknown, although a strong tradition beginning already with Clement of Rome about 95 lists the Apostles Peter and Paul as victims. Later tradition put their deaths on the same day and held that Peter was crucified head downward. The tradition of their martyrdom in Rome is of momentous import for Western history inasmuch as the apostolicity of the Roman See and all that it implied later rests largely upon it. Although recent archaeological exploration under St. Peter's Basilica has failed positively to identify Peter's remains, there is some evidence that the Apostle did come to Rome.

Those who assert that Nero's persecution reached beyond the confines of the city of Rome cite references in I Peter to provincial persecutions in Asia Minor, Pontus, Galicia, and Bithynia, but the letter may well be of later composition. Some cite Revelation and its gloomy picture as relevant, assuming that it was composed shortly after Nero's persecution and mirrors events at that time.

Whatever the details were, the persecution turned out to be a disastrous affair. It greatly shaped and determined the attitude of Rome toward Christians for two and a half centuries. Orosius in the early fifth century popularized the idea of ten persecutions against the Church. On the whole they were sporadic, localized, and often lackadaisically carried out by half-hearted Roman officials until 250 when Decius set afoot a universal dragnet by demanding certificates of sacrifice. Probably the worst period for Christians was from 303 under Diocletian and continuing under Galerius and Maximinus until 313 when the Edict of Milan gave official recognition to Christianity. The number of Christians executed in all the persecutions has been variously estimated as between ten thousand and a hundred thousand.

Pertinent Literature

Frend, W. H. C. *Martyrdom and Persecution in the Early Church*. Garden City, New York: Doubleday & Company, Inc., 1967.

Ever since 1890 when Mommsen's famous article "Crimes of Religion in Roman Law" appeared in the *Historische Zeitschrift*, a steady stream of scholarship has poured forth to investigate the legal basis of persecution of the Christians. The question is: what underlay the sudden crisis of 64?

W. H. C. Frend notes that the many theories advanced to explain the legal puzzle tend to fall into two groups which, strangely enough, often reflect national and denominational lines. Roman Catholic French and Belgian scholars seem generally to hold that after Nero's persecution Christianity itself was forbidden by a general law, often identified with the famous but nebulous "*institutum Neronianum*" of Tertullian. Once Christianity was declared an illicit religion, persecution for the name of Christian is naturally easy to explain. The fact that a *senatus consultum* concerning Christians might have been promulgated is an attractive theory. Such, indeed, had been formulated against Jews and worshipers of Isis. Yet there is no evidence of such a decree either in inscriptions or literature. Surely if Pliny had known of such a law, he would have spared himself perplexity over his procedures in Bithynia.

Surely Christian apologists would have mentioned it time and time again. Nor was there any early attempt to confiscate church property as would have been justified under such a decree. Moreover, one might well ask if Christians were important enough in Nero's time to warrant such attention.

English and German scholars have tended to stress the idea of mere police action in which individual Christians were punished locally through the power of *coercitio* presumably for such offenses as magic, superstition, or illegal assembly. *Coercitio* as an almost arbitrary exercise of *imperium* operated virtually outside ordinary forms of judicial procedure. Under it Roman magistrates could take almost any measure to keep order so long as they did not act contrary to custom.

The author appears to agree with the second thesis of police action. "What we see," he says, "in Nero's action is a brutal application of police administration . . . not the beginning of a policy launched by an edict." According to this theory the emperors intervened personally merely to regulate the exercise of this power locally. This explanation easily accounts for the localized and sporadic character of the early persecutions.

Though no definite rule appears to have been laid down by Nero against Christianity, Christians were nonetheless put on the defensive. If police action was not often initiated, Christians were thereafter susceptible to accusations initiated by delators so that investigation by a magistrate had to follow with defendant and accuser being forced to appear. Such procedure became standard by the second century, when mere accusation of the name "Christian" was sufficient to bring about indictment. It should, however, be remembered that persecution for the name alone does not necessarily imply the existence of a general law forbidding Christianity. It is more likely that the government operated on a general assumption that the supreme good was the public welfare, an end clearly threatened by any perverted religion with false oaths, contempt for official worship, and a penchant for secret assembly.

The author seems to be convinced that repercussions against Christians readily arose out of their close relationship with Jewish religion. Many accusations against Christians were identical to those made against Jews, the main complaint being that of obstinacy. It was easy for the Roman to transfer his hostility from the Jew to the Christian. Moreover when the Church claimed to be the true Israel, it exposed itself to Jewish as well as Gentile hostility. By claiming to be true Jews while refusing to accept the Jewish Law, Christians invited denunciation as schismatics by their adopted orthodox brethren. Christianity had indeed outlawed itself by denying national affiliation with Palestinian Jewry and at the same time repudiating the official gods of Rome to become *atheos*. Both Hermas and Origen realized only too well that if members of the new "third race" did not choose to honor the laws of the ruler of the world, they "must be prepared to leave his city."

Ramsay, William. *The Church in the Roman Empire*. London: Hodder & Stoughton, 1907.

This respected old book is one of the many which earned a high reputation before 1910 for trying to assess the basic character and meaning of the Neronian persecution.

Ramsay deduces that Pliny's letter of the early second century clearly reveals a situation where actions against Christians were habitual and stereotyped. The letter also shows, according to Ramsay, that no definite law against Christians had been promulgated, as it was later under Domitian for example, since it seems clear from Trajan's language that he is describing an unwritten policy or principle.

At this point the author sets out to explore the meaning, accuracy, and relevancy of Tacitus' remarks about the persecution by checking him against the only other available significant profane witness, Suetonius. He notes that Suetonius in speaking of Nero's punishment of Christians lists it among other police regulations, all of a character designed to maintain long-range order. In such a context where permanent regulation is implied, why would Suetonius single out the Christians for mention if their offense were regarded merely as an isolated incident? It seems obvious to Ramsay, therefore, that repression of Christians was meant to be a permanent policy along with the other accompanying regulations. When Ramsay studied Suetonius' report on the expulsion of Jews, and therefore supposedly of early Jewish-Christians, about A.D. 52 under Claudius, he notes that in this case the incident is stated in the context of other isolated events calling for only temporary police action. Obviously, Nero's policy was different.

Tacitus, he recalls, makes it clear that Christians were punished far less for incendiarism than for hostility to society and hatred of the world. These two accusations, in the author's mind, are not so much simultaneous as in series. In reporting that the crowds softened their attitude toward the Christians as having suffered too much or too unjustly for the fire, Tacitus shows that enthusiasm for the persecution based on this accusation died down. Nero then supposedly took up what Tacitus reports as a second accusation, that of turning people from their fathers' values, a sustained crime in contrast to the single offense of arson. Christians along with their magical practices, as permanent enemies of civilization, must be destroyed through a sustained attack by civilization.

Moreover, Tacitus cannot be referring to incendiarism when he reports that many Christians confessed. If they confessed to incendiarism, why did Romans tend to forgive them and in the long run blame the catastrophe on Nero? And how could a "great multitude" be guilty of arson? It is more likely that Christians were accused of general crimes against society. At this point Ramsay summarizes his position: "The persecution of Nero, begun for the sake of diverting popular attention, was continued as a permanent police measure under the form of a general prosecution of Christians as a sect dangerous to the public safety." In other words, persecution was not for the name "Christian"; rather trials were first held for incendiarism and only later for acts betraying a sustained willingness to tamper with the established customs of society.

The Neronian persecution ended with Nero's death; but the trials conducted during his reign established that certain acts such as secret assembly deserved death. Christians were regularly guilty of such acts. No formal edict or law was necessary; Rome merely set the precedent for its governors. Somewhere between 68 and 96 the attitude of the state became so fixed that proof of a definite crime was no longer required; the name "Christian" alone carried condemnation.

—*E. G. Weltin*

Additional Recommended Reading

Canfield, L. H. *The Early Persecutions of the Christians.* Vol. 138 in *Studies in History, Economics and Public Law* of Columbia University. New York: Longmans, Green, & Co., 1913. A study containing a useful history of scholarship on the Neronian persecution.

Guterman, S. L. *Religious Toleration and Persecution in Ancient Rome.* London: Aiglon Press, 1951. A well-annotated analysis of the reasons for Roman treatment of religion.

Hardy, E. R. *Christianity and the Roman Government.* London: George Allen & Unwin, 1925.

A standard treatise on Roman-Christian relations which agrees with Ramsay on the Neronian persecution.

Workman, H. B. *The Martyrs of the Early Church.* London: Charles H. Kelly, n.d. A short history of the persecution under Nero.

_____. *Persecution of the Early Church.* London: Epworth Press, 1923. A general work, larger than the one cited above.

STATEMENT OF TRAJAN'S RELIGIOUS POLICY

Type of event: Politico-religious: expression of Imperial attitude toward persecution of
  Christians
Time: c. 112
Locale: The Roman province of Bithynia in Asia Minor

Principal personages:
TRAJAN (MARCUS ULPIUS TRAJANUS), Roman Emperor 98-117
PLINY THE YOUNGER (CAIUS PLINIUS CAECILIUS SECUNDUS),
  Governor of Bithynia c. 111-114 with the title *legatus propraetore*

Summary of Event

Shortly after Pliny arrived in Bithynia he was confronted with numerous anonymous accusations against the Christians. Since he had no experience in dealing with this problem, he requested advice from the Emperor. The primary sources are Pliny's letter to the Emperor, and Trajan's reply in *Ep.* 96 and 97.

The Emperor is presented with three questions. First, should a distinction be made in age or sex, or "should the weakest offenders be treated exactly like the stronger"? Second, should pardon be given to those who recant, or must they be punished nonetheless for having been Christians? Third, does punishment attach to the mere name of Christian apart from the secret crimes allegedly committed by the new sect, or are Christians to be punished only for the actual crimes they may commit?

Pliny continues by reviewing the actions he has already taken against the Christians. Whenever accusations were made against them he brought them to trial. Some denied that they had ever been Christians, and they offered proof by worshiping with incense and wine before a statue of the Emperor; after they had reviled Christ, they were released. A second group admitted having been Christian but asserted that they had ceased to be such; these also were released after making offerings to the Emperor and reviling Christ. The third group, those who confessed to be-

ing Christians, were allowed three opportunities to recant, and those who refused were either put to death, or in the case of Roman citizens, remanded to Rome for sentencing.

Pliny also reported that his investigation of the Christians indicated they were a relatively harmless cult whose only guilt consisted in the habit of meeting "on a certain fixed day before it was light, when they sang in alternate verses a hymn to Christ, as to a god, and bound themselves by a solemn oath not to do any wicked deeds." The torture of two female slaves styled deaconesses revealed to the governor that the new religion was merely, "a perverse and extravagant superstition." The letter concludes with the observation that because of these stringent measures against the Christians, "the almost deserted temples begin to be resorted to, long disused ceremonies of religion are restored, fodder for victims finds a market, whereas buyers until now were very few."

Trajan's reply, embodying his statement of religious policy, is here cited in full. "You have adopted the proper course, my dear Secundus, in your examination of the cases of those who were accused to you as Christians, for indeed nothing can be laid down as a general ruling involving something like a set form of procedure. They are not to be sought out; but if they are accused and convicted, they must be punished—yet on this condi-

172

tion, that whoever denies himself to be a Christian and makes the fact plain by his action, that is, by worshiping our gods, shall obtain pardon on his repentance, however suspicious his past conduct may be. Papers, however, which are presented unsigned ought not to be admitted in any charge, for they are a very bad example and unworthy of our time."

The Emperor's reply placed the issue into the category of administrative procedure rather than Imperial law. Christians were not to be treated as common criminals, but if they menaced the peace and order of society they were to be punished. While the statement against anonymous accusations worked in favor of the Christians, it is clear that the open profession of Christianity continued to constitute an offense. This seems evident from the statement that a man convicted of Christianity "must be punished." Some historians see in this ambiguity the administrator's desire for peace and the prudence which would let sleeping dogs lie. On the other hand, the most famous criticism of this policy was Tertullian's diatribe, some years later, which scornfully exclaimed: "What a decision, how inevitably entangled. He says they must not be sought out, implying they are innocent; and he orders them to be punished, implying they are guilty. He spares them and he rages against them, he pretends not to see and he punishes" (*Apology* 2:8).

Pertinent Literature

Ramsay, William M. "Pliny's Report and Trajan's Rescript," in *The Church in the Roman Empire.* Ch. IX, pp. 196-225. London: Hodder & Stoughton, 1907.

Ramsay places the question in the larger context of unrest which had prevailed in Bithynia prior to Pliny's governorship. Pliny was sent by Trajan to restore financial and political stability in the province. The Christians represented a potentially disruptive force, and their repression was an administrative, not a legal, necessity. For this reason the Emperor permitted a degree of latitude to the local authorities to deal with each case as it arose.

The author insists that there was no express law or formal edict against the Christians in particular, nor were they apparently prosecuted for infraction of any specific laws of religion. They were judged and condemned by Pliny, with the later approval of Trajan, by virtue of the *imperium* delegated to the governor, to search out and punish all thieves, brigands, kidnapers, and fomenters of unrest. Even so, since the time of Nero the Christians had been classed as outlaws, *hostes publici,* and enemies of society and the government. The admission of the name Christian itself, therefore, entailed condemnation. This policy was already well established before Trajan took the purple.

Ramsay interprets Trajan's reply as a concession to the Christians. While the Emperor felt bound to carry out the established principle, he personally was opposed to it, and he suggested that Pliny ignore the Christians unless his attention was specifically addressed to an individual case by an accuser who appeared to demand Imperial interference. "Trajan's language is that of one who feels unable to contravene or to abrogate an existing principle of the imperial government, but who desires this principle to be applied with mildness and not insisted on." Ramsay believes that this view coincided with Pliny's thinking, and that the style of his letter to Trajan already suggested this solution to the Emperor.

There appears little concrete evidence to support the view of Eusebius, that a persecution of some magnitude occurred under Trajan. Rather it seems that Trajan's religious policy was on the whole successful in pre-venting large scale suffering by the Christians.

Canfield, Leon H. *The Early Persecutions of the Christians.* (Vol. 55 in *Studies in History, Economics, and Public Law,* No. 2.) New York: Columbia University Press, 1913.

Canfield's study begins with an investigation of the legal basis of the persecutions and ends with the attitude of Hadrian toward the Christians. Part II of the book contains primary source selections and source analyses for relations between the Church and the state up to A.D. 138. Chapter IV is entitled "Trajan and the Christians."

Canfield assumes that Pliny was simply following precedent by persecuting those Christians who were brought before him. Upon further investigation, "his conscience began to trouble him," when he realized the harmless nature of the sect. He then found it necessary to justify his action by emphasizing the Christians' stubbornness and inflexible obstinacy. When more and more accusations were made, the governor felt constrained to appeal to the Emperor for an opinion. Canfield agrees with Ramsay that the object of Pliny's letter "was to secure a modification of the whole imperial policy toward the Christians." Trajan was impressed by Pliny's suggestion, and his rescript indicated that henceforth a *laissez faire* attitude was in order so long as the Christians did not cause a disturbance. Both authors are also agreed on the possibility of anti-Christian feeling being generated by the business community in Bithynia, which according to Pliny's account had suffered losses from the conversion of large numbers to the new faith.

Canfield disagrees with Ramsay in one significant particular. He maintains that the rescript "is the first legal authorization of persecution, or at least the first that we know anything about." The rescript was therefore not to be considered merely as administrative policy, but it had the force of law. Christians were henceforth punishable for the "Name only," *nomen ipsum,* irrespective of other crimes which may have been associated with the sect. But anything like a general persecution was out of the question since Christians were not to be sought out.

The rescript was directed to a governor of a particular province, and its application could legally extend only to that province. But inasmuch as it was an expression of the imperial will, it would be respected wherever it was known. It soon came to widespread attention when Pliny's collected letters were published a few years later. — *Carl A. Volz*

Additional Recommended Reading

Frend, W. H. C. *Martyrdom and Persecution in the Early Church.* Oxford: Basil Blackwell, 1965. Frend believes that the justification for persecution of the Christians in Bithynia lay in their being classed as illegal Judaistic *collegia,* suspected of conspiratorial inclinations.

Grant, Robert M. *The Sword and the Cross.* New York: The Macmillan Company, 1955. Grant sees Trajan's religious policy as part of his larger concern to pacify and unify the empire.

Hardy, E. R. *Christianity and the Roman Government. A Study in Imperial Administration.* London: George Allen & Unwin, 1906, reprinted 1925. A treatment of the operation of the political machinery as it affected Christians.

Mattingly, H. *Christianity in the Roman Empire.* New York: W. W. Norton & Co. Inc., 1967.

Statement of Trajan's Religious Policy

An account of the difficulties between Christians and the state.

Sherwin-White, A. N. "Trajan's Replies to Pliny: Authorship and Necessity," in *Journal of Roman Studies.* Vol. 52, London: 1962, pp. 114-125. An examination of the correspondence in light of what is known of Roman imperial administration.

GAIUS' EDITION OF THE *INSTITUTES* OF ROMAN LAW

Type of event: Legal: development in the codification of law
Time: c. 165
Locale: Rome

Principal personages:
GAIUS, Roman jurist and author
JUSTINIAN, Byzantine Emperor 527-565, who imitated Gaius in his
work

Summary of Event

When Justinian in the sixth century published his monumental codification of Roman law known as *Corpus Juris Civilis*, he proscribed the use of any other legal texts. As a result the older collections lay unused and forgotten, falling prey during the course of centuries to the ravages of time. Since Justinian also ordered that all excerpts included in his *Code* should be altered if necessary to make them consistent with contemporary legal practice, it seemed impossible for modern scholars to ascertain the ancient texts. It was therefore of some importance to legal historians when B. C. Niebuhr, a German scholar of the early nineteenth century, discovered a fifth century text of the *Institutes* of Gaius, hitherto known only from fragments in the *Digest* (part of Justinian's *Code*) and barbaric codes of the sixth century.

Gaius, the author of this textbook of Roman law, is a shadowy figure. Although his *Institutes* was prescribed as a basic text in the law schools of the Western Empire and citations from eighteen of his works appear in Justinian's *Code*, he does not seem to have been cited by other jurists. From the text it would appear that the *Institutes* was compiled shortly after A.D. 162. Other than this dating, and the fact that he may have studied and taught at Rome, little else is known about Gaius. Even his complete name remains unknown.

Since it was meant to be a textbook, the work is devoid of penetrating analyses of law or profound solutions to complex legal problems. Nevertheless, it is important to legal historians and students for several reasons. It remains the only authentic work of classical legal scholarship still extant and unaltered by the ministers of Justinian. More than that, however, it provides insights into classical Roman law which would not otherwise be available. It is from the *Institutes* of Gaius, for example, that we obtain knowledge of the *legis actiones*, or "laws of actions," of ancient Roman law. Apparently in early Roman law a plaintiff could initiate an action or claim at law only by using one of the five distinct ritual modes, or *actiones*, recognized as legal. These ritual formulas did not cover, as might be expected, all possible situations; and even when the situation was covered by an appropriate action, the plaintiff had to take care to state his claim in words acceptable to the formula pertinent to his situation. Gaius gives a clear example of this anomaly when he states, in the *Institutes* 4:11, that "the actions of the practice of older times were called *legis actiones* either because they were the creation of statutes . . . or because they were framed in the very words of statutes and were consequently treated as no less immutable than statutes." He cites the case of a man who, when suing for the cutting down of his vines, would lose his claim if

176

he referred to "trees," since "the law of the Twelve Tables, on which his action for the cutting down of his vines lay, spoke of cutting down trees in general."

These actions were probably a form of verbal combat, the vestigial remains of a time when Roman society had recently emerged from a primitive state and was making its first attempts to regulate self-help. Although by Gaius' time the *legis actiones* were obsolete, his discussion of this ancient form of litigation is valuable for our knowledge of ancient Roman law and to our understanding of the reasons which underlay the development of the legal system and gave it form.

Even a cursory reading of Gaius' *Institutes* will indicate that it is the model followed by Justinian in his *Institutes* published as an introduction to his *Corpus Juris Civilis.* Justinian, following Gaius, divided Roman law into three main categories: the law of persons; the law of things; and the law of obligations. Although there is some overlapping, the first section contains those laws referring to people, the second refers to the rights and duties of persons, and the third contains laws relating to remedies, or the way in which rights and duties are to be enforced or protected. We would call this last section procedural law. What Justinian derived from Gaius he passed on to the world, for all legal systems are generally divided into these three categories. While Gaius was not clear about the divisions, he nevertheless bequeathed to us, through Justinian, a method of studying and teaching our law which has clarified it and made it more concise and manageable.

The *Institutes* of Gaius, therefore, offers us more than an opportunity to read an authentic document of ancient classical law; it allows us also to understand more about Roman law in general and our own approaches to modern law and legal philosophy.

Pertinent Literature

Zulueta, Francis de. *The Institutes of Gaius.* Text and Commentary. Oxford: The Clarendon Press, 1953, revised 1967. 2 vols.

Fundamental to an appreciation of Gaius is a knowledge of the text. Since few sources of Roman law are readily available in English for the student, the work of Zulueta provides a convenient edition of Gaius' *Institutes.* In fact, this clear translation, rendered difficult only by the subject itself, is indispensable for anyone wishing to come to grips with Roman law.

Zulueta also provides a companion volume to serve as a guide to, and discussion of, the text. The commentary avoids digressions into Roman legal history, which is left for the many general texts now available on the subject. To read the law of Gaius profitably, both volumes of Zulueta should be used simultaneously. Even then many students will find these volumes confusing since they presume some knowledge of Roman classical law.

In the *Institutes* IV:30-31 may be found Gaius' discussion of the formulary system. These sections, along with Zulueta's commentary, give valuable insights into the profound changes which affected the Roman system of pleading. Whereas the issue at court had previously to be formulated in *certa verba*, or ritual formula, the *Lex Aebutia* (c. 130 B.C.) and two *Leges Juliae* (17-16 B.C.) eventually replaced the formulary system, or "litigation by adapted pleading." In the latter method the phraseology in which the charge was couched was arrived at by means of rational discussion between the parties before a judge. The written document which resulted and on which the case was tried was thus adapted to the particular situation. Gaius explains that the old *legis actiones,* or ritual system, fell into disuse because "the excessive technicality of the early makers of the law was carried so far that a party who made the slightest mistake lost his case." Zulueta in his commentary notes that the formulary system arose in the praetor's court to provide remedies for situations where the law was inapplicable.

In these two volumes the reader will be able to see at work certain basic principles of Roman law which have been influential in legal history ever since. Justice and equity are apparent in the law as we have it in Gaius. Ulpian once wrote: "Justice is the art of doing what is good and equitable." Nowhere is this more apparent than in the transformation of the Roman method of pleadings. By the time of Justinian, bureaucracy and autocracy had eroded the vitality of Roman law, but in Gaius' *Institutes* this vitality is evident. Roman law was then a natural part of the social, human condition of Rome. Zulueta's book and its companion commentary give the student a totally authentic view not only of Roman law in its prime but also of Roman life and thought. Together, they open a window on the world of Rome and its law in the second century of the Christian era.

McDonnell, Sir John, and Edward Manson, eds. *Great Jurists of the World.* Vol. II of *Continental Legal History* series. New York: Augustus M. Kelley, 1968.

This volume contains a series of biographies of great lawyers. The first of these deals with Gaius. While this article is dated, having been originally published in 1914, it still provides the student with a generally good introduction to the man and his work. In discussing Gaius' life and his name, the various theories regarding his origins and his real name are examined. While such discussion may interest some, it reveals only the fact that most details about Gaius' life are still a mystery.

There is a section on the history of the *Institutes,* its barbarization by the Germanic peoples, its revival in the eleventh century, and its indirect influence on the French Civil Code of 1804. The story of the manuscript and its discovery illustrates the tenuous strands by which we are guided in our study of the past.

The final section of the article is reserved for an examination of the strengths and weaknesses of the *Institutes.* Clarity of expression and the logic of its arrangement mark the book. As the authors indicate, the *Institutes* is not a profound work of legal wisdom searching out the intricacies of Roman law; it is, as it was meant to be, a clear and simple exposition of the main rules of Roman law, to be used by the student as an introduction to the study of this complex legal system. It still serves that purpose today. — *J. A. Wahl*

Additional Recommended Reading

Buckland, William. *A Textbook of Roman Law from Augustus to Justinian.* 3rd revised ed. Cambridge: The University Press, 1963. A study that contains frequent references to Gaius' work.

Hazeltine, H. D. "Gaius," in *Encyclopaedia of the Social Sciences.* Vols. 5 and 6, pp. 544-545. New York: The Macmillan Company, 1932. This article summarizes, with brief bibliography, what we know of Gaius and his contribution to legal history.

Nicholas, Barry. *An Introduction to Roman Law.* Oxford: The Clarendon Press, 1962. A work

that discusses the history and impact of the *Institutes* on the work of Justinian.
Wolff, Hans Julius. *Roman Law: An Historical Introduction.* Norman: University of Oklahoma Press, 1951, reprinted 1964. Wolff emphasizes the importance of the *Institutes* as an aid to studying the rise of scientific jurisprudence in Rome.

FORMULATION OF ULPIAN'S DICTUM

Type of event: Legal: statement on theories of government
Time: c. 220
Locale: Rome

Principal personages:
DOMITIUS ULPIANUS (ULPIAN), classical jurist who was Praetorian
  Prefect in 222
ACCURSIUS, famous glossator and professor of Roman Law at
  Bologna
HENRY DE BRACTON, English jurist
HOSTIENSIS (HENRY DE SEGUSIO), influential canonist
BARTOLUS OF SASSOFERRATO, important Roman lawyer
BALDUS DE UBALDIS, Roman lawyer and canonist

Summary of Event

One of the most famous phrases in the *Digest* of Justinian's *Corpus Juris Civilis*, or Body of Civil Law, is Ulpian's statement concerning the origin of the Emperor's authority: "What pleases the prince has the force of law since by the *lex regia* which was passed concerning his authority, the people transfers to him and upon him the whole of its own authority and power."

Early Roman law asserted that law was an enactment of the whole people in assembly. In time, however, decrees of the senate were accepted as replacements for laws because of the impracticality of calling together and consulting the entire populus. By the first century A.D., however, the power of the *princeps* had so overshadowed the authority not only of the people but also of the senate that it could no longer be ignored. While it was an established fact of political life that imperial decrees were also laws, Ulpian attempted to protect the ancient popular rights by assuming that this authority rested on a grant of power by the people through a so-called *lex regia*. There is no evidence of such a law except possibly an extant *lex de imperio Vespasiani* (A.D. 69-70), whereby the Emperor Vespasian was granted sovereignty and in

which are mentioned the rights held by his predecessors. It is doubtful that any such formal grant was made later than that. In this fiction of the *lex regia* Ulpian clothed an absolutist reality with a veneer of constitutionalism.

Thus, two apparently contradictory concepts are contained in this one statement: unlimited imperial authority and the ultimate sovereign rights and power of the people. This opinion of Ulpian caused the Roman people no difficulty since the power of the Emperor was a fact, while the sovereignty of the people was a theory accepted by all, even the emperors.

But in the course of the Middle Ages two divergent traditions developed from Ulpian's statement: the absolutist and the constitutional concepts of monarchy. Ulpian's dictum did not create these terms of reference, but supporters on either side of the issue made use of his authority after the rediscovery of Roman law in the eleventh century.

In the twelfth century a doctrine of sovereignty arose which ascribed to the ruler an absolute plenitude of power; all inferior authority came by way of delegation. The adherents of this doctrine pointed to the first part of Ulpian's statement that the prince's will has the force of law. Not only was he unfettered by any statute but he could also apply or break them as he felt the circumstances warranted.

One such proponent was Henry de Bracton, a jurist of Henry II of England and a writer on English law, who concluded from the "quod principi" dictum that the king as supreme lawgiver could not be legally bound by any earthly authority or law even though he was morally bound to obey the law. Legally the ruler was an absolute ruler; morally he was a constitutional monarch.

Opposition to this exalted view of the monarchical office took the form of an emphasis on popular sovereignty. The proponents of this view also utilized Ulpian's dictum laying their stress on the second part. The king's power, according to them, rested on a grant of authority by the people. Should the people be convinced that he was not acting in their interests they could legally depose him and choose a new ruler.

Since both camps appealed with equal vehemence to Ulpian in support of their arguments, the discussion quickly began to revolve around the question of the nature of the cession authority to the king by the people. The proponents of the absolutist view, while conceding that a grant of authority had been made, insisted that it was irrevocable and complete. Not only were the people powerless to rescind the grant they had made; they, in fact, no longer possessed any legislative power. Among the advocates of this view was Accursius, who wrote what became the standard gloss, or commentary, on Justinian's Code, and Hostiensis, one of the foremost canonists of the thirteenth century. Hostiensis, who studied at Bologna and lectured in Paris, was particularly influential. He served Henry III of England and Pope Innocent IV, and became Cardinal Bishop of Ostia. His two commentaries on the Decretals, written between 1250 and 1271, assured his fame. Bartolus of Sassoferrato and Baldus de Ubaldis, two of the greatest Roman lawyers of the fourteenth century, also supported the absolutist powers of the prince.

The Enlightenment did much to settle the question by advocating the doctrine that the will of the people was the ultimate authority in government. Modern democratic countries have determined that in the final analysis Ulpian, though removed from us by many years, was nevertheless correct when he proposed that the ruler's authority was founded ultimately on the will of the people.

Pertinent Literature

Gierke, Otto. *Political Theories of the Middle Ages.* Translated by Frederic William Maitland. Boston: Beacon Press, 1958.

This book is an extract translated from a larger German work originally published in 1900; it is part of the German nineteenth century effort to claim some respectable inheritance in the predominately Greco-Roman and Judeo-Christian contribution to Western thought. Gierke believed and taught that the absolutism of Roman law and the resultant flavor of the legal and political institutions of Europe were moderated and transformed by Germanic concepts of popular sovereignty.

While this learned treatise is not a study of Germanic influences on law, it is clear that Gierke expects his readers to entertain certain assumptions. One concerns the character of law itself. As something rooted in a nomadic tribe and not in territory, law assumed a certain basic independence of time and place in the early German mind. It was not made by anyone but built into the very nature of things and so well understood that it could remain oral. New laws, when they were needed, were merely discoveries of laws already in existence in custom. The state existed only within the framework of preexisting law and indeed for the law's sake. This idea that the state's existence was bound up with, and regulated by, the law had to be modified in the face of other influences so that the state became a creature of need and necessity and its relation to law more creative than receptive. Yet the medieval world compromised on this point only so far; it continued to insist that the law was equal to the state and did not depend upon the state for its existence.

The idea that the ruler is subject to this law and cannot set aside what it guarantees, naturally follows. Kingship, then, is not a right but a duty, an office, a service leaving the ruler anything but absolute. Any violation of trust is tyranny and the perpetrator is subject to removal by the people. Indeed the best German law, according to Gierke, supports even the idea of the contract between state and people. The idea is obvious when one realizes that power escheats to the people when no rightful emperor exists. This dispensation came clearly into notice when Jurists had to find an explanation for the transfer of empire from the Greeks, through the Romans, to the Germans. The *consensus populi* mentioned in Charles the Great's coronation was the true act of transfer; the pope merely executed the will of the people. Elec-

tive monarchy, a dispensation under which electors act for the entire people of the realm, was a most fitting arrangement in the German medieval empire.

Another assumption dictated that law reflected the idea of primitive German fellowship with its sense of basic equality and its assumption that the right of the group as a whole takes precedence. The will of the people, then, is the source of temporal power and the ruler must consult with the assembly of the folk. The idea of lordship was encouraged partly by the patristic teaching of the Fall of Man.

Only in the twelfth century did emperorship begin to acquire absolutist overtones through jurists who claimed a plenitude of power similar to Roman caesars by citing Ulpian's dictum. Soon this absolutism began to attach itself to all monarchs, as kings argued that they were emperors in their own domains. This plenitude of power absolved them from subjection to the positive law while in scholastic terms they remained subject to divine law and natural law. Nonetheless, ideas of popular sovereignty, again based on another interpretation of Ulpian, did not die out. Thinkers such as Marsilius of Padua and William of Occam argued that the people could judge and depose a tyrant or a ruler neglectful of his duties. Presumably Gierke would agree that modern concepts of the state are in part a return to early Germanic contributions.

McIlwain, Charles Howard. *Constitutionalism: Ancient and Modern.* Rev. ed. Ithaca: Cornell University Press, 1947.

In this small but important book, Professor McIlwain offers two excellent chapters on constitutionalism in which he discusses the meaning and impact of Ulpian's dictum. While some of his theories have been savagely criticized, they still present challenging interpretations of the role of Roman law and

more particularly of Roman concepts of absolutism in the formation of Western political thought.

The author claims that, contrary to some modern writers, notably Gierke, Rome's major contribution was not limited to the absolutist maxim "What pleases the prince has the force of law." In fact, the strength of constitutionalism is reflected in the fact that it was not until the third century A.D. that we find such a statement. Even this statement by Ulpian is qualified by the words which follow it and state that the authority of the prince was the result of a *lex* of the people granting such authority. It is well to remember that in Roman law a *lex* was an agreement or contract binding two parties and that in public law it was a common agreement binding all the people. As McIlwain sees it, the political implications of Roman law and Ulpian's dictum are constitutional.

The author places a series of definite conclusions before the reader. The first and perhaps most important is that the true essence of the Roman political system and public law was constitutionalism, not absolutism. He claims that too much currency has been given to the first part of Ulpian's dictum and not enough to the fact that the people were the ultimate source of authority. His second conclusion is simply a statement that with the rediscovery of Roman law in the eleventh century and the study of the *Corpus Juris Civilis*, Roman political ideas and institutions had a great impact on the emerging states of Western Europe. McIlwain's third conclusion follows from the first two. The real influence of Roman law, as he sees it, was not in the movement towards absolutism witnessed after the Renaissance but in the strengthening of constitutionalism during the

Middle Ages.

The author studies this constitutionalism of the Middle Ages in the writings of Henry de Bracton, great English jurist of the thirteenth century. He discusses Bracton's treatment of Ulpian's dictum in some detail. Professor McIlwain asserts that whereas Justinian said that the prince's will had the force of law because (*cum*) all power had been conceded to him by the people, Bracton, by changing the translation, says the prince's will has the force of law together with (*cum*), or if it accords, the *lex regia*. The *lex regia* does not confer all the people's authority on the prince; rather it limits his authority to act in accord with the solemn promises made at the time of his coronation.

However, McIlwain sees a problem in that Bracton in other places says that the king has no peer on earth and is subject to God alone. The question whether Bracton was an absolutist or a constitutionalist is solved by distinguishing between government and jurisdiction. In government, that is, in the right of the king to preserve the peace and justice of the realm, the king has no peer. In jurisdiction, the individual application of law to particular circumstances, the king is bound by oath to proceed according to law. It is in this practical administration of the realm that McIlwain sees the great constitutionalism of England, a trait received from Roman law as much as from anywhere else.—*J. A. Wahl*

Additional Recommended Reading

Kern, Fritz. *Kingship and Law in the Middle Ages.* "Studies in Mediaeval History," Vol. IV. Translated by H. B. Chrimes. Oxford: Basil Blackwell, Ltd., 1956. A discussion of the Germanic contribution to medieval law.

Lewis, Ewart K. *Medieval Political Thought.* Vol. I. New York: Alfred A. Knopf, Inc., 1954. Selections of readings from various medieval authors who support popular sovereignty appear in this work.

McIlwain, Charles H. *The Growth of Political Thought in the West.* New York: The Macmillan Company, 1932. A study from ancient times to the fifteenth century, pointing out that medieval thought is a combination of elements.

Tierney, Brian. "Bracton on Government," in *Speculum*. XXXVIII, no. 2 (April, 1963), 295-317. Tierney shows that the only sanction on a king is a moral one.

Ullmann, Walter. *Principles of Government and Politics in the Middle Ages*. New York: Barnes & Noble, 1961. An excellent presentation of the ambivalence of medieval political theory.

INAUGURATION OF THE DOMINATE

Type of event: Constitutional: change in political theory
Time: 284
Locale: The Roman Empire

Principal personages:
DIOCLETIAN (GAIUS AURELIUS VALERIUS DIOCLETIANUS), Roman
    Emperor 284-305
MAXIMIAN (MARCUS AURELIUS VALERIUS MAXIMIANUS), Roman
    Emperor 285-305
GALERIUS (GAIUS GALERIUS VALERIUS MAXIMIANUS), Roman
    Emperor 293-311
CONSTANTIUS (FLAVIUS VALERIUS CONSTANTIUS CHLORUS), Roman
    Emperor 293-306

Summary of Event

The era of the Roman Empire has been traditionally divided into these two great periods: the Principate as founded by Augustus, and the Dominate as reconstituted by Diocletian. The difference in tone between the two periods is well indicated by their separate names: Principate, derived from *princeps,* or "first man," indicates that the emperor was, at least in theory, a constitutional magistrate. Dominate, on the other hand, taken from *dominus,* lord or master, acknowledges the fact that the emperor was an absolute ruler.

From the assassination of Alexander Severus in 235 to the accession of the Dalmatian peasant Diocletian in 284, the Roman Empire had been in a state of almost continuous anarchy. Thanks to assassinations and wars, only one of the more than twenty emperors who ruled during this period had died a natural death. Ruinous taxes, a plague that lasted from 253 to 268, wars with the Persians, and barbarian threats further afflicted the Empire.

In the face of these difficulties Diocletian effected a series of controversial reforms. Changes to make the army more mobile, arrangement for planned retirement of em-

perors after twenty years and for peaceful successions by trained caesars, and division of the state into four major districts with courts and capitals at Nicomedia, Milan, Trier, and Sirmium were ways in which Diocletian sought to eliminate some of the major difficulties. To facilitate collection of taxes and to curtail the power of provincial governors, Diocletian further divided the Empire for administrative purposes into twelve dioceses each under a vicar subject to the praetorian prefect of his respective Augustus or Caesar, and he enlarged the number of provinces to one hundred. In the new provincial arrangement military authority was separated from the civil, the former under *duces* or "dukes," the latter under *comites* or "counts." The old haphazard land tax was replaced with a new system based upon a division of land into *juga* of uniform value in each diocese and a similar division of men and animals into units known as *capita.* At stipulated periods praetorian prefects had to estimate the budget in terms of goods, and make an assessment, or *indictio,* according to *juga* and *capita.*

These reforms, however wise or necessary, were not made without cost. Already during the Severi, the emperorship and the state had been brutalized by falling under military domination. Liturgies had to be resorted to in order to bolster the flagging collection of taxes. Rich men and members of *collegia* were forced to provide free services and supplies in order to balance the budget. During the Severi, moreover, the classical age of Roman jurisprudence, law divorced both criminal and civil jurisdiction from vestiges of Republican institutions such as the senate of Rome, which under Diocletian became a provincial city. Ulpian's dictum well presaged the absolutism of Diocletian in asserting that the "will of the prince has the force of law." It was becoming more and more obvious that citizens were existing for the benefit of the state rather than the other way round.

Diocletian's reign can readily be seen as representative of this trend toward totalitarian control. The cost of supporting four elaborate courts and the enlarged army added to the burden of the already impoverished economy. Inadequate issuance of new gold and silver coins and over-devaluation of others encouraged rapid inflation. Consequently, in 301 Diocletian attempted to control the economy by issuing his famous Edict of Prices fixing the maximum that could be paid for all kinds of goods and services. Despite severe penalties, the law proved to be unworkable

and eventually had to be permitted to lapse. To prevent people from avoiding the more thorough collection of taxes, farmers became bound to their land and workmen to their trades; moreover, sons had to take up the same labors as their fathers, thereby creating a kind of serfdom in the country and a caste system in the cities.

Indicative of the new atmosphere, Diocletian introduced an elaborate ceremonial protocol into his court borrowed from Persian and earlier Hellenistic rulers. On formal occasions he wore a robe of purple silk and shoes adorned with jewels. He insisted upon being styled *dominus*, or lord; those admitted to his presence had to perform, now before a throne, the oriental *proskynesis*, or prostration, to kiss the hem of his robe. Many profess to see in the declining art of the period the trend toward domination by the emperor.

Finally, although not as an innovator, Diocletian took control over the consciences of his subjects. A conservative polytheist convinced that the prosperity of the state depended upon the favor of the gods, he issued decrees against Manichaeans in 297 and instituted the great persecution against the Christians in 303-304. This dragnet, which required all to display a certificate of sacrifice to the gods, came to a permanent end only with the Edict of Milan in 313 and the so-called "Peace of the Church."

Pertinent Literature

Mattingly, Harold B. "The Imperial Recovery," and W. Ensslin, "The Reforms of Diocletian," in *The Cambridge Ancient History.* Vol. XII, pp. 297-408. New York: The Macmillan Company, 1939.

Whether the good features of Diocletian's reforms could have been achieved without the imposition of so many burdens upon the citizenry is a debatable question. Both Mattingly in describing the character and rule of Diocletian, and Ensslin in recording his reforms, seem to feel that the Emperor's

positive contributions outweigh the negative contingencies involved in them. To his contemporaries, as recorded in the *Scriptores Historiae Augustae*, Diocletian was an "object of intense admiration," wise, subtle, and divinely favored. Even when he surrounded himself with kingly display and religious awe, he was constantly thinking of the welfare of the Empire. Since the Roman senate had lost its usefulness, the Imperial office had to be reinterpreted and made the center of national life; since neglect of the gods had been the cause of numerous disasters, reverence had to be shown again to them; since the problems of rule were too great for a single man, Diocletian had to choose men to assist him in this task, "and nothing showed his genius better than his power to choose them well."

Mattingly believes that history's favorable verdict on Diocletian is justified. His entire program was successful except for his religious policy, which Constantine handled better. But even here he is excused on the grounds that as an old man and an innate conservative, his love of the old religion could never permit him to accept the new. Otherwise, "he vindicated the majesty of Rome" by reasserting the supremacy of her arms throughout the Empire. More important, "he rebuilt the State on new foundations and gave her under changed forms a new lease of life." His ingenious system of government successfully circumvented the dangers which overwhelmed his predecessors, the ending of military anarchy being especially important.

Ensslin goes even further than Mattingly. He considers that, despite his innovations, Diocletian's government was markedly conservative. Following in the steps of his Illyrian and Pannonian predecessors and compatriots, Diocletian strove to maintain and

invigorate the idea of old Rome. As a rough soldier he was probably not inspired by any romantic attachment to the past glories of ancient Rome but convinced by his experience that affairs worked better when the emperors, the army, the civil service, and the people themselves were Roman in spirit, a spirit best expressed in the old religion and law. Consequently his rescripts show an attempt to check the further infiltration of Greek legal concepts into Roman law, and he insisted upon Latin being used as the official language of the state although his capital was far away in Nicomedia. He strove to win the protection of the gods by a revival of the old Roman piety and morality. Even his vicious attitude toward the Christians, assumed after an earlier period of toleration, is explained by his disappointed hopes that these people affected by a foreign superstition would change their ways and become good Romans.

The burdens which Diocletian imposed upon his subjects were inevitable considering the conditions of the times; his failure consisted only in being unable to train his subjects to take a personal interest in the political life around them. He was "the man whom the state needed," the first emperor "to gather together into a completed whole the various experiments and expedients of his predecessors." He managed to preserve civilization long enough by creating a firm basis for a new imperial system so that Christianity's Constantine could build upon it.

Rostovtzeff, Mikhail. *A History of the Ancient World.* Vol. II: *Rome.* Translated by J. D. Duff. Oxford: The Clarendon Press, 1928.

While Rostovtzeff does not deny that Diocletian was a great man, he prefers to dwell upon the deplorable conditions in the Empire which he feels were little alleviated by the Emperor. He aptly heads his chapter dealing with Diocletian: "The Military Despotism of the East." While he judges the Emperor's extensive program of reform generally prudent, he attributes whatever success it attained not to any outstanding genius on the Emperor's part but rather to the exigencies of the time out of which his program evolved. Not an innovator, Diocletian merely built into a legalized system what had grown up in the confusion of a weary and disgusted age. Included in this program was recognition of the

unmistakable trend toward the absolute character of the emperorship, which more and
more was copying the manner of the Sassan-
ian kings of the East. Diocletian's reforms
were, then, not chiefly concerned with the
welfare of the people but with the regeneration of the corporate state. "He sacrificed,"
says Rostovtzeff, "the interests of the people
to the public advantage more decidedly than
any of his predecessors." The army and the
Emperor dominated public life, and the army
was composed mostly of backward barbarian
troops, especially Germans, soldiers who were
the more highly prized in proportion as they
had less of an ancient civilization in their
background.

The burdens of military demands and of
administrative reforms as well as the cost of
new courts, buildings, necessary roads, forts,
and town walls all were aggravated by pecu-
lation on all sides. Consequently matters did
not improve much even after Diocletian reorganized the Empire. In a state already reduced to beggary, normal conditions were
only made less possible by Diocletian's efforts which laid additional imposts on the
people. The emperor merely succeeded in
giving "order and system to the oppression
and coercion by which the empire was governed in the third century." In simplifying
taxation he was merely adjusting it to the
demands of a primitive economic system in
an "impoverished and degenerate state."

Everywhere the citizen was subjected to
the service of the state. Town councils responsible for local taxes found their position
intolerable. By freezing to their trades the
working classes in industry and transporta-
tion, free Roman citizens were virtually con-
verted into state serfs. "Under Diocletian

and after him, the empire did indeed establish equality among most of its subjects, in
the sense that all alike were beggars and
slaves." Tillers of the soil fell more and more
in debt, landlords were ruined, and land went
out of cultivation. Since great officials with
influence at court often could evade taxes,
many took refuge on such estates "finding
slavery to a great man better than slavery to
the state." The Emperor became an Eastern
despot, an absolute ruler dominating "an om-
nipotent bureaucracy which suppressed every
trace of self government while professing to
retain it," and lording it over a population
of serfs who lived for the establishment.
The whole prospect causes Rostovtzeff to ex-
claim: "What a departure from the Graeco-
Roman ideals of freedom and self government."

Rostovtzeff maintains that those of Diocletian's reforms which were born out of existing demands, reforms in "administration,
judicial proceedings, finance, and military
organization" did, indeed, live to influence
following centuries. But Diocletian failed in
trying to reconstitute the central authority
by attempting to mix two incompatible elements: the "magistracy of the Roman people
and a despotism of the Eastern type." These
reforms failed even in his own lifetime so
that almost immediately after his abdication in 305 civil war broke out among the
very Augusti and Caesars he himself had
appointed. Moreover, his attempts failed to
coerce the Christian Church even though as a
state within a state it presented an intolerable
condition incompatible with the program of
the despotic and absolute submission which
he required of his subjects.

—*M. Joseph Costelloe*

Additional Recommended Reading

Anderson, J. G. C. "The Genesis of Diocletian's Provincial Re-Organization," in *Journal of Roman Studies.* XXII, 1932, 24-32. Documents the gradual development of certain military and administrative policies of Diocletian.

Jones, A. H. M. *The Later Roman Empire 284-602.* Vol. I, pp. 37-76. Norman: University of Oklahoma Press, 1964. A recent scholarly account based on cited original sources.

Van Sickle, C. E. "Diocletian and the Decline of the Roman Municipalities," in *Journal of Roman Studies.* Vol. XXVIII, 1938, 9-18. Argues that the fiscal burden of the Dominate, borne by the urban middle classes, led to a marked decline in the quality of municipal life.

Vogt, Joseph. *The Decline of Rome. The Metamorphosis of Ancient Civilization.* London: Weidenfeld and Nicolson, 1967. A laudatory account of Diocletian's program.

CONVERSION OF CONSTANTINE

Type of event: Politico-religious: legalization of Christianity in the Roman Empire
Time: October 28, 312
Locale: The Milvian Bridge, a few miles north of Rome

Principal personages:
FLAVIUS VALERIUS CONSTANTINE, Emperor in the West 312-324 and sole Roman Emperor 324-337
MARCUS AURELIUS VALERIUS MAXENTIUS, son of Maximian, former coemperor with Diocletian and self-proclaimed Roman Emperor 306-312
VALERIUS LICINIUS, coemperor with Constantine 313-324, who ruled the eastern part of the Roman Empire

Summary of Event

After the abdication of Diocletian in A.D. 305, at least eight rivals emerged to claim the Imperial title. By 312, only four remained: Maxentius and Maximinus Daia were aligned against Constantine and Licinius. When Constantine defeated Maxentius at the Battle of the Milvian Bridge and Licinius conquered Maximinus Daia, the two victors divided the Roman Empire between them. The division lasted for ten years until Constantine defeated Licinius in 324 and became sole ruler.

At noon on the day before the battle against Maxentius at the Milvian Bridge, Constantine, according to Eusebius's *Life of Constantine*, saw a sign appearing in the sky as a fiery cross with the legend: "Conquer by this." The same night the Christian God allegedly appeared to him in a dream and instructed him to place the Christian emblem on the imperial standards if he wished to be victorious. Eusebius claims that he heard the story from the lips of Constantine, but he wrote after the Emperor's death and he does not tell the same tale in his *Ecclesiastical History.* Anyway, Constantine placed at the head of his legions the *labarum* displaying the famous *chi rho*, two Greek letters (the first in the Greek word for "Christ") that combine to form a cross. Subsequent victory

against Maxentius convinced Constantine that the Christian God was more powerful than the classical deities worshipped by his rivals.

Whether the Emperor's conversion was contrived or genuine is still a matter of debate, but there can be no doubt that his rule was beneficial for Christianity. In 313, he and Licinius agreed upon the terms of the so-called "Edict of Milan," granting toleration to Christianity, reimbursing Christians for losses suffered in recent persecutions, and exempting the clergy from certain compulsory civil obligations. In 315, Constantine enacted legislation which prohibited retributions against Jewish converts to Christianity, and in 318, the Emperor ordained, in a precedent-making decree, that a civil suit might, with the consent of both litigants, be removed to the jurisdiction of a bishop, whose verdict would be final. By 321, the Church could inherit property and bishops could manumit slaves. Sunday was declared a holiday for Imperial employees. By convening church councils at Arles and Nicaea, Constantine set up ecclesiastical machinery for the adjudication of problems caused by dissenting groups such as Donatists and Arians. At the first ecumenical council the Emperor himself put his prestige behind the

190

famous *homoousian* formula, which has remained Christian dogma ever since. Associating his Christian piety with the welfare of the state, Constantine built basilicas, composed prayers, and paid for translations of the Christian Scriptures. Finally, he was baptized on his deathbed by Eusebius, Bishop of Nicomedia.

Christianity's sudden change in fortune from a persecuted, outlawed sect to a tolerated and favored religion posed special problems. The attitude of the Church toward the Roman Empire underwent a drastic change. The seventeenth chapter of Revelation, probably written at the end of the first century, is generally supposed to refer to Rome when it speaks of the woman "drunk with the blood of the saints," but Eusebius now saw the emperor as the viceregent of God. Nevertheless the dilemma had to be faced concerning where jurisdictional lines should be drawn between the Church and the state. Since Christians enjoyed political preferment in the Imperial government after the conversion of Constantine, the Church in the fourth century was inundated with large numbers of half-convinced pagans. This mixed blessing led to early reform movements in the Church and the institution of monasticism. The favored position of Christianity in the Empire

also led to a different interpretation of history; whereas Christians during the persecutions had looked for the immediate return of Christ and the establishment of the new Jerusalem to replace the vicious rule of Rome, it now appeared that the golden age had dawned. Eusebius saw in Constantine the fulfillment of God's promises to his chosen people through Abraham, but so sanguine a view of the state remained typically eastern; in the West a dualist attitude which held the Church and the state in tension was destined to become dominant.

Clearly the conversion of Constantine was a turning point in Imperial and Christian history which ultimately affected the entire Western World. Historians have variously interpreted the sincerity of Constantine's change of heart. One view holds that his conversion was motivated by political expediency in order that he might use the Church for purposes of state. The opposite position maintains that Constantine's acts can be explained only in the light of a genuine change of heart and full conversion. A mediating position attempts to postulate a gradual change in the Emperor from that of a deistic humanitarian trying to integrate Christianity with the current paganism, to one of nominal conversion by the time of his death.

Pertinent Literature

Burckhardt, Jacob. *The Age of Constantine the Great.* First published, 1852. English translation by Moses Hadas. New York: Doubleday & Company, Inc., 1956.

Burckhardt deals with broader issues than religious matters, but in dealing specifically with the question of Constantine's conversion he contends that many nonreligious factors helped the triumph of Christianity, and that Constantine used shrewd political judgment in his adoption of a persecuted religion.

Burckhardt maintains that Constantine was impressed with the unity, organization, and general morality of the Christians. He be-

came convinced that support for the *imperium* might be fashioned from this core group, that he could profit personally from growing public ennui with persecution, and that general sympathy for the Christians was growing. By championing the cause of this minority group, Constantine might also gain the support of the majority. Besides, the persecutions had not succeeded, and it was good politics to abandon an unsuccessful policy.

From 312 at the time of the Battle of the Milvian Bridge until 323, there was a growing estrangement between Constantine and his eastern colleague Licinius. The latter began a persecution since he viewed Christians, with some justification, as subversive elements. Consequently Constantine's war with Licinius could have had overtones of a moral crusade to release the Christians of the East from oppression.

Burckhardt believes that the pro-Christian legislation of Constantine in itself does not indicate the true religious convictions of the Emperor. The "Edict of Milan," he holds, merely gave the Church the same privileges that other recognized religions enjoyed in the Empire, and Constantine at no time showed disfavor toward non-Christians. He maintained the office and functions of the Pontifex Maximus, and his coins still carried the pagan *Sol Invictus.* The exemption of the clergy from the *munera sordida* was simply an extension to Christian clergy of the privileges already enjoyed by pagan leaders. The Sunday holiday may, in fact, be an argument in favor of the more skeptical interpretation, since the *dies solis* was hallowed for worship by pagan devotees of the sun. The account of the conversion as given by Eusebius, Burck-

hardt continues, came a quarter of a century after the alleged event, and Eusebius himself seems to be dubious about it. The inscription of the *labarum* on Constantine's triumphal arch appears to have been a later addition superimposed on an earlier inscription "I.O.M." (*Jupiter Optimus Maximus*). According to Burckhardt, the councils convened by the Emperor were not the result of his solicitude for the Church; rather, they issued from his desire to control a factious and potentially dangerous group.

Burckhardt and others who are critical of Constantine's brand of Christianity point to his personal life after 312 as evidence that no conversion took place. Shortly after the Council of Nicaea he had his son Crispus put to death, and soon afterwards he caused his wife Fausta to be drowned. Ultimately a "crowd of friends" succumbed to the Emperor's suspicious nature. He enrolled himself as a catechumen on his deathbed because his superstitious nature called for a dramatic act to stave off impending death. Because Burckhardt believes that Eusebius tends to disregard or explain away the Emperor's less godlike qualities, he refers to Eusebius as the first completely dishonest historian.

Jones, A. H. M. *Constantine and the Conversion of Europe.* (Teach Yourself History series.) 6th ed. London: The English Universities Press, first published 1948, reprinted 1964.

Like Burckhardt, Jones treats the entire era beginning with the crisis of the Empire under Diocletian, though he gives more attention to Constantine's religious policies. Jones insists that there is no reason to doubt the good faith of either Eusebius or Constantine. He claims that the Emperor unquestionably underwent a religious experience, if not a spiritual conversion. There was an actual apparition in the sky, a "halo phenomenon" of the sun, which to Constantine's imagination was deeply significant. Thus the conversion was genuine, or at least it was not contrived

for political purposes. It is true that the Emperor did not give strong evidence of uniquely Christian morality, but this was not unusual. Ethics played a small role in the religious attitude of the average Roman, whose religion was more in the nature of a contract with deity. In this case, the Christian God gave him a victory, and thereafter Constantine was pledged to support the new faith. There was a conversion in the sense that the Emperor's policies were directly influenced by his singular experience on the eve of the battle.

The legislation of Constantine, Jones maintains, was prompted by his gratitude to the Christian God. Although it is true that the Emperor's early attitude was one of toleration only, his later activities showed definite favoritism to the Church. His erection of basilicas, payment for translation of Scripture, bestowal of lands, and his intervention in ecclesiastical affairs all stemmed from his sincere espousal of Christianity. The relative freedom which was permitted to non-Christians came not from indifference but from the conviction that true religion cannot be coerced.

Jones sees no difficulty in reconciling Constantine's retention of pagan practices with his Christianity. Retention of the title Pontifex Maximus is hardly significant for it was merely a traditional appanage of the office of Augustus. Later emperors until Gratian, who were undoubtedly Christian, likewise retained its use. Because it entitled the holder to regulate religious practices in the Empire, it was as useful to a Christian as to a non-Christian ruler. Arguments from coinage are hardly conclusive, and the retention of the *Sol Invictus* should be interpreted more as evidence of Constantine's tolerant attitude toward non-Christians than as a sign of any inner pagan commitment. Finally, the murders perpetrated within his own family were certainly prompted by the political ambitions of Crispus and the intrigues of Fausta, so that these deaths were in reality the execution of traitors. Jones suggests that the reputation of Constantine may have been clouded by his non-Christian opponents in order to discredit Christianity. If indeed this be true, the case for Constantine's Christianity is strengthened by the attempt of his detractors to discredit the new faith.

Constantine regarded himself as being responsible for the inner well-being of the Church, especially for its unity. It was for this reason that he convened the first great ecclesiastical councils. He took a keen interest in theological questions, and he always spoke of himself as a Christian by using such phrases as "our most holy religion" and "our catholic faith." Deathbed baptisms were often the rule among fourth century Christians, and the Emperor's case was not exceptional.

Jones and those who agree with him about the sincerity of Constantine's conversion insist that as a tactical move it was politically unwise. The Christians constituted a small and despised minority in the Empire, and eight years of persecution had weakened their position still further. To identify with such a group made no political sense; therefore, the answer to the problem must be found by taking the account of Eusebius seriously.

—Carl A. Volz

Additional Recommended Reading

Alfoldi, A. *The Conversion of Constantine and Pagan Rome.* Translated by Harold Mattingly. Oxford: The Clarendon Press, 1948. A work that treats the religious development of Constantine.

Baynes, N. H. "Constantine the Great and the Christian Church." The Raleigh Lecture for 1929 in *The Proceedings of the British Academy.* XV, 1929, 341-442. A thorough treatment of the questions involved.

Doerries, Hermann. *Constantine and Religious Liberty.* New Haven: Yale University Press, 1960. A study concerned with Constantine's attitude toward non-Christians and heretics.

Eusebius. *The History of the Church.* Book 10. Translated by G. A. Williamson. Baltimore: Penguin Books Inc., 1965. A lucid translation from the *Historia Ecclesiastica.*

_____. *The Life of Constantine.* Translated by E. C. Richardson. Series Two, Vol. I of *The Nicene and Post-Nicene Fathers.* Grand Rapids, Mich.: Wm. P. Eerdmans Publishing Company, 1961. Original sources, excellently translated, for the conversion of Constantine and its consequences in the history of the Church during the period of his lifetime.

Lane Fox, Robin. *Pagans and Christians.* New York: Alfred A. Knopf, 1987. An account of the civic life of paganism and Christianity in the Roman Empire and of the triumph of Christianity with the conversion of Constantine I.

MacMullen, Ramsay. *Christianizing the Roman Empire (A.D. 100-400).* New Haven, Conn.: Yale University Press, 1985. A study of the growth of Christianity in the late Roman Empire, examining the process and types of conversion from the point of view of the non-Christian.

Parker, H. M. D. *A History of the Roman World from A.D. 138 to 337.* Pp. 238-309. New York: The Macmillan Company, 1958. This study includes useful information about the conversion of Constantine and its effect in the Roman world of his time.

INCEPTION OF CHURCH-STATE PROBLEMS

Type of event: Politico-religious: development of Western political theory
Time: 313-395
Locale: Roman Empire

Principal personages:
CONSTANTINE, sole Emperor 324-337
CONSTANTIUS II, son of Constantine, Emperor in the East, 337-350, sole ruler 350-361
CONSTANS, son of Constantine and Emperor in the West 337-350
GRATIAN, Emperor in the West 375-383
THEODOSIUS, Emperor in the East 375-395, sole ruler 393-395
ATHANASIUS, Bishop of Alexandria 328-373
AMBROSE, Bishop of Milan 374-397
HILARY, Bishop of Poitiers 353-367
AUGUSTINE, Bishop of Hippo 396-430, author of the *City of God*

Summary of Event

The institutions of the Church and the Empire could be correlated in three ways: they might coexist in total separation from each other; they could exist distinguished but not necessarily separated; or they could be fused. Although from the beginning the Church had recognized the existence and legality of the Empire by including prayers for the state and the welfare of its magistrates in its litanies, the Empire did not acknowledge the legality of the Church until the Edict of Milan in 313. Before that time there was no common ground of acknowledgment on which conflicts over jurisdiction could occur. The persecuted Church enjoyed freedom in its doctrinal formulations and juridical functions because Rome denied it legal existence. It was only with the coming of toleration that the Church and the state both found it necessary to define the limits of their respective jurisdictions. The history of the solution to the problem followed two major courses. Some fourth century Fathers were agreed that the two institutions must remain fundamentally separated, especially when matters of faith were at stake. Others developed the

idea that the Church was subject to the state in all things, especially when the state religion was Christianity.

One of the primary issues in the controversy concerned the emperor's prerogatives as *pontifex maximus*. In this capacity emperors, beginning in 12 B.C., had claimed jurisdiction over all religious activities in the Empire, displaying a special solicitude for the state cult. When Christianity succeeded paganism as the state cult, the question arose whether the new religion should be governed by the same public law that had controlled earlier pagan cults. Theoretically this problem could not arise until Christianity became the officially recognized state religion under Theodosius.

Historians of the crisis see the beginning of Church-state problems arising with the activities of Constantine *vis-à-vis* the Church. Not only did the Emperor favor Christianity, but he assisted the new faith by convening councils, by actively supporting its propaganda, and by threatening heretics with civil disabilities. At the same time Constantine disclaimed any rights of defining dogma or of judging bishops in matters of the faith. He did not aspire to act as Head of the Church. Yet under him the Church and state first acknowledged each other as legal and independent institutions and thus appeared the potential for a conflict of jurisdictions.

The relationship between the Church and the state came sharply into focus when Constantius II assumed ecclesiastical prerogatives which his father, Constantine, had disclaimed. He sought to impose an Arian creed upon the bishops, but some Western clerics protested that the *libertas* of the Church was being abused. The basis for Constantius' attempts at controlling Christianity was derived from the same constitutional rules which had placed state paganism under Imperial control. The incident called forth a number of statements from Athanasius, Hilary, and Ambrose on the proper relationship between the Church and the state. These Fathers admitted no other possibility than a true and complete separation.

Although church leaders protested the encroachment of the emperor in the spiritual domain, they allowed him extensive authority in civil jurisdiction. Included in these powers was the right of defending and propagating the faith and of taking action against non-Christian cults. The Church did not protest when Constantine sent the Arians into exile following the Council of Nicaea, and the majority of churchmen acquiesced in the practice of Imperial confirmation of conciliar decrees.

Gratian was the first Emperor to refuse the title of *pontifex maximus*, and henceforth the Christian emperors derived their claims to authority over the Church from the premise that their office was conferred directly by God for the welfare of the Church. With Gratian and Theodosius the Empire became legally Christian, and the issue of Church-state relationships became even more acute. The most dramatic fourth century confrontation between bishop and emperor occurred in the controversies between Ambrose and Theodosius.

By the end of the fourth century the principle of separation between the Church and the state was well established in the West, but the Church in the East tended to look to the emperor for guidance and approval in ecclesiastical affairs. The Western tradition of separation was bequeathed to the medieval Church largely through Augustine's *City of God*. Gelasius, who was Pope in the late fifth century, laid down the principle of two jurisdictions, spiritual and temporal, in a classic form frequently referred to by later writers.

Pertinent Literature

Morrison, Karl Frederick. *Rome and the City of God.* (Vol. 54 of the Transactions of the American Philosophical Society.) Philadelphia: The American Philosophical Society, 1964.

The first part of Morrison's essay deals with the legal principles involved. Fundamental to any consideration of fourth century ecclesiology is the fact that the Church considered itself an integral juridical body, a spiritually autonomous entity. The author attacks interpretations of this period which fail to grasp the fact that the Church had its roots in Judaism, and that as the "new Israel" it inherited Judaism's place in Roman law. From Jewish tradition Christianity inherited its hierarchy, councils, manner of worship, communal consciousness, suspicion of Greco-Roman culture, and its general attitude of autonomy. A consideration of the question cannot begin with the Church under Constantine but must take into account the self-consciousness of the Church from its very beginning. The author maintains that the Roman emperors respected the Church's claim to autonomy in matters of the faith, and wherever Imperial intervention in ecclesiastical affairs occurred until the time of Theodosius, it was invited by the Church, not imposed upon it. Prime examples of his thesis are the events surrounding the councils of Nicaea, Rimini, and Constantinople. At Nicaea and Constantinople the bishops were allowed complete freedom in the exercise of their powers. At Rimini, where Constantius II attempted to force an Arian creed upon the prelates, they responded with the assertion that no creed could be established by Imperial edict and that legal competence for such establishment lay only in episcopal jurisdiction. The trials of Athanasius are offered as further evidence of ecclesiastical autonomy in that trials of bishops could be conducted only by ecclasiastical law and before episcopal, not civil, judges.

On the other hand the Church readily acknowledged the competence of the state in civil matters. Athanasius admitted that his several banishments were legal and in the jurisdiction of the civil courts. These powers, civil and criminal authority, were said to be morally neutral, but they might be enlisted by the Church in the interests of its faith, discipline, administration, and laws.

In the second section of this study Morrison analyzes the theological principles of Athanasius, Hilary, and Ambrose as they related to the state. He cites numerous references from these Fathers to indicate their awareness of the Church as having received the legacy of Judaism, of its mystical and sacramental character, and of its supratemporal nature. He concludes his study: "The fathers of the fourth century did not attempt to correlate Church and Empire as one institution. With the precedent of the Synagogue ever before them, they rather sought independent juristic existence for the two, with the Empire guaranteeing the Church's integrity."

Greenslade, S. L. *Church and State from Constantine to Theodosius.* London: Student Christian Movement Press, 1954.

Greenslade begins his treatise with an analysis of Constantine's attitude toward the Church, which he claims was generally one of active intervention with the open consent of the bishops. Any theories of separation of the two institutions in this period would be anachronistic. The sons of Constantine followed his policies. The primary reason for tensions between the Church and the state after Constantine lay in the fact that administrative responsibility was divided territorially among his sons. The Eastern bishops were favorably inclined toward semi-Arianism, the Western bishops toward the Nicene formulas. Likewise, the rulers of the Empire, Constantius II in the East and Constans in the West, supported the views of their constituents. Therefore Constans' death in A.D. 350 resulted in sole rulership by an emperor sympathetic to the Arian cause, and the Western bishops were forced into a posture of defiance from which stance they developed their concept of separation of the Church and the state. Although Constantius II claimed jurisdiction in ecclesiastical affairs, "he was not simply a tyrant. On the whole the East was behind him. He consistently upheld the majority opinion." When Gratian and Theodosius established Christianity as the state religion and proscribed paganism, the Church was "profoundly grateful."

Greenslade next turns to a consideration of caesaropapism in the fourth century, and he maintains that its alleged evils have been overstressed. The emperor, representing the laity in the councils of the Church also represented the secular and natural order. Since God cannot be excluded from the governance of the secular order, neither is it proper to seek complete separation of the sacred from the secular. In this analysis the author offers his own opinions on the proper relationships as they should exist today.

The author next analyzes the statements on separation of the Church and the state coming from the fourth century, notably those of Athanasius, Martin of Tours, and Ambrose. The theory of separation, in addition to receiving support from these Fathers, was further enhanced as the Church developed its sense of autonomy through its councils, laws, hierarchy, and territorial divisions. The establishment of the appellate jurisdiction of the Bishop of Rome accelerated the Church's sense of independence from civil jurisdiction. It was in the West that the dualistic theory was stated most clearly. Greenslade again concludes with an observation which cautions against too great a stress on dualism in contemporary political thought. "The Church is somehow concerned with every action of the State which raises a moral issue, and that is, in the last resort, with almost everything."

In his concluding section Greenslade comments on the ascendancy of the Church in the West, referring especially to the controversies between Ambrose and Theodosius. He points to the difficulties involved in trying to maintain a strict separation of the Church and the state, and he closes with the hope that the extremes of theocracy and caesaropapism can successfully be avoided.

—Carl A. Volz

Additional Recommended Reading

Armstrong, Gregory T. "Imperial Church Building and Church-State Relations, A.D. 313-363," in *Church History,* XXXVI (March 1967), no. 1, pp. 3-17. A description of the policies which governed Imperial interest in building churches from Constantine to Julian.

Cranz, F. Edward. "Kingdom and Polity in Eusebius of Caesarea," in *Harvard Theological Review,* XLV (1952), pp. 47-66. An article showing that for Eusebius both the *ecclesia* and the Empire must be closely related since both are images of the kingdom of heaven.

Geanakoplos, Deno J. "Church and State in the Byzantine Empire: A Reconsideration of the Problem of Caesaropapism," in *Church History,* XXXIV (December 1965), no. 4, pp. 381-403. A study attempting to show that although Eastern emperors succeeded in controlling the administrative machinery of the Church, few tried and none succeeded in influencing Christian theology.

Loetscher, Frederick W. "St. Augustine's Conception of the State," in *Church History,* IV (March 1935), pp. 16-41. A treatise on Augustine's "dualistic" approach in separating the Church and the state.

MacMullen, Ramsay. *Christianizing the Roman Empire (A.D. 100-400).* New Haven, Conn.: Yale University Press, 1985. A study of the growth of Christianity in the late Roman Empire, examining the process and types of conversion from the point of view of the non-Christian.

Setton, K. M. *Christian Attitude Toward the Emperor in the Fourth Century.* New York: Columbia University Press, 1941. This work is a minor classic in the field.

Williams, G. H. "Christology and Church-State Relations in the Fourth Century," in *Church History,* XX (September-December 1951), no. 3, pp. 3-33, and no. 4, pp. 3-26. A treatise maintaining that the Christian's theology of the divine and human natures of Christ had a direct influence on his conception of the emperor's role in the natural order.

FOUNDING OF CONSTANTINOPLE

Type of event: Political: establishment of Roman capital in the East
Time: 324-330
Locale: Constantinople

Principal personages:
CONSTANTINE, sole Roman Emperor 324-337

Summary of Event

Constantine the Great (c. 280-327) is remembered for three major achievements: the liberation and legal recognition of the Christian Church, the stabilization of the Imperial currency on a gold standard, and the founding of a capital which was destined to last for a thousand years as the economic and political center of the Byzantine Empire. During most of that time it was an intellectual and artistic center as well, recognized even by Western Europeans as a focal point of civilization.

Constantine started to build the city in 324, shortly after his victory over his rival Licinius. He cannot have failed to recognize the excellence of the site he had chosen. Built on the site of ancient Byzantium, Constantinople could be made almost impregnable, surrounded as it was on three sides by water: on the north by the Golden Horn, a bay seven miles long; on the south by the Sea of Marmora; and on the east by the Bosphorus. Standing at the crossing of two of the most important trade routes of the world, Constantinople commanded communications between Europe and Asia, and also controlled trade between the Mediterranean and the Black Sea. From Constantine's point of view, the location had the advantage of being strategically placed midway between the frontiers bounded by the Danube and the Euphrates. It was thus more centrally located than Rome and was situated in the more developed and prosperous part of the Empire. Byzantium had long been recognized as

an ideal location for a fortress. In the Peloponnesian War (431-404 B.C.), Greek rivals tried to secure it because it held the key to Athens' grain trade, on which her survival depended. Philip of Macedon (359-336 B.C.) and Alexander the Great (336-323 B.C.) saw Byzantium as the gateway to Asia. At least one Roman emperor before Constantine considered the old Greek city a danger to his security and withdrew its privileges. Constantine, on the other hand, found Rome with its Republican traditions uncongenial. By his time the Oriental concept of sovereignty prevailed, and he wanted a center of administration far removed from a scene hallowed by the memories of an aristocratic senate.

Constantine called his capital "New Rome," but it soon came to bear his own name. Although the inhabitants called themselves Romans, the new capital had none of Rome's constitutional prerogatives; that is, it was subject to a proconsul, and had no quaestors, tribunes of the plebs, or praetors, nor did it have a workable senate. It was, constitutionally, only one of several Imperial residences, such as those at Sardica and Nicomedia in the East, and Milan and Trier in the West. Actually, it was intended as the normal residence of the emperor and was built on a scale more magnificent than that of the other Imperial capitals. For over two centuries Constantinople was culturally a Roman city, in which the court and a large proportion of the population were Latin-speaking. The citizens of Constantinople considered themselves Romans by nationality, and as late as the twelfth century it was the boast of aristocrats that their ancestors had arrived with Constantine.

On May 11, 330, six years after it was chosen as the site of "New Rome," Constantinople was dedicated to the Holy Trinity and the Mother of God. The work of building the city had been hasty and somewhat careless. To offset this flaw, Constantinople was adorned and enriched with artistic and literary treasures sent at the Emperor's command. There was, for example, the famous bronze serpent from Delphi commemorating the Greek victory over the Persians at the Battle of Plataea in 479. To keep alive the Hellenistic culture, libraries were built and filled with Greek manuscripts.

Positive efforts were made to stimulate immigration to the new city. Settlers were encouraged by land grants on condition that they build and maintain suitable residences. This measure was aimed chiefly at the affluent. Beginning in May, 332, free daily bread was given to eighty thousand inhabitants. The purpose of this program was not to care for the indigent, but to stimulate immigration.

From the beginning, Constantinople was a Christian city, although concessions were made to pagans who lived and worked there. Pagan temples were erected to serve the many construction workers, but the city never had an official pagan cult. On the other hand, Constantinople was filled with magnificent places for Christian worship, dramatically expressing Constantine's concept of the Church as an arm of the state.

Pertinent Literature

Vasiliev, A. A. *History of the Byzantine Empire 324-1453.* Madison: University of Wisconsin Press, 1952.

This work by an eminent Russian scholar has been periodically revised since the first English edition appeared in 1929. Since that time, there have been French, Spanish, and Turkish editions. This printing incorporates the findings of much research, some of which is presented in the first chapter, dealing with tools and the history of Byzantine studies in the West and in Russia. The book is excellently annotated throughout, with a good index and an extensive bibliography.

As the title indicates, Vasiliev uses the date of the founding of Constantinople as a starting point for his study of the Byzantine Empire, thus highlighting the importance he attaches to the establishment of the new capital. He treats the foundation of the city in the context of Constantine's relations with the Church, so that the connection between the Church-state problem and the decision to establish a new capital is unmistakably clear.

Constantine played the leading role in the Council of Nicaea, which dealt with the Arian heresy. This long struggle with the Arians was a major threat to the unity and stability of the Empire in the East. In the course of this struggle, Constantine may have come to a realization of the need for an administrative center close to the scene of the struggle, but one which could not be identified with any religious faction.

Vasiliev calls the foundation of the new capital "the second event of primary importance during Constantine's reign, next to the recognition of Christianity." He traces the ancient history of the city and also discusses earlier Roman intentions to transfer the capital to the East. According to the Roman historian Suetonius, Julius Caesar wanted to move from Rome to Alexandria or to Ilion on the west coast of modern Turkey; some emperors spent long periods in the East, to the neglect of Rome. Byzantium itself, at the end of the second century, was the victim of the revenge of the Emperor Septimius Severus, who sacked the city and almost completely destroyed it because of aid it had given to his rival, Pescennius Niger.

Tradition surrounds the selection of the site with legends of supernatural intervention, important because they support Constantine's alleged claim to have been guided by divine power in his choice of the location. Not all historians agree that Constantine should be given much credit for making Constantinople the leading city of the Empire. Vasiliev calls attention to the German scholars Ernst Stein and O. Seeck, who play down the importance of the founding of Constantinople, and Ferdinand Lot, who says that the city was born out of a despot's caprice

arising from intense religious exaltation. Vasiliev's own opinion is that Constantine had the "insight of genius" and was well aware of the political, economic, and cultural advantages of the city. He concludes his treatment with a quotation from another Russian author, Th. I. Uspensky, who holds that of all Constantine's achievements, the founding of Constantinople was the greatest. His edict of religious toleration was not Constantine's greatest service, since the recognition of a victorious Christianity was inescapable sooner or later. "But by his timely transfer of the world-capital to Constantinople he saved the ancient culture and created a favorable setting for the spread of Christianity." Unfortunately such an interpretation leaves the author with little to say about the administrative machinery of the new capital.

Lot, Ferdinand. *The End of the Ancient World and the Beginnings of the Middle Ages.* New York: Barnes and Noble, Inc., 1953.

The edition here cited is a reprint of a work published originally in French in 1926. While historical research since that time qualifies much that Ferdinand Lot has to say on the period from the third to the seventh century, his keen analysis of the interplay of historical forces continues to command attention. Lot is no mere chronicler of events. Aiming to assess the influence of events on human psychology, individual and collective, he maintains that men of the seventh century, for instance, contemplated the world entirely differently from those of the third or fourth century, and again have so changed since ancient times that there is no longer a thought in common.

Lot sees the Roman Empire from a Western viewpoint, so his approach to the era of Constantine provides an instructive contrast to that of a Byzantine historian like Vasiliev. Lot is more interested in the Roman Empire as dying under Constantine than as beginning a new phase of an Eastern rule destined

to endure for more than a thousand years.

He is in the tradition of those who see Christianity as a cause of the decline and fall of Rome, and therefore it is the religious significance of Constantinople's foundation that most impresses him. He dwells on the early accounts describing Constantine's alleged divine inspirations and also analyzes the effect of Constantinople on the development of Rome in the West. Old Rome, abandoned by the Emperor, was left to the Church, and the Bishop of Rome's power rose until it became the supreme authority in Western Europe. Lot also sees from the beginning of the "two Romes" the roots of the schism between the Church in the West and the Church in the East. Ironically, he notes that Constantine's design, aimed to promote a unity of faith, was a large factor in its division.

He poses a series of questions regarding the founding of Constantinople, and his answers are unconventional. Recognizing the importance of the event because it displaced the axis of the Roman world, Lot asks why Constantine set up a competitor with Rome. He discounts the proffered reason that Republican memories annoyed the Emperor. Nor does he find military reasons satisfactory, since the greatest dangers were on the Danube and Rhine frontiers. Above all, Lot rejects the view that sees Constantine endowed with insight into the consequences of the choice, for "that would be to imagine that he was gifted with so penetrating a vision of the future that no man has been able to equal him." Besides, he argues, if Constantine could

have seen the future, he would not have chosen Constantinople, for Constantine wanted a "new Rome," and Constantinople became a Greek, not a Roman, city.

"Constantinople," he concludes, "was born on the whim of a despot who was prey to intense religious exaltation. Nevertheless few concerted measures of statesmanship have had more important and more lasting results." The most important result was that Greek civilization was saved by the city which was at once an impregnable fortress and a center of administration in the economically viable part of the Empire. — *Mary Evelyn Jegen*

Additional Recommended Reading

Burckhardt, Jacob. *The Age of Constantine the Great.* Translated by Moses Hadas. New York: Pantheon Books, 1949. A modernized version of a nineteenth century work in German.
Diehl, Charles. *Byzantium: Greatness and Decline.* Translated by Naomi Walford. New Brunswick: Rutgers University Press, 1957. A study containing much material on Constantinople, particularly in its development after the time of Constantine.
Jones, A. H. M. *Constantine and the Conversion of Europe.* New York: Crowell, Collier & Macmillan Co., 1962. A treatise which recognizes Constantine's design to found the city as a symbol of the break with the pagan past.
_____. *The Later Roman Empire 284-602—A Social, Economic and Administrative Survey.* Oxford: Basil Blackwell, 1964. 4 vols. A standard reference on the late Empire, and a good guide to sources.
Ostrogorsky, George. *History of the Byzantine State.* Translated by Joan Hursey. New Brunswick: Rutgers University Press, 1957. The author, a leading German authority on the institutional life of the Byzantine Empire, includes a useful bibliography.

BATTLE OF ADRIANOPLE

Type of event: Military: beginning of the great Germanic invasions
Time: August 9, 378
Locale: Adrianople

Principal personages:
VALENS, Roman Emperor in the East 364-378
GRATIAN, Roman Emperor in the West 367-383
FRITIGERN, leader of the Visigoths
SEBASTIAN, commander of the Roman infantry
LUPICINUS, Roman official of the province of Moesia

Summary of Event

For almost two years rebellious Visigoths had spread death and destruction throughout the Roman provinces that comprised the area of modern Bulgaria. The Emperor Valens was in residence at Antioch pursuing his campaign against the Persians, and it was there in 376 that he learned of the disastrous breakdown of his agreement with the Visigoths. Without undue haste he arranged a truce with Persia so that he might deal with the Germanic threat; it was not until April, 378, that he departed for Constantinople. Dissatisfied with the efforts of his commander Trajan against the Visigoths, he replaced him with a capable officer recently arrived from the West, Sebastian by name, who had a distinguished military record. To him the Emperor entrusted a selected infantry force which Sebastian quickly whipped into shape and then led off towards the troubled provinces. He experienced no difficulty in clearing the countryside of the roving bands of marauders, but he was not prepared for a major engagement. The Emperor himself, with additional veteran troops, left his headquarters near Constantinople at the end of June, and advanced toward Adrianople to join his general in preparation for a decisive blow.

Fritigern, the Visigothic leader, became alarmed. He realized that his scattered countrymen, impeded by the presence of their wives, children, and possessions, were highly vulnerable. They were more like a nation on the move than an army. Fritigern therefore ordered his people to concentrate near Cabyle, and at the same time he sent out agents to enlist auxiliaries for the impending clash with the Romans. Bands of Huns and Alans from beyond the Danube joined him, and a wandering contingent of Ostrogothic cavalry under Alatheus and Saphrax promised to do the same. He had already recruited runaway slaves and a variety of discontented Roman subjects, and while these additions to his fighting force swelled his numerical strength, the diversity of their interests and their undisciplined nature placed heavy demands on Fritigern's leadership. Food supplies were uncertain since the Germans were living off the countryside, and time worked against them.

Unfortunately for the Romans, the Emperor threw away his advantages. Reinforcements from the West led by his nephew the co-Emperor Gratian were marching eastward; a small advance unit in fact reached Adrianople about August 7 while Valens and his officers were discussing strategy. Some urged caution and delay until the Western army arrived. Sebastian and others, however, favored an immediate attack, and their advice confirmed Valens' own inclination. He had been incorrectly informed that the Visigoths numbered only about ten thousand men. No figures are available about the numerical strength of either side, but the Roman army probably totaled at least twenty thousand. At the same time, unknown to Valens, the Germans actually outnumbered the Romans. Possibly Valens was also motivated in his decision by jealousy. Gratian had shortly before achieved a notable victory over the Germans in the West, a feat which Valens seems to have desired to emulate. To wait for the Gallic reinforcements would mean sharing the glory of victory rather than enjoying it alone. Whatever the reason, he decided on an immediate offensive.

While these councils were being held, Fritigern sent a Christian priest as an envoy to negotiate with Valens. He promised peace in return for a guarantee of land in Thrace for the Visigoths to settle upon as their own, together with an adequate food supply. In effect this had been Valens' original agreement with the Germans two years earlier, so that Fritigern asked little more than what had been previously conceded. Yet Valens rejected any talk of a truce or treaty. Perhaps he felt that the rebellious depredations of the Germans could not be left unpunished. Perhaps, too, he doubted Fritigern's sincerity, for the Visigoth leader was awaiting the arrival of the Gothic cavalry of Alatheus and may have been stalling for time.

Early on the morning of August 9, 378, the Romans broke camp and advanced eight miles out from Adrianople to within sight of the Visigoths. Fritigern had drawn up his forces in a defensive position with his wagon train forming a circle enclosing his noncombatants and supplies. Tired from their morning's march, the Roman soldiers also suffered from the summer heat as well as from the smoke and heat of the fires that the Visigoths set in the surrounding fields to confuse and discomfit them. A second offer of negotiations from Fritigern induced Valens to dispatch one of his officers towards the Visigothic camp for a consultation, but before he could reach it some of the Roman troops impetuously opened the attack.

The details of the battle cannot be reconstructed accurately. The Germanic army, largely cavalry, overwhelmed the Roman infantry, who evidently broke under the shock and the superior numbers of the Visigoths. By nightfall scarcely a third of the Romans survived. Among the slain were Valens and Sebastian. The Emperor's body was never recovered. Two stories circulated about his death: one that he had been killed by an arrow while fleeing in a band of common soldiers, the other that he had been carried wounded into a farmhouse which the Visigoths destroyed by fire, not knowing the identity of the Romans within who refused to surrender.

Fritigern's victory at Adrianople did not solve his problem. Even with numerical superiority the Visigoths could not follow up their success properly because they lacked equipment and knowledge to conduct siege operations. Hence they could not strike at the towns where Roman wealth and power were concentrated. Two days after the battle they tried to take Adrianople itself, but had to abandon this vain effort. They soon made their way southward and reached the outskirts of Constantinople before retiring.

Essentially the Visigoths desired land on which to settle and make new homes for themselves, but they could attain their objective only by coming to terms with the Roman authorities. Shrewdly understanding this aim, the new Emperor of the East, Theodosius, combined diplomacy with military pressure and subdued the barbarians with a treaty in 382. They received what they desired and also the right to rule themselves. They agreed to pay an annual tribute in return for peace, and guaranteed to serve in the Roman army whenever called upon to do so.

There were two results of the Battle of Adrianople. First, the Visigoths became the first German tribe to win territory within the Empire and a degree of autonomy that placed them generally beyond the government's control, thereby portending the future dismemberment of the Roman Empire; and second, the destruction of a Roman army on its own soil demonstrated the deterioration of the once powerful legions, thereby encouraging the Visigoths themselves and later other Germanic tribes to risk further campaigns against Rome. The period of the peaceful penetration of the Empire by the Germans thus came to an end, and the age of invasions by conquest and force began on the battlefield of Adrianople.

Pertinent Literature

Marcellinus, Ammianus. *The Histories.* Translated by J. C. Rolfe. (The Loeb Classical Library.) Cambridge: Harvard University Press, 1956. 3 vols.

The thirty-first book of the contemporary history by Ammianus Marcellinus is the main source of information about the Battle of Adrianople and the Visigothic rebellion. Ammianus, a soldier by profession, pays close attention to military events and narrates them fully. As a Roman he regards the Visigoths as barbarian foes, yet he soundly castigates his own countrymen and unhesitatingly blames them for the Visigothic war.

Utterly terrified by the Huns who had recently subjugated their Ostrogothic kinsmen, and despairing of their own ability to protect themselves, the Visigoths were near panic and sought safety within the Roman Empire. They congregated along the north bank of the lower Danube and petitioned the Emperor for refuge. No thought of harassing the Empire had entered their heads; rather, they saw it as their only salvation and protection. Reckoning the number of potential recruits for the army and the savings in taxes, Valens agreed to grant the Visigoths land on condition that they accept the obligation of military service. By this time many Germans were serving in the armed forces of the Empire, so there was nothing new in such an arrangement. The Visigoths accepted Valens' terms, and he ordered the officers along the frontier to ferry them across the wide river and guide them to their new homes.

The officers entrusted with this task, especially the Count of Thrace, Lupicinus, took advantage of the situation to abuse the Visigoths. By selling provisions at exorbitant prices and even taking their children as slaves in exchange for bread, the Romans reaped huge profits. Ammianus states simply that "their treacherous covetousness was the cause of all our disasters." Compounding their wickedness, they ignored Valens' instructions to disarm the Visigoths and take hostages from them, and they allowed unauthorized warlike bands of Ostrogoths to enter the Empire.

Perhaps to placate the chieftains Alavivus and Fritigern, Lupicinus invited them to a banquet in Marcianopolis as the immigrant train approached that town. When some of the Visigoths meanwhile tried to enter the city to purchase supplies, the Roman soldiers, on Lupicinus' orders, prevented them. Arguments led to blows and a riot developed. Learning of the tumult during his banquet, the Count rashly ordered the massacre of his guests' bodyguards waiting in the courtyard. The Visigothic leaders rushed to the aid of their screaming men. Many were slain, apparently including Alavivus, but Fritigern escaped and raised the banner of revolt. The Visigoths had reached the breaking point. Lupicinus rushed out against them but his soldiers were cut to pieces. These incidents occurred either late in 376 or early in 377.

The Romans made another mistake at Adrianople, where several contingents of Visigothic mercenaries were stationed. These mercenaries loyally held aloof from their countrymen's revolt until the magistrate of the city tried to have them slaughtered. He, however, only convinced the trained warriors that they should join the rebels who were now looting and murdering about the countryside. Slaves and downtrodden people from all over the province similarly flocked to join the Visigoths.

From Antioch in 377 Valens dispatched new commanders, first Trajan, then Saturninus, and finally Sebastian, to suppress the rampaging barbarians, but they could not cope with the Germans' guerrilla tactics. At least one pitched battle was fought at Ad Salices in the region now known as the Dobrudja, but it ended in a draw. In the West, the Emperor Gratian prepared to bring reinforcements but an incursion of the Alamanni, who had learned of the Visigothic war and hoped to profit from it themselves, temporarily pinned him down in Gaul. No choice remained for Valens but to come north with his veteran legions and take personal command. When he arrived during the following summer, however, he displayed no better generalship than his subordinates, and led the Romans to the disaster at Adrianople which Ammianus describes as the greatest catastrophe to Roman arms since Cannae.

Thompson, E. A. *The Visigoths in the Time of Ulfila.* Oxford: The Clarendon Press, 1966.

Few historians have undertaken the difficult and demanding task of writing about the early history of the Visigoths. Thompson's book has merit because he accepts the challenge and succeeds in exposing the life of these barbarians so that the reader may understand their side of the story. He limits himself to their history before they came to live within the Empire, the most obscure phase of their history. His method consists of collating all available scraps of evidence— literary, archaeological, and theological— and integrating them into a meaningful portrait of the tribe.

In the last century B.C., the combined Gothic peoples crossed the Baltic Sea from Sweden to Poland. Remaining along the lower Vistula for two centuries, they then moved southeastward. By the middle of the third century, they occupied the Ukraine and began to harry the Empire. In the 270's, the emperor Aurelian evacuated Dacia (modern Romania and Transylvania) and some Goths occupied it so that they split into two main divisions, the Visigoths settling west of the Dniester River and the Ostrogoths to the east.

On three occasions during the fourth century the Visigoths went to war against Rome: during 332, the 340's, and 367-369. On the last occasion the Emperor Valens invaded their territory, ostensibly to punish them for supporting an attempted usurpation of his power but actually to forestall a possible Visigothic irruption across the Danube. These hostilities created bad feeling between the two peoples.

Nevertheless, Roman influences made themselves felt on the economic life of the Visigoths as they became sedentary and developed commercial contacts with the Mediterranean world. Visigothic craftsmen, drawing on native talent as well as Roman inspiration, demonstrated considerable skill. Early in the fourth century Christianity penetrated Gothia, associated with the work of the so-called Apostle of the Goths, Bishop Ulfila. A descendant of Christian slaves, Ulfila composed the Gothic alphabet and translated the Bible into their language, but he and his fellows suffered exile in 347-348. They found shelter among the Romans. A second persecution of Christian Visigoths occurred in

369-372, and produced a number of martyrs. Yet Christianity of an Arian type became the Visigoths' national religion after 382. Thompson interprets the two persecutions as instinctive reactions against the gradual Romanization of their lives. Nevertheless, through Ulfila the Goths achieved literacy and a more advanced culture.

The Visigoths did not develop a monarchy; they adhered to a loose form of organization that only in time of stress evolved into a confederation under a chieftain, known as a judge. Authority resided in an assembly of the people. As their social and economic life advanced they became less democratic, and property holders emerged as the dominant class. Athanaric was their acknowledged leader at the time of the Hunnish crisis, but his failure caused the Visigoths to turn to Alavivus and Fritigern. After a long tribal discussion the decision was taken to appeal to Valens for protection and a new home. Athanaric, Valens' opponent in the previous war, preferred to take refuge in the Transylvanian highlands when the majority of his people crossed the Danube in 376. He was reconciled to Rome some time after the Battle of Adrianople as part of Emperor Theodosius' scheme for achieving peace through conciliation. —*Raymond H. Schmandt*

Additional Recommended Reading

Baynes, Norman H. "The Dynasty of Valentinian and Theodosius the Great"; M. Mantius. "The Teutonic Migrations, 378-412"; and Martin Bang. "Expansion of the Teutons (to A.D. 378)," in *The Cambrige Medieval History*. Vol. I, pp. 183-276. Cambridge: The University Press, reprinted 1964. These chapters contain a detailed, scholarly treatment of the events at Adrianople and those preceding and immediately following it.

Bury, J. B. *The Invasion of Europe by the Barbarians*. New York: Russell and Russell, reissued 1963. The military and political side of the invasions are discussed, together with their impact on Rome.

Jones, A. H. M. *The Later Roman Empire 284-602*. Norman: University of Oklahoma Press, 1964. A social, economic, and administrative survey of the Empire during its later stages.

Thompson, E. A. *A History of Attila and the Huns*. Oxford: The Clarendon Press, 1948. The Huns impinged on the Visigoths only briefly but they shaped for all time thereafter the history of the Germanic peoples; this interesting volume deals with an important part of that story.

PROMULGATION OF THEODOSIUS' EDICTS

Type of event: Politico-religious: issuance of Imperial decree establishing Nicene Christianity
Time: 380 and 392
Locale: The Roman Empire

Principal personages:
THEODOSIUS, Emperor in the East 379-395, sole ruler 392-395
GRATIAN, Emperor in the West 375-383
VALENTINIAN II, Emperor in the West 383-392

Summary of Event

The reign of Theodosius brought to a close the turbulent fourth century controversy over the nature of the Trinity. Basically the question revolved around the issue of relationships within the Godhead. Arius had said that the Son and the Holy Ghost were inferior to the Father, whereas the bishops assembled at Nicaea in 325 had affirmed equality of Son and Father. In succeeding years many of these bishops also agreed that the Holy Ghost shared essential deity with the Father and the Son.

After the death of Jovian in 364, the Empire was again divided politically, this time between Valentinian (364-375) in the West and Valens (364-378) in the East. The Western Emperor was little inclined toward interfering in Church affairs, but in the East Valens adopted a modified form of Arianism and harassed Christians who adhered to the Nicene formula. Gratian (375-383), who succeeded Valentinian in the West, supported the Nicene faith and began to place both heretics and pagans under civil penalties. When Valens died in 378, Gratian appointed Theodosius to succeed him. Theodosius, a Spaniard, was sympathetic to the Nicene views espoused by most Western bishops. At the same time a Nicene group was also emerging in the East, and Theodosius evidently felt the time was ripe for his own vigorous participation in the controversy among the Christians. He issued his edict of February 27, 380,

from Thessalonica. It has come to be known as *Cunctos Populos* from its opening words. The text of the edict is translated as follows: "It is our pleasure that all the nations which are governed by our clemency and moderation should steadfastly adhere to the religion which was taught by St. Peter to the Romans; which faithful tradition has preserved; and which is now professed by the pontiff Damasus and by Peter, Bishop of Alexandria, a man of apostolic holiness." In accordance with the teachings of the Gospel and of the early apostles, he enjoined belief in the sole deity of the Father, the Son, and the Holy Ghost, "under an equal majesty and a pious Trinity." Only followers of this doctrine could assume the title of "Catholic Christians"; all others were judged extravagant madmen, and were branded with the "infamous title of heretics." Their conventicles should no longer be called churches and they could expect to suffer the penalties which the emperor, under divine guidance, would deem justifiable. Thus by Imperial edict orthodox Christianity was established, and deviationists were threatened with penalties. Besides establishing Nicene Christianity as the standard, the edict, according to many, is an early step in establishing the Roman Church as sovereign in orthodoxy.

Although Theodosius took a rigid attitude toward Christian heretics, he allowed considerable latitude to non-Christians during the

208

first twelve years of his reign; but in 391 two edicts were issued against the pagans, and the following year a more comprehensive law was promulgated. In this decree, which has come to be known as *Nullus Omnino*, he ordered that no one was to kill innocent victims in the worship of idols, nor was anyone henceforth permitted to venerate *lares, genii,* or *penates.* The reading of entrails was likewise forbidden, and he encouraged informers to reveal infractions of the law. Idol worship was ridiculed as a violation of true religion. Houses where pagan rites were conducted were to be confiscated, and a fine of twenty-five pounds in gold was to be imposed on all who sacrificed to idols or circumvented the law. The edict concludes with threats against officials who might be lax in enforcing this law.

Theodosius' solicitude for Christianity was not confined to the promulgation of these two edicts. By *Nullus Haereticis* in 381 he ordered that there be "no place left to the heretics for celebrating the mysteries of their faith," and he went on to assign the name Catholic only to those who believed in the Trinity. Heretics were forbidden to conduct assemblies within the limits of towns. During the next two years the Emperor set aside wills of apostate Christians, and he denied them the rights of inheritance. Likewise his attitude toward pagans resulted in the laws of 391 which prohibited sacrifices and the visiting of shrines. Possibly as a result of these laws the great temple to Serapis in Alexandria was destroyed about 391.

The two most significant confrontations of the Church and the state which occurred during Theodosius' reign were his convocation of the Second Ecumenical Council at Constantinople in A.D. 381, in which the Emperor gave the force of civil law to the conciliar canons, and his several disputes with Ambrose, the Bishop of Milan, in which the Emperor acquiesced to the churchman. These events, taken together with the edicts of 380 and 392, make the reign of Theodosius crucial in the establishment of Christianity as the state religion and in the domination of the Eastern Church by civil authority.

Pertinent Literature

King, N. Q. *The Emperor Theodosius and the Establishment of Christianity.* Philadelphia: The Westminster Press, 1960.

This book represents the best and most carefully documented treatment of Theodosius available in English today. In it the author treats successively the Emperor's background, his attitudes toward Christians, heretics, and pagans, and his general policies as lord of the Roman world.

As to *Cunctos Populos*, King styles it "a magnificent trumpet blast" and "as with most trumpet blasts, nobody paid any attention once the noise ceased." Nevertheless the law gives us some valuable clues to the thinking of Theodosius, and since it came early in his reign it resembles an election manifesto outlining future policies. The law clearly gives evidence that citizenship and orthodoxy, imperially dictated right belief and Catholicism, are being aligned. The Emperor believed that he had received his power from heaven, and as God's agent it was his responsibility to foster correct belief and worship.

King speculates on the background of this edict. He suggests that the sudden change in his fortune, from obscure country gentleman to lord of the Roman world, caused the Emperor to turn to religion. The reason for choosing Nicene Christianity may lie in the fact that he was a Westerner, and that his Western colleague Gratian was active in supporting that faith. More important, however, was the baptism of Theodosius by Ascholius, Bishop of Thessalonica, a Nicene in belief, when the Emperor was taken seriously ill early in his reign. In fact, the edict was published only one month after his baptism. "His baptism so early in his career as emperor meant that during the greater part of his reign Theodosius was pledged to Christ in a way in which Constantine and Constantius II had not been." Soon after this event the Emperor turned out the Arian Bishop of Constantinople, Demophilus, and installed the more orthodox Gregory Nazianzus in his place. A portent of the Emperor's thinking lay in his use of military force to effect the transfer.

King stresses the difference between Theodosius' two anti-heretical laws, that of 380, *Cunctos Populos* and 381, *Nullus Haereticis.* In the former the Emperor, in typically Western style, stressed the unity of the Godhead. In the latter he allowed for greater personality of the three entities comprising the Godhead. King surmises that the shift is indicative of the influences surrounding the Emperor, and it is perhaps a subtle manifesto of independence from the Roman and Alexandrian usages.

When King asserts that the edict was ignored once the noise had died, he means that penalties were not always meted out to heretics. The law had its effect on the majority of the population not so much because of the penalties attending its infraction but more because it was now clear that the road to Imperial preferment and civil concord lay in

accepting the Nicene faith.

King demonstrates that, before 391, Theodosius exercised a mild attitude toward pagans. Had the Emperor been hostile toward them from the beginning, the violent laws of these years would hardly have been necessary. Although antipagan laws existed between 379 and 391, King shows that they were aimed at abuses of morality and at black magic connected with pagan worship. The attack against paganism, when it came, was simply an extension of the Imperial policy: one God, one religion, one Empire. However, it was probably the praetorian prefect of Egypt, Cynegius, who was the prime instigator of the laws against the pagans. King expresses regret at laws which dealt the death blow to a religion "dying already of decrepitude," a religion not devoid of nobility. The author exonerates the Emperor of the destruction of the Serapeum, and he concludes, as do most writers on this subject, that the contradictory elements in Theodosius' policies— persecution of heretics, toleration of pagans, and lack of enforcement of the penalties for heresy—were due to laziness, or duplicity, or both. King also points out that the "persecution" of paganism by Christian emperors can in no way be compared to earlier persecutions of Christians. Since no Christian laws went so far as to order the death penalty or even physical punishment for the pagans, no pogrom of pagans was ever officially endorsed comparable to those directed by Decius or Diocletian against the Christians.

Huttmann, Maude Aline. *The Establishment of Christianity and the Proscription of Paganism.* New York: Columbia University Press, 1914.

This treatise deals with the period from Constantine to the accession of Justinian in 527, with chapters 5 and 6 concerned specifically with Theodosius' religious policies. The book is primarily a collection of the most significant laws dealing with the Church-state issue, together with a commentary.

Huttmann emphasizes that antiheretical and antipagan laws had already been passed by Gratian in the West before Theodosius came to power, and it is probable that the Eastern ruler was influenced by Western policies. The author also points to the early baptism of Theodosius as a possible explanation for his activity against heretics in 380. The disestablishment of paganism in the East effected by two laws passed in 391 and the edict of 392 was, according to the author, simply an amplification of the earlier prohibitions. The destruction of the Serapeum is put at 389, with Cynegius receiving most of the blame for the affair. One reason for Theodosius' sudden aversion to paganism after twelve years of toleration may be discovered in the political situation in the West. Gratian was succeeded by his brother Valentinian II (383-392), but the real power lay with Arbogast, a general. By 390, Arbogast had usurped most of the Imperial prerogatives in the West, and in 392 he was instrumental in having Valentinian II murdered. A usurper, Eugenius, allowed himself to be proclaimed emperor, and together with Arbogast bid for the support of the pagans by restoring their ancient rights of worship. The fact that Theodosius' edict of 392 coincided with the revival of paganism in Rome under the usurper Eugenius may indicate more than a purely religious motivation. The defeat of the Western usurpers in 394 was taken by the Christians as a judgment of God on paganism and a vindication of orthodoxy.—*Carl A. Volz*

Additional Recommended Reading

Boyd, William K. *The Ecclesiastical Edicts of the Theodosian Code.* New York: Columbia University Press, 1905. A typical commentary on the Code of Theodosius II, containing primary texts of the edicts of 380 and 392.

Greenslade, S. L. *Church and State from Constantine to Theodosius.* London: Student Christian Movement Press, 1954. A well-known account of the fourth century experimentation in Church-state relations.

Lietzmann, Hans. *The Era of the Church Fathers.* Vol. IV of *A History of the Early Church.* Translated by Bertram Lee Woolf. London: Lutterworth Press, 1961. A study stressing that Theodosius' religious policy reflected his desire for political unity and control.

Momigliano, Arnaldo, ed. *The Conflict Between Paganism and Christianity in the Fourth Century.* Oxford: The Clarendon Press, 1963. In one of eight essays, Herbert Bloch sees in the edict of 392 the logical result of Theodosius' gratitude for the forgiveness granted to him by Ambrose the previous year.

EXCOMMUNICATION OF THEODOSIUS

Type of event: Politico-religious: critical incident in relations between the Church and the
state
Time: 390
Locale: Milan

Principal personages:
AMBROSE, Bishop of Milan 374-397
THEODOSIUS, Emperor in the East 379-395, sole ruler 392-395

Summary of Event

In 388, a confrontation took place between Theodosius, Roman Emperor in the East, and Ambrose, Bishop of Milan, in which the latter successfully used the veiled threat of excommunication to gain his objective. The Bishop of Callinicum, a small town on the Euphrates, had permitted some Christians to burn a synagogue at the same time that a gang of monks had destroyed a Gnostic (Valentinian) chapel. Theodosius determined that the Bishop must make restitution at least of the synagogue, but Ambrose insisted that a Christian bishop could not use his resources for a non-Christian cause. Theodosius agreed with this logic and ordered that Imperial funds be used for the purpose. The Bishop again intervened by arguing that this course of action would be tantamount to Imperial adoption of Judaism as the state cult, and that a Christian emperor ought not to engage in such action. Again the Emperor acquiesced, but only after Ambrose preached a sermon in his presence threatening to stop the celebration of the Eucharist until the Emperor disassociated himself from the Callinicum affair. Historians are generally agreed that in this instance the Bishop misused his influence and thwarted the cause of justice, but it was no doubt his success with the Emperor at this time which encouraged him to take action against him again two years later.

In the summer of 390, a popular charioteer in Thessalonica was imprisoned for gross immorality by the commandant of the town, an Imperial official. A mob appeared at the jail demanding the release of the prisoner, and when they were refused, the furious citizens murdered the commandant and dragged his body through the streets. When Theodosius, then residing at Milan, heard of the riot, he determined to make an example of the Thessalonians' disrespect for Imperial officials. He invited the people of Thessalonica to attend games in the Circus, and at a given signal soldiers rushed in and massacred seven thousand persons. Although the Emperor thought better of his drastic decree and sent another to countermand it, it arrived too late to prevent the tragedy. Shortly afterwards, Theodosius reflected his own horror of the precipitous act by issuing a law which provided that all sentences of death should henceforth be suspended for thirty days and then be reconsidered.

About September 10, Ambrose wrote with his own hand a secret letter of excommunication intended for the Emperor's eyes alone. In the corpus of Ambrosian epistles it is *Letter 51*, which most historians (excepting Gibbon) agree is a masterpiece of tact and pastoral concern. After rehearsing the melancholy affair, the Bishop calls to mind precedent for royal penance from the Old Testament. "Are you ashamed, sir, to do as David did, who was a prophet as well as a king, and an ancestor of Christ?" The Emperor should not take it ill if the same words were addressed to him which the prophet addressed to David: "Thou art the man." Ambrose professed no intention of confounding the Emperor but only a desire to induce him, by citing royal precedent, to remove the curse of his sin from his Empire. The Emperor was told he must humble his soul before God. As a mere man to whom temptation had come, he must conquer it. Only tears and penitence could take away his sins. Ambrose assured the Emperor that he enjoyed the Bishop's love, affection, and prayers, but that even so he must follow Ambrose's instructions. If the Emperor refused he could at least pardon Ambrose for preferring God to the state.

Theodosius made no reply, but he authorized Rufinus, Master of Offices, to negotiate a compromise with Ambrose. But the Bishop remained firm in his demands. By the end of October the Emperor had agreed to do penance, and for some weeks he presented himself at the church as a public penitent; he laid aside his Imperial robes; he prayed and wept; he abstained from Communion. The public absolution was pronounced upon him by Ambrose at the Christmas Eucharist.

For the first time in Christian history, a bishop claimed power to judge, condemn, punish, and pardon a prince, thereby forcing him to submit to spiritual authority. The incident marks the beginning of a new relationship between the Church and the state.

Pertinent Literature

Dudden, F. Homes. *The Life and Times of St. Ambrose*. Oxford: The Clarendon Press, 1935. 2 vols.

Dudden's work remains the most comprehensive treatment of Ambrose available in English today. Chapter 15 of vol. 2 considers Ambrose's relationship with Theodosius.

Drawing on all the primary accounts of the incident, Dudden first attempts to reconstruct the event. He discounts later dramatic recitals of a personal confrontation between the Emperor and the Bishop at the church door as improbable, it being unlikely that Theodosius, knowing Ambrose's resolute nature, would have defied him openly. Nevertheless, it seems certain that for some weeks the Emperor did resist the Bishop and refused to submit to public humiliation. By mid-October, Rufinus was authorized to negotiate a compromise, which came to nothing. By the end of the month the Emperor was willing to do as the Bishop required. The period of penance was shortened to a few weeks, and the solemn readmission took place at Christmas.

The story of Theodosius' penance, says Dudden, is honorable to each of the principals concerned. The action of Ambrose was not simply an arrogant display of sacerdotal authority, but the vindication of divine and human laws against one who had offended both. On the other hand, Theodosius' penance was not craven submission to the demands of an intruding hierarchy but a recognition of the fundamental principles of religion and morality. The primary motivation on the part of both men was religious.

In his commentary on the Callinicum affair, Dudden suggests that Theodosius' submission to episcopal demands may also have been politically motivated. Having only recently arrived in Italy where he was not yet firmly established, he dared not risk antagonizing a prelate who had the power of stirring up the entire Christian population.

Whatever Theodosius' motivation, Dudden marks the event as a turning point in the history of the Church by establishing a precedent for sacerdotal supremacy over civil authority. It also marked a change in the relationship between Ambrose and the Emperor. Theodosius seems to have taken the Bishop more and more into his confidence after 390, particularly about legislation against pagans and heretics. Far from resenting the Bishop's imposition of penance, the Emperor admired him for it and is reported to have said: "I know no one except Ambrose who deserves the title of bishop."

Paredi, Angelo. *Saint Ambrose—His Life and Times.* Translated by M. Joseph Costelloe. Notre Dame: University of Notre Dame Press, 1964.

Chapter 14 of Paredi's biography is entitled "The Penance of Theodosius." Paredi, unlike Dudden, occasionally takes the side of the Bishop against the Emperor, although in the Callinicum affair he admits that "even saints can make mistakes."

The author rehearses the details of the incident. Although the letter of Ambrose to Theodosius did not explicitly excommunicate the prince, its effect was the same. Paredi suggests that Ambrose's recollection of a dream, in which the Emperor approached the church but the Bishop was unable to celebrate the Holy Mysteries in his presence, was a delicate way of telling Theodosius that he was excommunicated. Although we are ignorant of the Emperor's immediate reaction to this letter, Paredi sees in the legislation of Theodosius on August 18, 390, which suspended death penalties for thirty days, a gesture of his remorse which he hoped would suffice to keep him in a state of grace in the eyes of the Church.

Before the end of November, Theodosius was ready to submit. That he presented himself at the entrance of the church as if to challenge the Bishop's authority and that he was turned away, Paredi regards as legendary. The reconciliation took place at Christmas, 390, with Theodosius receiving absolution and readmittance to the sacraments. Paredi sees the significance of the incident in the fact that Theodosius was the first monarch in history to acknowledge publicly that he too was subject to the eternal laws of justice; a Christian bishop succeeded at the same time in establishing the right of judging and absolving kings. He points to Ambrose's actions as a symbol of the primacy which law and reason must have over brute force, and he reminds his readers: "It was the Catholic Church in the person of one of her bishops that affirmed this principle, which alone makes life worth living." —*Carl A. Volz*

Additional Recommended Reading

Ambrose. *Letter 51. Early Latin Theology.* Edited by S. L. Greenslade. Vol. V of *The Library of Christian Classics.* Edited by John Baillie, John McNeill, and Henry Van Dusen. Philadelphia: The Westminster Press, 1961. Ambrose's letter of excommunication is included in this primary source of Ambrose's letters translated into English.

Greenslade, S. L. *Church and State from Constantine to Theodosius.* London: Student Christian Movement Press, 1954. This work sees in the Theodosius-Ambrose incident the germ of the medieval conflict between the papacy and the Empire.

King, N. Q. *The Emperor Theodosius and the Establishment of Christianity.* Philadelphia: The Westminster Press, 1960. A study maintaining that Theodosius' humility and repentance were his greatest achievements.

Lietzmann, Hans. *The Era of the Church Fathers.* Vol. IV of *A History of the Early Church.* Translated by Bertram Lee Woolf. London: Lutterworth Press, 1961. The author believes that "a straight line runs from Milan to Canossa," though in 390, neither side was aware of the implications.

Morrison, Karl F. *Rome and the City of God: An Essay on the Constitutional Relationships of Empire and Church in the Fourth Century.* Transactions of the American Philological Society, Philadelphia, 1964. This essay studies Ambrose's actions in the light of legal justification.

Paulinus the Deacon. *The Life of St. Ambrose.* Translated by F. R. Hoare. *The Western Fathers.* New York: Harper and Row (Harper Torchbook 309L), 1965. Chapter 34 offers a brief account in which Theodosius is said to have undergone public penance.

Sozomen. *Church History.* Vol. 2 in Series 2 of *Nicene and Post-Nicene Fathers.* Grand Rapids: Eerdmans Publishing Company, 1957. Book VII, 25, describes the misery caused in Thessalonica by Theodosius' decree.

THE SACK OF ROME

Type of event: Military: barbarian expedition of plunder
Time: August 24-26, 410
Locale: Rome

Principal personages:
ALARIC, leader of the Visigoths 395-410
STILICHO, Vandal general in control of Rome as Regent for
    Honorius 395-408
HONORIUS, Emperor in the West 395-423
JEROME, scriptural scholar who popularized the idea that the sack
    of Rome meant the destruction of civilization
AUGUSTINE, Bishop of Hippo 395-430, who wrote the *City of God*
    to refute charges that Christianity was responsible for the
    decline of Rome

Summary of Event

When the Emperor Theodosius died in A.D. 395, the breakup of the Empire into eastern and western halves was inevitable. From that time onward, the civil rulers in the West were under the power of barbarian leaders. The sack of Rome by the Visigoths under Alaric in 410 should be seen as one episode in the final stages of the disintegration of the united Empire.

Theodosius' successors were his sons: Arcadius, aged eighteen, who became Augustus in the East; and Honorius, a mentally-retarded child of eleven, designated Augustus in the West. Actual rule in the West was in the hands of the army under the leadership of a Vandal, Stilicho, chosen by Theodosius as Regent for Honorius.

Alaric, a leader of the Visigothic allies of the Romans, took advantage of the death of Theodosius to make a bid for power in the Balkans and southern Greece. Stilicho tried to stop him in the North, but was deflected by an order from Arcadius to lead his army back to Constantinople. Later, Stilicho managed to come to terms with Alaric in Greece. Alaric and his Goths settled in Epirus, and Alaric had the satisfaction of receiving the title *Magister Militum* or "Master of the Soldiers" from the Eastern court, a title which was tantamount to official recognition as a military dictator.

In 401, Alaric first invaded Italy but was forced to withdraw by Stilicho. Stilicho checked a similar attempt in 403. For a time, Alaric joined forces with Stilicho to help him in taking Illyricum, which the Vandal leader was attempting to restore to Honorius. However, news of an uprising in Gaul caused Alaric to sense an opportunity for advancing his own cause. He hurried north, demanded employment for his troops, and succeeded in obtaining four thousand pounds of gold from the senate. His adviser in this negotiation was Stilicho, who soon after, in 408, was killed by enemies in court, an imprudent action accompanied by an antibarbarian purge in which soldiers along with their wives and children were brutally murdered. The result was that barbarian troops defected to Alaric.

With Stilicho out of the way, Italy was defenseless, and Alaric had his opportunity to strike at the heart of the Western Empire. He demanded lands and supplies for his men. Honorius refused and barricaded himself at

Ravenna, northeast of Rome. In 408, and again in 409, Alaric and his Goths marched on Rome. The first time he was bought off, but the second time he set up a rival emperor, Priscus Attalus. By this time, however, Honorius, having secured supporting troops from the Eastern Empire, refused to capitulate, and internal dissension between Alaric and his puppet Attalus led to the latter's deposition.

Finally, on August 24, 410, Alaric, with about forty thousand Goths, seized Rome and plundered it for three days. The actual physical destruction was relatively slight, but the impression on contemporaries was shattering. It was the first time in over eight hundred years that Rome had been taken by an enemy. It appeared that an era or even a civilization had come to an end. When the news reached Bethlehem, the scriptural scholar Jerome wrote that all humanity was included in the ruins of Rome. Augustine was moved by the event to write his great masterpiece of political and historical theory, the *City of God*, in which he answered those who charged that Christianity was the cause of Rome's decline.

After his attack on Rome, in which he took the Emperor's sister Galla Placidia as one of his own prizes, Alaric attempted to invade Africa, the granary of Italy, but failed when his ships were wrecked in a storm. He died soon after and was buried in the Busento River by followers who were afterwards slain lest anyone should know the exact location of the body and desecrate the remains.

If Alaric had any consistent policy, it seems to have been the acquisition of lands in the Empire, preferably in Italy, where his people might settle. In this attempt, he failed. Another aim, according to Jordanes, historian of the Goths, was the union of the Goths and Romans as a single people. In this, Alaric was unrealistic in terms of his own time, though later generations saw the assimilation of the two peoples in Spain and southern Gaul. Alaric's successor, his brother-in-law Ataulf, led the Goths into Gaul and from there into Spain, where Ataulf died in 415. The next Visigoth leader, Wallia, negotiated with the Romans and was given lands in southern Aquitania, in Gaul, in 418. Spasmodic struggles between Goths and Romans continued for another sixty years, but by 477 the Goths' sovereignty in southern Gaul and Spain was assured.

Pertinent Literature

Jones, A. H. M. *The Later Roman Empire 284-602—A Social, Economic, and Administrative Survey*. Oxford: Basil Blackwell & Mott, Ltd., 1964. 4 vols.

The reader looking for a detailed narrative of Alaric's sack of Rome will not find it in this book. Instead, he or she will find research on almost every aspect of Roman life during the period of interaction between Rome and the barbarians, a long-drawn-out process in which the sack of Rome in 410 was one important episode.

Jones' work is not a history of the later Roman Empire, but a social, economic, and administrative survey. It is the fruit of a life of research, and will remain a standard work of its kind. The work is excellently documented. The entire third volume is given to annotations, appendices, and an index; a fourth volume contains maps to accompany the text.

Jones does not accept a clear-cut terminal date for the Roman Empire in the West, and since he writes specifically of the Empire and not of the successor barbarian kingdoms, his emphasis is on elements of continuity rather than on those of change, which, of course, affects his view of the sack of Rome in 410.

Actually, Jones does not describe the sack of Rome by the Visigoths at all, but handles it in a single sentence: "Infuriated, Alaric for the third time marched on Rome, and this time entered into no negotiations, but sacked the city." References to the chief primary sources will supply the reader with further details. Jones' work is valuable in the description of Alaric's movements from the death of Theodosius in 395 to the attack on Rome, emphasizing the fact that Alaric advanced his own interests and those of his people by playing off one government against another. Jones is able to show that it was the friction between the government of the East and that of the West which gave Alaric his opportunity.

While Jones' work lacks the color that comes from a more biographical treatment of a historical subject, it does provide details that make a remote episode more understandable. For example, he mentions that in the antibarbarian purge which followed the death of Stilicho, an estimated thirty thousand barbarians joined Alaric. Some of these were *foederati*, or free allies, and others were barbarian slaves who used the occasion to escape from Rome. Such an easy change of allegiance was not unusual in the period under consideration. Jones' chapter on the Roman army is essential to an understanding of the actual participants of the struggles between Roman and barbarian, at least on the Roman side.

In the final chapter of the second volume, the author takes up the problem of the decline of the Empire, and here assesses the place of the barbarians as a factor in the fall of Rome. After a caveat that all historians who have discussed the decline and fall of the Roman Empire have been Westerners, who dismiss the fact that the Roman Empire did not fall for another thousand years, he does agree that the sack in 410 came as a great shock to Christians as well as to pagans. The fall of the Empire in the West had as its major cause the barbarians. Jones comes to this conclusion on the basis of his comparison of conditions in the East and West, and after he has given deserved attention to other interpretations, from the ancients through Gibbon and Marx. The internal weaknesses of the Empire cannot have been a major factor, Jones claims, because the East had the same weaknesses (political, economic, and moral) and in some cases to a far greater degree, but survived because the East was strategically less vulnerable to external attack. "This suggests that the simple but rather unfashionable view that the barbarians played a considerable part in the decline and fall of the empire may have some truth in it." For Jones, it is a major truth in the explanation of the decline of Rome, though his work focuses on the Roman rather than on the barbarian elements of the story.

Perowne, Stewart. *The End of the Roman World.* New York: Thomas Y. Crowell Company, 1966.

Perowne is the author of four other books on what he calls the "spiritual evolution of the Roman world." In this, his latest study, his aim is to review the various reasons given for the decline of Rome, to test their validity, and finally, to come to some conclusions about the way Rome lived on in succeeding generations.

In the introduction to this work, Perowne traces the history of the problem of the decline and fall of Rome from Petrarch in the

fourteenth century to the monumental work of A. H. M. Jones today. It was Petrarch who made the sack of Rome in 410 the signal event for the boundary between "ancient" and "modern" history. Perowne observes: "The year 410 became to Roman history what 1066 was to be for English history, the Great Divide." Perowne reviews the main lines of interpretation of the subject of Rome's decline, through Flavio Biondo, the fifteenth century humanist, Macchiavelli in the sixteenth century, Montesquieu, Gibbon, and Voltaire in the eighteenth, and the Marxist interpretation beginning a century later. The nineteenth century historians, with their more exact methods of research, emphasized anew the role of the Germanic barbarians in Rome's decline and fall. Finally, Perowne calls attention to three new factors in twentieth century studies of the problem: the developing understanding of Byzantine civilization, the role of non-Germanic tribes (notably the Slavs and the Huns), and finally, the school of historians who see little or no break between old Rome and the new West. These last come to their conclusions by emphasizing elements of cultural continuity rather than political aspects of the problem.

Within this broad perspective, Perowne still sees the sack of Rome by the Visigoths as an event of signal importance and gives it an entire chapter in his book. He begins by stating that there is no single occurrence in the history of Rome more difficult to evaluate, not only because of the long history of interpretation of the event, but also because certain assumptions are not in accord with the facts.

Alaric, Perowne insists, was no savage. He was driven from blackmail to violence by the obstinacy of Honorius, which prevented a rational solution. The death of Stilicho was a particularly unfortunate event, for had he lived, the affair might have been "realistically" settled.

Perowne believes that Alaric's capture of a starving Rome was a hollow triumph for the Visigoth chief. He plays down the amount of loot carried off by the Visigoths in three days, insisting that the picture of the barbarians carrying off wagonloads of removable goods, as described by Gibbon, could hardly be true in famine conditions when beasts as well as men were starving.

The author makes much of Alaric's nobility, shown in his clemency and in the control he kept over his own men. He cites several examples of their restraint, and quotes at length from Augustine's *City of God* to show how Augustine compared Alaric favorably with a barbarian chief who had attempted to sack Rome only a few years earlier. For Perowne, Alaric is almost an English gentleman.

The author finally poses the difficult and obvious question: Why was the sack of Rome by Alaric considered "as traumatically final" both by contemporaries and by historians for centuries after? He gives three reasons. First, Jerome, a contemporary writing from Bethlehem, popularly equated the fall of the city with the fall of civilization. Jerome was a scholar held in high repute, and his interpretation was widely accepted on his authority. Second, the disaster of 410 was preceded and accompanied by a flow of refugees from Rome who supported the view propagated by Jerome. Finally, there was the shock of the novelty of the event. Rome had long stood as the symbol not only of stability, but of civilization itself, and the city had not been occupied by an enemy for eight hundred years. To men living in 410 and long after, the impossible had happened. Perowne's conclusion is in keeping with his approach to the study of Rome, which is concerned chiefly about the extent and manner in which the "idea of Rome" has been perpetuated in history. Thus his final words are understandable: "The real significance of the year 410 is neither material, nor physical, nor political: it is spiritual, and of all ills, spiritual ills are the hardest to bear, the least easy to cure."

—Mary Evelyn Jegen

Additional Recommended Reading

Boak, Arthur E. R., and William B. G. Sinnigen. *A History of Rome to* A.D. *565.* 5th ed. New York: The Macmillan Company, 1965. A useful handbook.

Chambers, Mortimer. *The Fall of Rome—Can It Be Explained?* New York: Holt, Rinehart and Winston, 1963. A presentation of differing interpretations of the decline of Rome emphasizing economic factors.

Gwatkin, H. M., and J. P. Whitney, eds. *The Cambridge Medieval History.* Vol. I: *The Christian Roman Empire and the Foundation of the Teutonic Kingdoms.* New York: The Macmillan Company, 1924. Chapter Nine, "The Teutonic Migrations, 378-412," by M. Manitius, presents a detailed account of Alaric's career.

Lot, Ferdinand. *The End of the Ancient World and the Beginnings of the Middle Ages.* New York: Barnes and Noble, 1953. A discussion of the interaction of Romans and barbarians from the fourth century to the eighth.

Previté-Orton, C. W. *The Shorter Cambridge Medieval History.* Vol. I: *The Later Roman Empire to the Twelfth Century.* Cambridge: The University Press, 1953. A valuable reference work for study of the barbarian migrations.

Randers-Pehrson, Justine Davis. *Barbarians and Romans: The Birth Struggle of Europe,* A.D. 400-700. Norman: University of Oklahoma Press, 1983. A history of the early Middle Ages, tracing the interrelationship between the Romans and the German barbarians and showing how the new Europe emerged from the fusion of these two cultures.

VANDAL SEIZURE OF CARTHAGE

Type of event: Military: capture of leading Roman city in North Africa
Time: 439
Locale: Northwest coast of Africa

Principal personages:
GAISERIC, King of the Vandals 428-477, leader of attack on
    Carthage
WALLIA, Visigoth leader 415-418, authorized by Rome to attack
    the Vandals in Spain
COUNT BONIFACE, Roman governor in Africa 425-431, who is
    supposed to have sought the Vandals as allies in rebellion
GALLA PLACIDIA, Regent 423-455 for the Emperor Valentinian III,
    against whom Count Boniface rebelled

Summary of Event

Driven west by the swiftly moving Huns, the Vandals crossed the Rhine near Mainz in A.D. 406, for several years ravaged Gaul, and at one point seemed about to cross the English Channel and invade Britain. Instead, they crossed the Pyrenees and settled in Spain in 409, and in 411 became *foederati*, or official allies of the Romans. The Vandals remained in Spain for twenty years, but the Roman-Vandal peace was an uneasy one, broken in 416 when Rome authorized the Visigoths under Wallia to attack them in the name of the Emperor. The Vandals suffered severely under this treatment but recovered their strength within a decade.

In 429, under their king Gaiseric, the Vandals crossed to North Africa, lured by the prospect of controlling the rich grain lands there. Conditions in Africa made an invasion an attractive prospect to the enterprising Vandals, because the local ruler, Count Boniface, had rebelled against Galla Placidia, Regent for the child Emperor Valentinian III. It cannot be proved that Count Boniface actually invited the Vandals as allies; nevertheless, when they came, an estimated eighty thousand strong of whom fifteen to twenty thousand were fighting men,

they found further advantages in the restlessness of the native Berbers and in the turmoil fomented by the religious discord of the Donatists, a group of schismatic Christians.

Though Gaiseric did not capture any of the chief cities then, he did ravage the country and defeat Boniface's troops in battle in 431. He also laid siege to Hippo for fourteen months, during which time the city's great bishop, Augustine, died. Finally in 435, a peace was concluded by which the Vandals were permitted to settle in Numidia.

In 439, Gaiseric threw off the Roman yoke and seized Carthage, the leading city and key to the control of North Africa and the Mediterranean. Next, a fleet was organized to operate off the Sicilian coast. In 442, Rome acknowledged the independence of the Vandal kingdom.

For the next century, the Vandals under Gaiseric and four of his successors ruled independently in North Africa, holding Sicily, Corsica, and Sardinia as well, and thus controlling the Mediterranean. In 455, when the Emperor Valentinian III was assassinated, Gaiseric descended upon Rome. The Vandals spared the buildings and monuments but otherwise plundered the city's art treasures.

The Vandals continued to administer the rich, grain-producing North African territory in much the same manner as had the Romans, even using the same administrative personnel. The significant differences were to be seen in the confiscation of large landed estates, which now became properties of the Vandals, in the independent stance towards the Roman Emperor in Constantinople, and in the religion of the people. The Vandals were Arian Christians, and Gaiseric and several of his successors waged bitter persecution against the non-Arian Christians; they were largely successful in destroying orthodox Christianity and replacing it with Arianism. This hollow victory proved to be the seed of the Vandals' own undoing.

Vandal control of Africa came to an end when the Emperor Justinian decided to reincorporate the western portion of the old Roman Empire and to enforce orthodoxy throughout his dominions. Belisarius, Justinian's general, defeated the Vandals at Ad Decimam and soon after captured the Vandal king Gelimer, thus bringing Vandal rule in Africa to a close. The Vandals who survived became slaves of the Romans and as a people disappeared from history.

Although the Vandals held North Africa for more than a century, their influence was more negative than positive. They made little or no lasting cultural contribution to North Africa and left almost no records. The coming of the Vandals marks the denouement of Roman culture in North Africa, which had been among its most advanced areas. The career and writings of Augustine of Hippo serve as a reminder of the achievements and potential of North African civilization, had the Roman-Christian synthesis there survived the barbarian onslaught. Justinian's recovery in 534 proved ephemeral, for North Africa soon succumbed to another shock of invasion when the Moslems took over the region in the seventh century, permanently to destroy the unity of the Mediterranean area economically, religiously, and politically.

Pertinent Literature

Gwatkin, H. M., and J. P. Whitney, eds. *The Cambridge Medieval History.* 2nd ed. Vol. I: *The Christian Roman Empire and the Foundation of the Teutonic Kingdoms.* New York: The Macmillan Company, 1924.

The Cambridge Medieval History remains a standard source for the story of the barbarian kingdoms in Europe. The section on the Vandals in Africa, by the German scholar Ludwig Schmidt, gives a well-rounded picture of the political and social institutions of the Vandals from the time of Gaiseric until their defeat by Justinian a century later.

Gaiseric's seizure of Carthage on October 19, 439, was recognized as the beginning of their rule in Africa by the Vandals themselves, even though the Romans did not acknowledge their independent rule until 442. The legal dating in Carthage began from 439, and October 19 was considered New Year's Day.

As Schmidt points out, there is ample evidence that other barbarians recognized the power of Gaiseric's kingdom. One king of the Visigoths, Theodoric, sought an alliance by marrying his daughter to Gaiseric's son. Aetius is to be given credit for bringing an end to the coalition achieved through this marriage alliance, by proposing an even more advantageous marriage between Gaiseric's son and a daughter of the Emperor Valentinian III. While this marriage did not take place, negotiations brought the Romans and the Vandals closer together so that they maintained friendly relations until 455.

Carthage remained the center of Vandal rule in Africa, and there is sufficient evidence to make possible a detailed picture of the Vandal kingdom there. The Vandals kept the Roman division of the land into provinces, along with much of the machinery of government as the Romans had developed it. On the other hand, the Romans were looked upon as conquered subjects, and marriage between Romans and Vandals was forbidden. In sharp contrast to this treatment, the Moorish tribes were allowed more independence. Schmidt is of the opinion that had the Moors been given less freedom, the Vandals in Africa might have developed a high degree of culture and civilization. He observes: "The destruction which befell the works of ancient civilization in Africa must be placed to the account of the Moors, not of the Vandals."

An important feature of Vandal rule to which Schmidt gives particular attention was the manner of succession. Gaiseric considered himself the originator of a dynasty and looked upon the kingship as a property which he could hand on in his family. He further established the principle that the crown should pass to the eldest of his male issue. Should a son be too young to rule personally, the throne was to pass to a nephew. The Vandal kingdom was not only the first but also, for a long time, the only state which achieved a permanent rule of succession. In an absolute way, the king controlled appointments, justice, the army, the assembly, finance, police, and the Church. If there was a theory underlying this government, it was that royal power came from God.

The secret of the Vandals' success lay in the speed of their military operations; they even constructed a navy of small, fast cruisers with a capacity of about forty persons. Soon after Gaiseric's death, a military decline set in. Schmidt attributes this fact to the enervating effect of the hot climate and the luxurious way of life the Vandals adopted when they inherited one of the richest parts of the Empire.

Bury, J. B. *The Invasion of Europe by the Barbarians.* New York: Russell and Russell, 1963.

This book, a reprint of a work first published in 1928, is still an important contribution to the subject. While not one of Bury's major works, it contains some bold interpretations based on his highly specialized research into problems of the late Roman Empire. This is particularly true of his assessment of the significance of the Vandal kingdom in Africa.

Bury accepts without question the claim that Count Boniface invited Gaiseric into Africa, a claim which more recent historians have questioned. Bury also is a propagator of the Vandal image as that of particularly ruthless barbarians: "The Visigoths were lambs compared with the Vandal wolves." Gaiseric, "unquestionably the ablest" among contemporary barbarian kings, was a man "of astute and perfidious diplomacy."

These observations are, however, peripheral to Bury's main thesis concerning the Vandals, which holds that the increase of barbarian power and the corresponding decrease in imperial control not in Africa only but also throughout the Western Empire, "was largely conditioned by the existence and hostility of the Vandal power in North Africa."

The influence of the Vandals was negative. Because the Vandals controlled the corn supply of Italy for a hundred years, they prevented the Roman government from vigorous action in Gaul and in Spain. Bury's argument is that had the Vandals not been there, and had the Romans continued to hold Africa, a strong Roman government would have had the means to check Germanic expansion.

Seen from the side of the Germans, the Vandal naval power in the Mediterranean acted as a "powerful protection for the growth of the new German kingdoms in Gaul and Spain, and ultimately helped the founding of a German kingdom in Italy, by dividing, diverting, and weakening the forces of the Empire."

Had the Vandals been peaceful settlers, their effect would have been less; but, as Bury points out, they were hostile and aggressive. Besides their actions in the Mediterranean, they interfered in affairs between Rome and other barbarian peoples. For example, when the Huns under Attila invaded Gaul, Gaiseric exerted pressure on Attila to fight against the Visigoths, though in this case the urging may have been unnecessary.

In Bury's view, then, the Vandals are the key to an understanding of the decline of Rome and the rise of the barbarian kingdoms in Western Europe. Even though this interpretation is too simple an explanation, it provides an approach to interpreting a historical phenomenon which will remain baffling on account of its complexity and the paucity of sources. — *Mary Evelyn Jegen*

Additional Recommended Reading

Jones, A. H. M. *The Later Roman Empire 284-602: A Social, Economic and Administrative Survey.* Oxford: Basil Blackwell, 1964. 4 vols. The standard work on the subject; the fourth volume contains a set of excellent maps.

Perowne, Stewart. *The End of the Roman World.* New York: Thomas Y. Crowell and Company, 1966. A study particularly directed toward the elements of Roman survival.

Randers-Pehrson, Justine Davis. *Barbarians and Romans: The Birth Struggle of Europe,* A.D. *400-700.* Norman: University of Oklahoma Press, 1983. A history of the early Middle Ages, tracing the interrelationship between the Romans and the German barbarians and showing how the new Europe emerged from the fusion of these two cultures.

BATTLE OF CHÂLONS

Type of event: Military: engagement of Roman barbarian army with the Huns
Time: 451
Locale: Near Troyes, France

Principal personages:

AETIUS, Roman general in control of Gaul *de facto*
GALLA PLACIDIA, Regent, 423-455, for Emperor Valentinian III,
 who tried to break Aetius' power
ATTILA, leader who unified the Huns 434-453
GAISERIC, King of the Vandals 428-477, who incited Attila against
 the Visigoths
THEODORIC, King of the Visigoths, 419-451, and ally of Aetius

Summary of Event

When Valentinian III became Emperor in the West in 423, he was a child of five under the regency of his mother, Placidia, sister of the Emperor Honorius. The able Roman general Aetius, chief supporter of a rival claimant to the Imperial throne and leader of an army of Huns serving as mercenaries, was bought off with a command in Gaul in exchange for dismissing his army.

Aetius complied, but as master of the situation in Gaul he remained a threat to the Emperor. When Placidia tried to reduce his power by relieving him of his office of Master of the Soldiers, Aetius appealed to the Huns and with their help was able to win his reappointment in 433. For the next twenty-one years he was, in effect, an independent ruler in Gaul, demonstrating his power by receiving ambassadors and signing treaties.

Aetius continued to rely on Hunnish mercenaries in his struggle against various groups of barbarians: Franks, Burgundians, and Goths. During this period, while Gaul remained Roman, the Vandals took over North Africa, and the Saxons occupied Britain.

When the many separate groups of the Huns were united under the magnetic leadership of Attila in 444, the relationship between Aetius and the Huns changed. Work-ing from a base in the Balkans, in what is now Hungary and Romania, Attila succeeded in exacting an annual payment of more than two thousand pounds in gold as a price for maintaining peace. In 447, he invaded Imperial territory across the Danube and made peace only on condition that the Romans evacuate a strip along the south side of the river. The Huns continued to seek more lands in the West; their pretext for further invasion was the Roman refusal to accede to Attila's demand for the hand of the Emperor's sister, Honoria, with half the Western Empire as her dowry.

Even though Aetius was desperately short of troops in the face of the Hunnish threat, he decided to resist his former allies. He carried off a remarkable diplomatic achievement by making an uneasy alliance with the Visigoths, who were such traditional enemies of Rome that Attila had counted on their benevolent neutrality, along with support from the Franks. The Vandal king Gaiseric cleverly managed to incite the Huns against the Visigoths, who were his own enemies.

The actual battle between Aetius and Attila was fought on a plain near Troyes. The Hunnish forces, mainly cavalry, were flanked by troops of subjugated German tribes. Aetius arranged his own forces with his picked Roman troops and some Gothic allies on the left flank, and his allies from the Alans, barbarians whom he did not trust, in the center.

Attila failed to get possession of a high position commanding the battlefield, and directed his attack against the right flank of the enemy, composed of the Visigoths under their King, Theodoric. The battle was not a clear victory for either side, and there were heavy casualties. Finally, the Huns were driven back to their camp and eventually withdrew from the area unmolested.

The battle is variously known as the Battle of Châlons, the Battle of the Catalaunian Fields, the Battle of the Mauriac Plain, and the Battle of Troyes, all names referring to places near which it was fought. It has also gone down in history as the Battle of the Nations, because it has been portrayed by some historians as a battle of the united tribes of western Europe against the Asiatic menace, or even as a struggle of civilization against barbarism. This interpretation is unwarranted. There were Germanic barbarians on both sides, the union of forces under Aetius was ephemeral, and Attila himself was not a rude savage. The significance of the battle lies more in its importance as an episode illustrating the complexity of relations between Rome and the Germanic peoples in the last generation of the Roman Empire in the West.

Pertinent Literature

Previté-Orton, C. W. *The Shorter Cambridge Medieval History.* Vol. I: *The Later Roman Empire to the Twelfth Century.* Cambridge: The University Press, 1952.

Previté-Orton discusses the Huns and the Battle of Châlons in the chapter, "The Crumbling of the Empire in the West, 395-476." In this treatment, the activities of the Huns serve as a foil to illustrate the independent development of the Empire in the East and in the West, or the two empires, as the author prefers to call them even at this relatively early period. Attila's career up to the Battle of Châlons is developed in considerable detail, following the account of Priscus, a Greek who accompanied an embassy from the Byzantine court to Attila's in Hungary in 449. Attila himself is depicted as "a ruthless, destroying conqueror, a genius of rapine and war . . . an absolute ruler [who] had little idea of government beyond conquest, slave-hunting, and looting."

Attila's exploitation of the eastern half of the Empire led to a treaty in 434 by which the leader of the Huns received an annual tribute of seven hundred pounds of gold, or in Previté-Orton's terms, an "annual black-mail." When the East could not or would not pay, and also refused to hand over refugees upon demand, Attila retaliated by invading the Balkans.

In the West, Attila broke off his old friendly relationship with Aetius for several reasons, both real and alleged. For Previté-Orton, the real cause was Attila's imperialism. Having reached the Rhine, the Baltic Sea, and the Caspian Sea, Attila in 441 sought to despoil the still wealthy Roman Empire itself. As a pretext for Attila's move into Gaul, the author discusses the fact that the Franks were fighting among themselves, one group appealing to the Huns for help and another seeking help from Aetius. Gaiseric, the Vandal leader, complicated the picture by urging the Huns to fight against his enemies, the Visigoths. The story that Attila invaded Gaul because he was refused the hand of Valentinian's sister is, according to Previté-Orton, at best but a flimsy pretext and certainly not the actual cause of hostilities.

The account specifies various Germanic barbarians who fought on Attila's side, including Gepids, Ostrogoths, Thuringians, Rugians, Sciri, Heruli, Burgundians, and the Ripuarian Franks. Attila tried to persuade Aetius that he was really attacking the Visigoths and merely using Roman Gaul as a route. On the other hand, he told Theodoric, leader of the Visigoths, that he was merely invading Roman territory.

In the actual battle Aetius forced the issue only after he had seized a high position which commanded the scene of the battle. Attila, meanwhile, had already carefully moved his own army to a plain where his horsemen would be able to operate to best advantage. While some authors see Châlons as a drawn battle, Previté-Orton describes it as a victory for Aetius, inasmuch as Attila, who was the aggressor, did not renew the conflict. The question whether the engagement was one of the decisive battles of the world remains open

for consideration. On the one hand, Aetius did not stop Attila's activities; the year after Châlons, the Huns invaded Italy, and although Rome was spared, Aquileia, Milan, and Pavia were plundered. On the other hand, after his major encounter with Aetius, Attila never again risked a pitched battle; he died in 453 while he was preparing another invasion of the Balkans, but no sooner was Attila gone than the Germanic tribes subject to him revolted. The Huns were crushed in a battle at Nedao in Hungary, and played no further role in the Western Empire, though they continued to serve as mercenaries in the East.

Previté-Orton notes the irony in the fact that the removal of the Huns was fatal to Aetius. Left with neither mercenaries nor an enemy, that is, with neither an army nor the chance to prove himself a hero, Aetius soon became a victim of intrigues in the court and was stabbed to death by the Emperor himself.

Fuller, J. F. C. *A Military History of the Western World.* Vol. I: *From the Earliest Times to the Battle of Lepanto.* New York: Funk and Wagnalls, 1954.

In the chapter on "The Battle of Châlons or of the Mauriac Plain, 451," the author centers his attention on the Huns and the significance of their defeat. It is Attila, their leader, and not Aetius, the victorious Roman general, who is of chief concern to Fuller.

In this chapter, the author works from Ammianus Marcellinus, from the epic-like Gothic History of Jordanes written about a hundred years after the Battle of Châlons, and from several nineteenth century historians. Fuller offers few results of recent research on the Battle of Châlons. The account itself traces the movements of the Huns into Western Europe and the complex entangling alliances of the Romans, Huns, and various Germanic tribes who became involved in the battle on either side.

Fuller's account mentions the famed legend of Saint Geneviève, who saved Paris after

Rheims, Metz, Cambrai, Mainz, and Strasbourg had been sacked as Attila and his horde had moved West, and the similar story of Saint Aignan who saved Orléans.

Fuller suggests in a footnote that the strangeness of Attila's escape after his defeat indicates collusion between Attila and Aetius. He reasons that Aetius, as well as Attila, was in a difficult situation, since Thorismund, the new leader of the Visigoths, could not be trusted to maintain an alliance with the Romans. It was only at the last minute that the Visigoths under Theodoric had been prevailed upon to join forces with the Romans, their recent enemies. Jordanes recounts how Aetius, hoping to keep Thorismund at a safe distance, urged him to return to his own dominions to enforce his power and position in the face of his brothers. Even though assured of victory against Attila with Thorismund out of the way, Aetius needed to preserve the Hunnish leader as a possible threat against Ravenna. In this way Aetius would make himself indispensable to the defense of Italy. According to Jordanes' account, Aetius became separated from his men in the confusion during the night following the battle, and during this interval, Attila was able to save himself by returning to his well-fortified camp. Fuller suggests that far from losing his way on the night of June 20-21, Aetius paid a secret visit to Attila to arrange the whole incident of the withdrawal with him; otherwise, it is hard to explain why Attila did not attack Aetius after Thorismund left, or why Aetius did not follow up Attila's retirement and cut off his foragers.

In keeping with the general approach of his military history, Fuller is not content to interpret the Battle of Châlons merely as a significant check on the ravages of the Huns, but as a victory of European civilization over that of Asia. "It was not a Roman victory or a Teutonic victory, but a victory of both peoples combined over Asiatics, as Salamis had been a victory of both Athenians and Spartans over Persians." Once again faced with a clash of West and East, Europe and Asia, Europeans settled their private quarrels to

face a common foe. Few historians will see the battle in such panoramic perspective.

Fuller further emphasizes the growing power of the Church under the papacy as the only agency which maintained institutional continuity in the period of extreme disorganization following the Battle of Châlons, an event in itself symptomatic of continuing disintegration within the Empire in the West. The partly historical, partly legendary, accounts of Saint Geneviève and Saint Aignan, and especially of Pope Leo, who was credited with having saved Rome from the ravages of Attila, reflect the Church's position of leadership even in war. War was now seen by the semibarbaric Christians of Western Europe as something which could be averted by an appeal to the supernatural.

As a final observation, Fuller recalls the legend of Attila in the Western European cultural tradition. When one wants to insult an enemy, he calls him a Hun, while Attila himself has gone down in history as the "Scourge of God" and appears as Etsel in the *Nibelungenlied*. The Battle of Châlons is doubly significant in the history of Western civilization as an event and also as the basis of legend.

—*Mary Evelyn Jegen*

Additional Recommended Reading

Boak, Arthur E. R., and William B. G. Sinnigen. *A History of Rome to* A.D. *565.* 5th ed. New York: The Macmillan Company, 1965. A useful handbook.

Gordon, C. D. *The Age of Attila.* Ann Arbor: University of Michigan Press, 1960. For the most part this book translates contemporary sources and adds a commentary.

Lot, Ferdinand. *The End of the Ancient World and the Beginnings of the Middle Ages.* New York: Barnes and Noble, Inc., 1953. A study of the interaction of Romans and barbarians from the fourth to the eighth century.

Randers-Pehrson, Justine Davis. *Barbarians and Romans: The Birth Struggle of Europe,* A.D. *400-700.* Norman: University of Oklahoma Press, 1983. A history of the early Middle Ages, tracing the interrelationship between the Romans and the German barbarians and showing how the new Europe emerged from the fusion of these two cultures.

Thompson, E. A. *A History of Attila and the Huns.* London: Oxford University Press, 1948. One of the few books on Attila in English by a specialist in the field.

MAGILL'S HISTORY
OF
EUROPE

CHRONOLOGICAL LIST OF EVENTS

Volume 1

III

Volume 2

CHRONOLOGICAL LIST OF EVENTS

Volume 3

Volume 4

CHRONOLOGICAL LIST OF EVENTS

CHRONOLOGICAL LIST OF EVENTS

Volume 6